Lifelines

Culture,

Spirituality,

and Family Violence

Lifelines

Culture, Spirituality, and Family Violence

UNDERSTANDING THE CULTURAL AND
SPIRITUAL NEEDS OF WOMEN
WHO HAVE EXPERIENCED ABUSE

Reinhild Boehm
Judith Golec
Ruth Krahn
Dianne Smyth

THE UNIVERSITY OF ALBERTA PRESS

Published by

The University of Alberta Press
Ring House 2
Edmonton, Alberta, Canada T6G 2E2

Copyright © The University of Alberta Press 1999

ISBN 0–88864–312–8

Canadian Cataloguing in Publication Data

Main entry under title:

Lifelines

ISBN 0–88864–312–8

1. Victims of family violence—Services for—Canada. 2. Victims of family violence—
Counseling of—Canada. 3. Abused wives—Canada—Case studies. 4. Abused wives—
Counseling of—Canada. I. Boehm, Reinhild, 1944–
HV6626.23.C3L53 1999   362.82'92   C98–911112–1

Printed on acid-free paper. ∞

Printed by Hignell Printing Ltd., Winnipeg, Manitoba, Canada.

Printed and bound in Canada.

Financial assistance for the research for *Lifelines* provided by Department of Canadian Heritage,
Status of Women Canada.

The University of Alberta Press gratefully acknowledges the support received for its publishing
program from The Canada Council for the Arts. In addition, we also gratefully acknowledge
the financial support of the Government of Canada through the Book Publishing Industry
Development Program for our publishing activities.

THE CANADA COUNCIL | LE CONSEIL DES ARTS
FOR THE ARTS | DU CANADA
SINCE 1957 | DEPUIS 1957

To Gita Das

whose ideas, energy, and passion

gave birth to this book

Contents

Preface   xi
Acknowledgments   xv
Lifelines' Voices   xvii

THE BEGINNING...   1

1   UNDERSTANDING THE NEEDS OF ABUSED WOMEN:
     The Missing Link   3
          Spirituality   4
          The Women's Movement   6
          Aboriginal Inspiration   8
          Women's Shelters in Transition   9
          Bridging the Secular and the Spiritual   10

2   THE WOMEN'S STORIES:
     Where Does Strength Come From?   13
     WOMEN WHO WROTE THEIR STORIES   15
          In Answer to Psalms 55   25
          Why Is God White?   27
          Escape   30
          My Beautiful Golden Bones   38
          From Fit to Free   43
     WOMEN WHO TOLD THEIR STORIES   46
          Loss and Ritual   49
          Learning to Cry   56

ONTENTS

The Violation of the Veil 62
Spiritual Awakening 67
STRENGTH COMES FROM WITHIN 74

3 VOICES OF WOMEN OF FAITH:
Personal Views on the Diversity of Culture,
Religion, and Background in Canada 75
Otter Woman Speaks 78
Buddhism for Monday, for Tuesday, for Wednesday... 81
From the Pulpit—A Word or Two on Christianity 86
Views of a Hindu Woman 102
A Woman as Rabbi—A Message of Hope 113
A Voice From the Muslim Community 133
WOMEN OF FAITH 143

4 CONVERSATIONS WITH FRONT-LINE WORKERS:
The Issue of Family Violence as Seen by Individuals
Who Work for Community Service Providers 145
Views of a Chinese-Canadian Counsellor 149
Changing Together: A Centre for Immigrant Women I 155
Changing Together: A Centre for Immigrant Women II 164
Catholic Social Services 167
Mennonite Centre for Newcomers: Centre for
Survivors of Torture and Trauma 171
Edmonton Community Services: A Partner in
the Spousal Abuse Follow-Up Team 174
Edmonton Police Service: A Partner in the
Spousal Abuse Follow-Up Team 185
Safe Place Women's Shelter 190
WIN House Women's Shelter 195
FRONT-LINE IMPRESSIONS 198

5 WHERE HAS *LIFELINES* LED US?:
Openings and Closings 201
Opening the Door 201
Lifelines—A Collection of Voices 202
Understanding Multiculturalism 204
Addressing Human Spiritual Need 205
Lifelines as a Catalyst 206
Hope and Healing 207

APPENDICES:

Tools for Helping, Healing 209

APPENDIX 1 A FEW TOOLS FOR BEGINNING 211

APPENDIX 2 ENABLING ACTIVITIES 214

EA# 1 Self-Affirmation 215

EA# 2 Self-Visualization 216

EA# 3 Centring: Awakening Yourself 217

EA# 4 Cultivating the Ability to Experience Joy 218

EA# 5 A Self of One's Own 219

EA# 6 Choosing Your Mantra 220

EA# 7 Your Evolving Inner Spirit 221

EA# 8 A Room of One's Own 222

EA# 9 Praying Your Spirituality 223

EA# 10 Centring: Creating 224

EA# 11 A Garden as Dwelling Place 225

EA# 12 Comparison of Assertive, Nonassertive,
and Aggressive Behaviours 226

EA# 13 Community as Dwelling Place 227

EA# 14 Centring: Traditioning 228

EA# 15 Exploration of Spirituality as Traditioning 229

EA# 16 Centring: Transforming 230

EA# 17 Taking Time for Mourning 232

EA# 18 Our Experiences of Bonding 233

EA# 19 The Experience of Birth 234

EA# 20 Labelling Emotions: Positive Words 235

EA# 21 Labelling Emotions: Negative Words 236

APPENDIX 3 INSPIRATIONAL WORDS 237

The Pathway to God 237

A Prayer for Strength 238

Prayer of Forgiveness 239

Prayer 240

The Woman's Drum 241

Saraswati 242

Sunlight 243

APPENDIX 4 WHAT PLACES OF WORSHIP AND COMMUNITIES
CAN DO ABOUT FAMILY VIOLENCE 244

APPENDIX 5 THE CANADIAN CHARTER OF RIGHTS
AND FREEDOMS 246

BIBLIOGRAPHY 247

Preface

Survivors of spousal abuse inevitably fail to find the answers they seek in the realm of reason as they try to make sense of their pain and suffering. *Lifelines* is intended to help those who need answers. Its primary focus is the healing power of spirituality, a process that often evolves through pain and mental anguish. *Lifelines* offers a celebration of healing, a message of hope, and a way of helping.

This book is intended to be a tool for those who encounter or are affected by abusive relationships. It offers a selection of stories, experiences, and views on the issue of family violence to help the reader identify both the positive and the negative effects of religious and cultural beliefs and to provide some insight and encouragement for those dealing with it.

Lifelines addresses family violence and spirituality in a community and cultural context. It is a collection of knowledge, experiences, and impressions of people who have discovered that the process of healing is dependent on one's spirituality and inner strength. We gathered these stories and experiences through a number of steps. First, we talked to women from various cultural backgrounds who had been abused. Several told their stories in their own words. Next, we attempted to outline the issue of family violence as perceived by women of faith from various cultures. The last step was to discuss and record the cross-cultural experiences of people involved as service providers, counsellors, or care-givers in the area of family violence.

We are aware that our writing has been influenced by our own individual experiences, backgrounds, cultures, and beliefs. Within these limits we have tried to give voice to the wisdom of all the women we had the privilege of listening to, those who shared their intimate feelings and their deepest anguish, their pain, their tears, their joy, and their laughter. Without their thoughtfulness, their reflections, and their analytical skills, this book would not have been possible. Our thanks to all of them.

WRITING *LIFELINES*

Once the need for the book was endorsed by the community and the funding put into place, an editorial collective (the authors) was called together to shape the direction, define the content, and to take on the responsibility of writing various sections of the book. Together, we bring to the book experience with women's shelters, an awareness of the issue of family violence in the immigrant community, expertise in qualitative research methodology, a dedication to feminist consciousness, a commitment to the solution of family violence, and a thirst for a better understanding of the spiritual condition of humankind.

By opening up the issue of the spiritual needs of abused women, *Lifelines* hopes to bring a wider understanding of this aspect of the healing process. In its centre are the stories of the women themselves, women from various cultural and religious backgrounds. In exploring this issue we invited women who have experienced spousal abuse to tell their stories in writing and through personal conversations. These women came to us through women's organizations, women's shelters, counselling agencies, and immigrant service agencies. The process and method we used to assemble the material was a qualitative one. The material collected differs from the social science prescribed practice of choosing a random sample in order to arrive at a representative view of the subject in a tightly described community. Rather, we hoped to approach the subject from the viewpoints of the individual, the women who have experienced family violence, those who are front line workers in social services, and members of specific faith communities.

Through the editing process, we have made every attempt to retain each woman's voice. The material was edited for readability and clarity and then given back to each person who was interviewed or who wrote her story. Some women requested that we take out comments that had the potential to offend others. In some cases, we did this ourselves. However, each participant had the opportunity to review and comment on her contribution. We believe that the voices heard accurately reflect the attitudes and experiences of the women, who clearly wanted to be heard. They do not pretend to speak for all women of a given community or culture or country. And they do not speak for all women of a given faith.

The women's stories emphasize the spiritual needs of women who have been abused. The stories also provide new insights and hope for shelter workers, members of faith communities, and others interested in women's issues. The stories of the women are framed by "Voices of Women of Faith," an overview of the perceptions of women who are members of various faith communities. In addition, we talked to the service providers, "Conversations with Front-Line Workers," to gain an understanding of how shelter workers and other counsellors define their own roles in addressing the needs of abused women. Workers from a variety of religious backgrounds serving in mainstream as well as ethnic and newcomers' organizations were interviewed.

Since this book is but a beginning exploration into this topic, we chose to interview predominantly women in order to capture women's perspective. We feel that the entire community, both women and men, will benefit from this approach because it validates women's realities and increases understanding of their spiritual space. We are confident that, in the wake of this first attempt, other voices will continue to inform the community and to broaden the views presented here.

Acknowledgments

We wish to express our deep appreciation to those individuals who shared their stories, experiences, knowledge, and insights in order to make this book possible.

We thank those in the community who had faith in our work, the service providers:

Catholic Social Services
Changing Together, Centre for Immigrant Women
Chinese Community Members
Hindu Community Members
Indo Canadian Women's Association
Mennonite Centre for Newcomers: Centre for the Survivors of
    Torture and Trauma
Native Student Services, University of Alberta
Safe Place Women's Shelter

Edmonton Community Services
Edmonton Police Service
WIN House Women's Shelter

We are indebted to individual members of several faith communities who shared their personal views, experiences, and knowledge:

An Aboriginal woman
A Buddhist woman
A Christian woman
A Hindu woman
A Jewish woman
A Muslim woman

and to our funders for their support and understanding:

Department of Canadian Heritage
Status of Women Canada

We extend a very special thanks to the women who wrote or told their stories. These women were asked to remember painful times. They shared their pain in order to help others. They were, by turns, reflective, rueful, ambivalent, ironic, observant. Some were bitter and angry, but most were accepting and insightful. Most of their names do not appear here. Names have been changed to protect the privacy of the women.

We would also like to thank others who have helped us in the early stages, Lu Ziola, Melanie Eastley, Natali Rodrigues, and Naomi Marathalingam.

Finally, the Faculty of Extension at the University of Alberta contributed time and resources to our project and we appreciate the support of our colleagues at the University.

Lifelines' Voices

Each woman's story is preceded by a few words about her, a brief glimpse of who she is. Some of the stories were written by the women and others were told and transcribed from tapes. The stories have been rewritten or edited and were approved for publication in the present form by each individual storyteller. These women are the true authors of this text.

ABOUT THE VOICES OF WOMEN OF FAITH

These are the voices of women in the community who have first-hand experience with abused women and their families. Each is a member of a specific culture and a specific religious community although they do not assume to represent those communities. Their comments are their own personal views on the diversity of culture, religion, and upbringing that have influenced women they know in the context of their lives in Canada. Each of these women has counselled many others, whether formally or informally.

ABOUT THE FRONT-LINE WORKERS

These individuals talk about their experiences in dealing with abuse in relationships between women and men from the viewpoint of community service providers. They have had direct contact with abused women and their families and communities in times of crisis and beyond. Although the names of the organizations and agencies they work for are included, these people are stating their own views.

ABOUT THE AUTHORS

REINHILD BOEHM, PH.D., is an anthropologist and the Director of the Millwoods Welcome Centre for Immigrants. She is the former Director of the Women's Program, University of Alberta. Dr. Boehm's doctoral study and other scholarly writing explores women's spirituality and the role of religion in community development. She is a member of the Action Committee Against Family Violence in the Immigrant Community and was president of Edmonton Women's Shelter Society. Dr. Boehm's publications include *In the Name of Religion: Impact of Fundamentalism on the Status of Women* (1994) and "Spirituality" in *Pathways to the Community: A Program for Federally Sentenced Women Who Act Violently* (1996).

JUDITH GOLEC, PH.D., has a nursing background and teaches in the areas of qualitative methodology, the social-psychology of health and illness, social organization of health care, sociology of mental illness, and the sociology of deviance at the University of Alberta. Dr. Golec was president of the Board of the Edmonton Women's Shelter and is a member of the Indo Canadian Women's Association. Dr. Golec's publications include "A Contextual Approach to the Social Psychological Study of Disaster Recovery" in *The International Journal of Mass Emergencies and Disaster*.

RUTH KRAHN received an undergraduate degree in English at the University of Alberta. Ruth is a fiction writer whose work has appeared in publications such as *PRISM International, Grain, Prairie Fire, Fiddlehead*, and the *New Quarterly* and in the anthologies of *Alberta Bound, Alberta Rebound*, and *Boundless Alberta*. Her nonfiction has appeared in the journals *Event* and *The Road Home*. She teaches writing for the Women's Program, University of Alberta and works as an editor for the Edmonton-based literary magazine *Other Voices*. Ruth is currently working on a novel.

DIANNE SMYTH is a writer and editor with an Bachelor's degree in the social sciences from the University of Alberta (1993). Dianne's publications include *Newcomer Suicide Prevention Project, Immigration Culture, and Suicide* (1995); *Pregnancy and Childbirth Experience in the Indo-Canadian Community* (1995); *Culture, Health, and Healing, Establishing Intercultural Health Care in Canada* (1994); *Project Management for Program Delivery: Trainers' Manual and Course Manual* (1998); and *Social Justice and Peace Towards Women's Human Rights* (1999). Dianne is a member of Changing Together, Centre for Immigrant Women and is the professional development co-ordinator for the Editors' Association of Canada, Prairie Provinces Branch.

The Beginning...

The truth is that much of story comes from travail: theirs, ours, mine, yours, someone's we know, someone's we do not know far away in time and place. And yet paradoxically, these very stories that rise from deep suffering can provide the most potent remedies for past, present, and even future ills.

Clarissa Pinkola Estes

The stories in *Lifelines*, arising from deep suffering, tell of universal spiritual need and the power of healing it provides.

The idea for this book slowly germinated and evolved from work done by the Action Committee on Immigrant Women and Family Violence and its interfaith sub-committee, and the Women's Program, Faculty of Extension, University of Alberta. A series of conferences, workshops, and meetings raised the question of the "spiritual" needs of victims of spousal abuse.

People began to ask, "If the need for culturally specific spiritual counselling arises, is it effectively dealt with in places of worship, in women's shelters, in service providing agencies, and in the health care system?"

This question was the catalyst that clearly identified the need for a book on this subject. Thus *Lifelines* was born.

Understanding the
Needs of Abused Women

The Missing Link

1

In our fervent attempt to understand and answer the anguished cry of abused women, those of us who care and help may have overlooked a vital component in the healing process—a missing link.

Women's shelters and other organizations in the community that are set up to help women deal with family violence issues have made huge strides in enabling and empowering women to get to safe ground. The physical needs of the abused woman are addressed by the safety the shelters provide during the most dangerous times. Her emotional needs are met by counselling throughout her stay in the shelter. Coping strategies provide her with the means to develop rational responses to her situation and with tools to deal with her future. The empowering process within the shelters and community organizations provides a holistic way of coping, a way to meet a woman's physical, mental, and emotional needs. So what is missing?

When one's body is in pain, the mind and heart are deeply anguished. Sometimes, the only hope is found in the spirit deep within. Spiritual affirmation of self is a deeply felt human need. What has slowly disappeared from the work of the shelters and the community is the attention to the spiritual needs of the abused woman.

SPIRITUALITY

What do we mean by "spiritual" needs? As editors and authors we struggled with this concept because it is so personal to each of us. However, we agreed that spirituality is a universal human gift connecting us to the mystery of creation and defining our place within it. We acknowledged our connectedness to the mystery at the centre—god, goddess, creator, higher power—the unnamed one.

This is where we started when we began talking to the women as they revealed their stories. As they talked to us our understanding of the word "spiritual" evolved and emerged from their stories. We encourage the readers of this volume to take the same path.

All over the world people have been inspired to think deeply about the mysterious force that gives us energy, hope, and courage to live through the most difficult circumstances. In Paleolithic times, long before writing evolved, images of the divine often took feminine shapes. Even today, though we may have forgotten the precise meaning these images had for their creators, they still imbue a sense of awe and intuitive connection to the power of life and the will to live.

Women on every continent are starting to come back to these ancient images and to connect their spirituality to the strength and energy flowing from the god and goddess symbols. Aboriginal groups all over the world, including Canadian

First Nations, are attempting to revitalize the spiritual traditions of ancient times through dance, song, and story.

But among those groups where writing evolved, the story of creation, the meaning of life, God's plan for us, and the divine rules and laws were committed to sacred texts. Today we recognize, amongst many others, five major religious streams with written traditions: Islam, Christianity, Judaism, Hinduism, and Buddhism. Within each of these there are countless regional and cultural variations. Each religion is set in a particular social environment satisfying the unique needs of the people adhering to its tenants. Sacred scripts are interpreted and reinterpreted into laws and codes of conduct. These provide guidelines for appropriate social behaviour. They describe the role of genders, for example, "the honourable man" and "the good woman," as well as the hierarchy within the family structure including the child's place and other culture-specific role definitions.

All world religions share this belief and transform it through their sacred writings into an understandable text by which we interpret reality. Which part of the world we live in, which age we are born in, what gender we are born to, what society and culture we share, and what religious beliefs we adhere to all influence our behaviour. Priests, imams, ministers, rinpoches, gurus, rabbis, elders, and other religious leaders have put their spin on the sacred texts by interpreting and translating them into rules and guidelines to shape our spiritual awareness and growth and our understanding of our place and role in the world as men and as women. All major religions have over time adopted patriarchal structures. As a result, the position of women has been universally devalued often contrary to the wisdom of the sacred texts.

Today, most of the world religions are headed by men. Women have increasingly been placed in a subservient role in terms of the religious hierarchical structure and in the family order as well. If spiritual leaders, decision makers, and the wider population would take it upon themselves to revisit and read the scriptures, sacred texts, and other ancient primary sources, placing this information in the context of the times, they might be surprised by the status, power, and influence of women throughout history. Most of us do not do that very often. And so women all over the world have absorbed the message that they are less valued than men and that women are at fault if family life does not succeed or if it turns violent. Female infanticide, abortion of female fetuses, circumcision of female children, the deliberate rape of women during war, and many other systemic abuses and violent acts against women demonstrate their lesser worth. Such systemic and accepted abuse of women creates a mind-set that easily triggers domestic abuse.

Many women have told us of their spiritual anguish in the midst of experiencing spousal violence. The comfort that they hope to derive from their faith communities and their religious leaders is often missing. Cases of family violence are often seen as blights on the good reputation and on the image that religious or cultural communities have of themselves. Women who have experienced abuse in a relationship often feel excluded, ashamed, and powerless, unable to access the help and support they need. It is telling in this context, that only 2.5 percent of spousal abuse survivors stated, in a recent research report,* that they had sought spiritual guidance.

THE WOMEN'S MOVEMENT

All over the world, the bodies of women have been much maligned, often being thought of as a possession for the pleasure of men. Women have become increasingly alienated from their bodies that tragically are often the target for male

---

* Safer Cities Initiatives, Edmonton Police Service & Community and Family Services, 1994, *Family Violence: Follow-Up Team Implementation/Expansion Phase Research Report and Findings*, Edmonton: City of Edmonton.

aggression. *Hurt a woman's body and you erase her spirit.* One might wonder if this is the underlying motive behind spousal abuse.

Yet, many believe that the body is the seat of the divine spark in us. The women's movement has re-appropriated the female body for women and fostered an awakening of the female spirit within. Spiritual awakening begins with the recognition of the body as essentially good. This awakening allows a woman to centre herself, to listen in quietness to her inner voice, to affirm her worth as a member of the community of beings.

We often perceive the body, mind, and spirit as separate entities, but they could also be seen as parts of an integrated whole. Their boundaries are permeable. A defiled body can be consecrated by the purifying power of spirit. From classical Greece comes the story of the goddess Hera. The legend tells how each year the goddess bathed in a sacred stream and thus recovered her virginity, her state of purity. In many religions sacred water symbolizes the purifying and pacifying power of the spirit.

The belief in a spiritual self helps us to see ourselves, as well as others, as worthwhile persons irrespective of social and physical identity. When people do not focus on their spiritual selves, they often feel they have no inherent worth. This sometimes translates into feeling that they are "nobody" or "nothing." Their abusers also tend to treat them with contempt. Often, even the people who care, think that nothing can help the abused woman because she lacks hope and courage.

Family violence can only be fully overcome when women everywhere take their place next to men as full spiritual partners and are recognized as equals in religious organizations. This book is intended to raise awareness of a woman's spiritual needs during the period of violence, so that women's shelters, faith communities, service providers, and health professionals can understand her pain and longing and can think about the contributions they can make towards her healing.

In the face of Canada's multicultural nature, the protection of privacy laws and the respect for all religious persuasions have acted in tandem to draw a veil over the issue of spiritual needs of victims and survivors of family violence in shelters. Shelter workers find themselves ill prepared to deal with the vast array of beliefs of the women in their care. Religious groups may find it difficult to locate their followers in a shelter. The women themselves may find it impossible to reach out to their faith community in the midst of crisis, when safety issues, children's needs, financial considerations, and legal implications are foremost in their minds.

ABORIGINAL INSPIRATION

Through our collective experience, we have begun to realize the wisdom and healing Aboriginal people have achieved through their myths, ceremonies, and spiritual traditions. We have all been inspired by Native women's shelters where older women in the community (and sometimes elders*) contribute to a woman's spiritual growth beyond the experience of violence.

Aboriginal communities in Canada have long recognized that women who experience violence and abuse need balance and harmony. Treatment involves the whole person, the body, the mind, the emotions, and the spirit. Consulting elders, story telling, and healing circles are all integrated into the healing process of the individual woman. Healing includes the woman, her family, and her community. This process often occurs during the time that she may be finding sanctuary in a shelter. Even in mainstream shelters an elder may be called in to assist a Native woman in her journey. Her spiritual aspects are seen as central pathways to healing and as a way of reconnecting the woman to herself, her family, and her community.

---

* An "elder," in the context of this book, refers to a learned and acknowledged spiritual leader or a person of considerable influence within a specific Native community. An elder is considered, by the community, to be "one who knows."

The example of the Aboriginal communities initiatives, in these instances, has inspired us to attempt to come to terms with the spiritual needs of other shelter users who do not have the privilege to have an elder or a community to draw on.

WOMEN'S SHELTERS IN TRANSITION

When we attempted to address the question of what was missing in the helping and healing process, we kept coming back to the issue of spirituality. But we had to ask ourselves, "Who can accompany the women in the shelters on their journey to spiritual growth?" Shelter staff have been trained in crisis intervention and appropriate empowering methods. But shelter workers have enough demands on their time without adding another responsibility to their duties. Further, one must not lose sight of another very important point. Each woman's spirituality, both the shelter worker's as well as that of the abused woman, is such an intensely personal experience that anyone not specifically trained in spiritual counselling might shy away even from trying. Then there are the multitude of beliefs, customs, and rituals that colour the tapestry of Canadian religious life and that can discourage exploration by even the most courageous among us. Apprehension about creating misunderstandings (or being misunderstood) or of intruding on a woman's privacy hinders the worker's efforts to help empower a woman to get to safe ground. Does the helping process even allow for recognition of a woman's cultural and spiritual needs? Should it?

In the last few decades, public awareness of the magnitude of family violence in Canada has increased substantially. The Royal Commission Report on Family Violence in Canada of 1993 publicly addresses this issue. This report initially resulted in additional funding for shelters from private organizations and from government departments. Administrative services were put in place and, initially, governments contributed substantially to the operations of women's shelters. With government involvement levels of education and training for shelter workers rose with simultaneous increases in complexity of administration and reporting lines within the sheltering organizations. What started as a self-help movement of women helping women has, over the past quarter century, become a complex web of organizations ruled by policies, procedures, union agreements, and a bureaucracy to operate it. This is not to downgrade the necessity for, or achievements of, women's shelters. Their underlying strength is their continuing commitment towards providing safety and empowerment for those experiencing violence in relationships.

The first shelters were operated by women helping other women, many involving coalitions of church groups, social service agencies, and philanthropic organizations. The shelter movement historically evolved from women's growing understanding of their position in society. Legal and counselling services are provided, often on a voluntary basis, by caring individuals and organizations. The community at large has donated both time within the shelters and valuable goods for shelter shops, which assist the women to get a material head start. As a result of this widespread movement and the exposure of the underlying problem, fewer men and women are now willing to condone spouses being abused in the place that should be the safest place on earth, the home.

With more research into the roots of family violence it has become clear that all levels of Canadian society are affected; rich and poor, rural and urban, new and established. This systemic problem needs the broadest societal commitment in order to be rectified.

BRIDGING THE SECULAR AND THE SPIRITUAL

But where does the victim's spirituality fit in? A few very fundamental steps could open a whole new world of understanding between shelter workers and women in an abusive situation. For instance, in shelters and in counselling agencies a worker could address the woman's cultural and spiritual background. Does she want to talk about it? Can someone from her faith community be contacted? Is there some culturally appropriate reading, music, or relaxation technique that might help? Is there a quiet room available to her for prayer or reflection?

The ancient concept of sanctuary could also be drawn on. In many religions a person could be protected from persecution or pursuit by surrendering to the Divine in a sacred place. In today's secular world, a shelter offers physical safety. It offers an environment conducive to reducing confusion, fear, and anxiety. But it seldom offers help that allows a woman to focus on her inner self. Can shelters also become sanctuaries that bridge the secular and spiritual worlds?

The following stories tell us, in the voices of women who have survived family violence and in the voices of those who come from a variety of faith communities and in the voices of those shelter workers who care, that we are joined by the invisible bond of the same spirit that makes us sing and dance and cry and laugh all in different ways, all in the same ways.

The Women's Stories

Where Does Strength
Come From?

2

We learn from each other. It is our collective experience that gives us wisdom. By listening to the women who are willing to share their stories in *Lifelines,* we hope that each of us can draw from their strength when we need it. The stories presented here are told by individual women, each one drawing on her own inner strength to cope with, or leave, an abusive relationship.

The idea for *Lifelines* was preceded by several workshops and conferences that identified a need, a missing link, in the intervention and treatment of women who had experienced or were experiencing family violence. These previous events and consultations indicated that the cultural and spiritual needs of abused women were not fully understood and were not being adequately addressed by service providing agencies and religious institutions.

We talked to and listened to people from different cultural and religious backgrounds, and in the process undertook a qualitative and informal study on culture, spirituality, and family violence. We set out to discover where inner strength comes from in the women faced with abusive situations. Six of the major faiths represented in our diverse Canadian population—Aboriginal, Buddhist, Christian, Hindu, Jewish, and Muslim—are the focus of our conversations. We learned that many women draw upon inner spiritual resources, some from formalized religious teaching, others from cultural experiences.

Women Who Wrote Their Stories

Old things, unnamed, lie strong
across my heart.
This is from where my strength
comes.

Adrienne Rich
Sources *(1984)*

To collect women's stories for our study, our first step was to offer a free writing course, through the Faculty of Extension at the University of Alberta, to any woman who had suffered deep pain in a personal relationship and who wanted to write her story. Posters were placed where people from different cultures and religions gathered.

About fifteen women initially responded and came to the first class. They were told that some of the stories would be included in *Lifelines* and that parts of others would be mentioned as well. During the course of the writings it became apparent that those whose chose to tell their stories were predominantly Christian and born in Canada. If we were to get representation from the immigrant community, including other religions, we would also need to create an environment where women could tell us their stories rather than attempt to write them. It was evident that those whose first language was other than English were not totally comfortable writing about their experiences in English.

The second stage included extensive interviews. These were arranged through the same agencies that had put us in touch with those who took the writing course, generally organizations that were service providers in the community.

As a result we eventually used a poem, four written stories and four spoken stories. Some of the women dropped out of the course along the way and some asked for their interviews to be withdrawn from publication. Others requested that substantial parts be deleted either because they were too personal or because they might appear judgmental or condemning to readers unfamiliar with certain cultural beliefs and practices.

In Guyana, where Clare grew up, God was white. Being white was where it was at. Clare says, "This suggestion of racial superiority instilled in me a devaluing of myself and my own race, my people. I grew up with this confusion, feeling that being 'white' was something which I had to aspire to."

Diane, who grew up in Alberta, was not subjected to any religious influences as she grew up. She remembers envying friends who were raised in Christian households and feeling that she was missing something, that she was an outsider. As a young married woman she found herself in a foreign country, isolated from family and friends, with an abusive husband and no emotional support. Her mother-in-law, a witness to the abuse, was herself a victim of her son's rampages. She simply counselled her daughter-in-law to pray. When Diane told her she had no God, her mother-in-law responded by saying that it did not matter and gave her a prayer book, written in Spanish, which was intended especially for abused wives. In it were prayers asking God to help the wife change as the abuse she suffered at the hands of her husband was her fault.

Pushpa's childhood in India, along with her education at exclusive girls' boarding schools and university, prepared her for a life of privilege. At age twenty-one she had everything—youth, beauty, economic freedom, and a prestigious position. After immigrating to Canada, many things changed for Pushpa. Her husband, unemployed, powerless, and lonely himself, began to exercise power over Pushpa and soon was a stranger to her. She became just another "visible minority woman" trying to make ends meet, alone. Pushpa says, "I have been deeply lonely and I have had to struggle alone." Finding the goddess and identifying and trusting her inner strength has paved a new path for Pushpa.

Nineteen years old, with a newborn baby, Francine trusted and respected all adults. Adults were always right. Her marriage was going to last forever. Ten years later, Francine was on her own with three young children. Her abusive husband had left her for a woman eleven years younger than she was. She had never had a job because she was not supposed to work outside the home. She had barely finished high school when she married.

After her husband left, Francine had to work as a waitress in the evenings so she could be home during the day with her youngest child. Her problems did not end there. Her second husband, now in prison for his crime, sexually assaulted her young son for two and a half years without her knowledge. Francine says, "I continue to suffer the pain of not being accepted in my community and my church because of my feelings towards this man."

An abusive husband tells his wife Nadia that she is overweight and unattractive and that nobody would want her. Yet he gets jealous if she is friendly towards another man. He tells her, "I have no problems with sex. It must be your problem. There's something wrong with you if you're not getting anything out of it."

He then rapes her in a drunken oafish way. He wants her to stop dancing because it is "exhibitionistic." But dancing is not just a hobby for her. It is her career, her identity. She is a dancer. This is the kind of emotional and physical abuse Nadia suffered in her marriage relationship.

These are just a few of the stories told by a group of women meeting Saturday mornings to talk and write about how they found the strength to go on during times of adversity. Most of us expect to find safety and privacy within the family unit. When it betrays us, feelings of isolation, loneliness, sadness, and bewilderment result. Where did these women find the strength to go on? What helped? To whom or what did they turn? Was the church or faith community there for them?

Some are still trying to make sense of what happened to them. One of the women in the group says organized religion was not part of her childhood or adult experience. She came because she wanted to figure out what it was that helped her survive. For some women the very idea of going for help and spiritual affirmation to someone in the church is foreign.

Clare says that although she was Catholic, it did not count because she was not "white." She did not even think of turning to anyone in the religious community for help when her family was in crisis. Even though her mother was "the backbone of the church," the church was still a somewhat alienating place. It was a place for important people—white people—not a place where Clare would think of going with her problems.

When she did finally talk to her parish priest, she soon realized that to question him on anything he said or did was a sin. And when he spoke to her it was in a condescending manner. She felt like a five-year-old child. He did not acknowledge her as a grown mature person. This made Clare very angry and she writes:

> A person is better off examining their doubt
> God is within myself
> is not a person
> not a he
> and not white

Francine spoke bitterly about seeking help in her religious community. She felt rejected because she was not willing to forgive her husband. She says that she eventually made a conscious decision—by herself—not to let hurt overcome her.

> I did not want to become someone twisted with bitterness and self-pity... I have cried many rivers... I have sat in the darkness outside under a blanket of stars and cried and pleaded with God....After many sessions out there on the deck, seemingly talking to myself, I have received peace and serenity.... I can still love! I don't hate. What a wonderful uplifting feeling...

Several women expressed the sentiment that they survived in spite of the church. They had received the distinct message that maintaining the forms of religion was more important than dealing with individual needs.

Nadia says she always felt odd in her Ukrainian National Orthodox church. It was an overtly patriarchal and traditional religion (although she certainly never got this idea from her father). The church was full of third generation Ukrainians.

When Nadia takes her daughter to be christened in the Orthodox church (carefully chosen by her mother), the priest stops her at the door murmuring politely, "Please wait here and I will call you. No, you may not come in yet, not until the holy sacrament of baptism has been completed." Nadia, remembering this as if it is happening again, writes:

> He takes the baby from my arms and leads everybody into the sanctuary. I am left alone in the anteroom numb and unbelieving. Suddenly I am sick and hot with incredulous fury. No one even said anything!

Only after the holy sacrament of baptism is completed is Nadia invited to enter:

> He says a prayer over me and brings me right in, up to the steps. I kneel on the stairs, he says some other prayer, he puts his hand on my head. Then I am allowed to go up the steps right to the doors of the ikonostasis, and pick up my child from the floor where he has placed her in another bit of symbolism I am beyond trying to understand.

This alienating aspect of the church, in which unspoken rules seem to dominate, often at the expense of people's feelings, was common to many stories.

And yet this same woman is haunted by the majestic liturgy in the traditional church and remembers stories of strong Ukrainian poets in the Ukraine, one of whom was a woman. They were revered. Only recently has she realized that her father was an artist like herself.

Charlotte writes:

> i was brought up by people with answers
> when I was asked later for my questions
> i had none on my tongue they were buried
> deep in my soul
> and inquiring through my body
> my questions without words
> for whose language
> i had only a child's dictionary
> whose fury both infuriated me
> and made me afraid
> they wanted out
> i feared consequences

It soon became apparent that not one woman in this group could express satisfaction or had a positive story to tell concerning religion's role in her recovery, survival, journey towards understanding—or healing. Nobody could name anyone from a religious fellowship or community who had helped her. Nobody could say that a priest, minister, sheik, or holy person had been there for them. No woman wrote about a person in the faith community to which they belonged simply listening to them without judgment. No one spoke or wrote about ever being encouraged to tell what had happened to them. They did not appear to encounter any spiritual leaders who were aware of the healing component of telling one's story. One woman's defiant words illustrate this point.

I want to tell one story.
Mine.
I want an audience, here in the same room,
the person here to listen to me.

She spoke of never having had a connection with a faith community. She says she had to find her own spiritual way, that it was within herself that she found strength and power. That was where she had to find it, in the absence of all other help.

The most positive comment concerning the church's influence on a woman's life came from someone not in the Saturday morning group. Laura had joined a Mennonite church as an adult and was able to tell her story of abuse to the congregation on a Sunday morning. Laura readily admitted that she was able to do this from her secure position within the fold, where she was an active respected person. She didn't think she would have been able to do it had she not been an insider or if the abuse she suffered as a child had occurred at the hands of someone in the church.

Laura spoke of being well connected, her parents-in-law being church stalwarts, when she first began attending. Perhaps, she speculated, it was easier for church members to accept her and therefore, much later, her story. Besides having relatives in the congregation, she and her husband have two children. They both work as teachers, they are traditional, a known and acceptable entity. They socialize with other young couples in the congregation.

The church community has provided Laura with many opportunities she otherwise would not have had. She has learned about music and history and has grappled with faith issues. Laura has good friends in the church, friends of different generations, belongs to women's groups, and thinks it is a positive place for her kids. It is a meaningful place for her. But she sees how this comfortable place she is in is also a weakness of the church, that "we minister only to the strong, we preach to the converted."

Many of these women "hit rock-bottom" before turning to spiritual help. Pushpa, who thinks that religion hurts women, spoke of being dazzled by the beauty and rituals of the Catholic Church at a young age. She married a Hindu and forgot all about religion when she was happy lecturing and having children. But her marriage soon dissolved, and after difficult lonely years in a new country she considers herself to be a skeptic—says she tries to "cover all the bases." Pushpa has since found her own spiritual self through reading ancient Hindu philosophy and learning about the goddesses.

It seems as if almost all these women, alone and desperate, had no alternative but to call on some inner reserve of strength. Nonetheless, almost all of them wrote that, in situations of extreme danger or anxiety or depression, what stands out in their memories are the small human kindnesses and the slightest indication that others validated their actions. Diane, desperate and alone in Mexico, after eight years with an abusive partner, found the strength to begin her long journey back to Canada after talking to two women friends. Rhonda remembers a kind word from her normally emotionally-absent mother. Lorna remembers being held in the arms of a mother or mother-figure. Pushpa remembers and misses powerful figures in her past, her mother-in-law, her mother, and mother India.

Asked what they would have needed in their times of deepest despair, several women mentioned "naming." Charlotte, an abused lesbian, says it this way:

> what I needed was a Namer, someone
> who had the power to name
> my story, every time my church said
> i was an issue not a person.
> i needed someone to remember. i have a name
> i wanted the homophobia to stop
> hurting words
> pervert
> sinner

All the women, without exception, expressed wrath. Their words were:

anger
hatred
rage
fury
resentment
darkness

They are angry at their abusers and they are angry and disappointed about how their faith communities failed them. They are not done, not done telling, not done making changes, not done finding their strength. After an angry outburst one woman says, "Collect myself. Centre myself. I know I don't have to keep feeling this way." Another admits:

I shake inside.
It actually chokes me to try to bring my feelings to the surface.

They are tired of being victims. In response to an Adrienne Rich poem, Charlotte writes:

if i am "wood with a gift for burning"
i choose to be the burning bush
that confounded Moses
if i were to suggest we burn all those
bits of the old rugged cross beloved
of those who would hang on to an
instrument of torture rather than
rejoice at an empty tomb
i might well be the wood
of a dory cast adrift
and gain all the moods of the sea
for my lover

Many spoke of loneliness and aloneness. Their problem was often perceived, by these women and by their families, as a private matter. Some even kept it a secret, alone. Some initially blamed themselves for what happened. But all got beyond that. Many discovered inner strength, often because they were so completely desperate there was no alternative.

Almost all recalled a specific incident concerning their abuse, a single vivid horrific encounter that became the central image for what happened to them. Certainly all remembered a single person, a being who abused them, often wanting to confront this person with words. Clare describes, in a letter to her father, what happened forty years ago:

> Daddy!
> It's so good to see you. All these years I have been holding this terror inside of me,...

Writing it down, telling her life story, has been therapeutic for Clare. After the writing class one day, Clare says that she feels like she was freeing up her feelings while writing the letter. She says that it felt good, that she was touching on something she had tucked away deep inside. Clare now thinks that she must revisit her trauma and speak with (write to) the other characters about this incident.

Many of the women in the writing class tell of seeking refuge and finding meaning in artistic pursuits such as painting, dancing, or music. However, although these women continue to experience despair over unresolved pain from time to time—"I am a lamb of your flock yet lost"—most are also experiencing feelings of calm mature acceptance.

In Answer to Psalms 55

i find people like me
brave spirits

Charlotte

Give ear to my prayer O God...
attend unto me and hear me
i make a noise
and wings of a dove
when i was 13
i was a boy soprano
i sang O for the wings of a dove
in my boy soprano voice
the song has often been with me
on difficult days
i have always loved the psalms
they so often railed at the Holy One
demanded that if this be love
that love be manifest
if this be power great enough to save
that it save those singing for help
or look like a fool and a braggart
and a liar

"O for the wings
for the wings of a dove
far away far away would i roam"
i have roamed far way
half way around the world away
from family
from the quintessential Canadian
church of the middle road
to a global church
started by hurting-people like me
people on the margins of the middle road
in the middle of the road
i find people like me
brave spirits
who walk and have time
to wonder at a dove
what it might feel
like to have wings of a dove…

Charlotte

Why Is God White?

Experiencing loneliness is
a good thing for me. It gives me
time to focus on my life's journey—
a journey I will take alone.

Clare

*Clare was born in Guyana and
has a Master's degree in
theological studies. She is now in
her middle years and has lived
in Canada for some time.*

Clare's letter to her dead father…

18 November 1995

Daddy!

It is so good to see you. All these years I have been holding this
terror inside of me, it was ripping my insides apart. I was terrified of
you. I was afraid of your terrible abusive temper.

I remember clearly the day when you invited the neighbours over to
our house, telling them to sit down; then you called Mummy and told
her to sit down. We were in our sitting room. I was about nine or ten
years old. Do you remember why you invited these people over? Well I
do. Your reason for inviting these people over was to whip my brother.
Yes, you remember him. He was the eldest of your children. We called
him Stevie. You whipped and whipped and whipped him. Yes, I was
looking on and I was hurting inside. I wanted God to kill you right then

because I was hurting inside for what you were doing to my brother. He was crying and you would not stop beating him.

Yes, you remember these people were sitting there and looking on. No one said a word. They were adults, grown up people who could have held you down and taken the whip away from you, but they did nothing. When Stevie was almost to the point of death, I heard Mummy say—do you remember what she said?—I remember it clearly. She said, "Paulo! (as that is what she called you) are you going to kill him now?" That was when you stopped beating Stevie. Do you remember?

I have developed a hatred toward you over all these years for what you did to my brother. Do you remember why you beat Stevie? I do. He and other students went to visit a war frigate which came into port in the Demerara River. During this visit he fell and the white suit he was wearing got very dirty from the grease on the ship deck. He came home and told you what had happened. This beating that you gave him was your response to his falling and getting his clothes dirty.

Why did you become so cruel? I remember the good days we had together, when I was much younger. I believe these good days lasted until I was about seven years old. After that you became a tyrant. I had to protect myself from you and your very bad temper, so I erected a wall between myself and you. I became very hardened, had no emotions in my dealings with you.

I am glad that I had this time with you today and you seem to be willing to have further visits with me. This is only the beginning.

So long...until next time...

Clare

God was white where I grew up. So was the Virgin Mary, so was the Baby Jesus. In my country, Guyana, the leaders of the church were all from the mother country, England. Every single priest and bishop who ministered at the church was white. I could see just by looking at them, and at the pictures and statues in the church, that being white was where it was at. This evidence of racial superiority instilled in me a devaluing of myself and my own race, my people. I grew up confused about the message—the greatness of being white—always feeling I was inferior because I was not of the right colour. This devaluing of self was continually reinforced as everything in the church pointed to the ideology of a white God. Being white was something I had to aspire to become.

My childhood memories centre around growing up in a home which was a patriarchal bastion. My father was the sole authority in the household. He fervently believed that his children must grow up to become independent people.

In his misguided efforts to ensure this, he became very abusive and violent towards us, his children and his wife.

I remember that it was a sin to question my parish priest on anything that he said or did. He was the supreme being whose every word I had to believe. When I told the priest years later about the beatings my husband gave me, he spoke to me as if I were a five-year-old child. He did not acknowledge me as a grown mature person. This made me very angry. He is encouraged by the authority of his position—to treat me as a child.

Expressing my anger, in the company of my women and men friends has been a liberating process for me. I came to recognize and appreciate my mother's strength and influence rather late in life. I began to realize that the strength I have now came from seeing my mother raise eight children. She had to be a strong woman to do this job for which she sacrificed her profession as a teacher. Her home became her classroom, where she toiled to feed, clothe, and house eight children and a husband. This was no easy feat. Yet she did it all with such calmness and dignity. She had to be a strong person inside in order to do this. Her inner strength is what kept her going. My strength comes from her, my one and only mother.

If I am lonely now it is because I choose to be lonely. I came into this world alone and I will be leaving it alone. Experiencing loneliness is a good thing for me. It gives me time to focus on my life's journey—a journey I will take alone.

I am tormented and angered by those of us who sit and watch our fathers abuse our mothers or any of our brothers or sisters and do nothing about it, those of us who go to church and follow the teachings of the church without questioning these teachings, those of us who abuse our children so that our children will adhere to the rules, those of us who feel that we are superior to other people, those of us who preach that one race is more intelligent than another, those of us who decide what is good for other people, those of us who decide how much money a family needs to live in poverty, and those to whom we relinquish our dignity.

But maybe, just maybe—those of us who detest patriarchy and all it stands for, those of us who long for the good old days, those of us who long for a society to be made up of more caring people, those of us who long to give expression to our feelings, those of us who want to be responsible for our own lives, those of us who are tired of being told what they must do, those of us who are fed up with feeling that things are hopeless, those of us who demand to be free of oppression, those of us who know what it is to be voiceless, those of us who want to help others find their voice, those of us who demand to be listened to—can make a difference. Those of us who have suffered abuse in the hands of our loved ones, those of us who have survived, and those who have silently witnessed must speak out now.

Clare

Escape

Diane

Diane, who is thirty-one years old, was born in Canada in a small town in Alberta. She has a university degree in nursing.

Writing about this feels good.
It's empowering to write it down,
It gives me some kind of strength,
Almost with every word I feel my ball of light,
my self, showing through
The darkness almost gone.

I remember the first time I was raped by my husband, although I wouldn't have called it rape back then. In fact I wouldn't have called it rape until I found the strength to leave this relationship. It was just after Easter 1988. I had injured my back at work, nursing, and was on workers' compensation. I had been prescribed Tylenol #3's but couldn't take them because the codeine made me ill. So I was in absolute agony as the injury involved some fractured vertebrae and torn muscles all along the lower back. When my husband got home from work, he wanted to have sex with me. I refused, said I was in too much pain. He said it was my duty, his right, that if I didn't he'd get it somewhere else. He told me it would make me feel better. Then he called me names, sometimes screaming at me, sometimes almost in tears, telling me I was such a cow, so fat, I disgusted him, how could anyone be turned on by me. This went on for hours, his ranting and raving and threatening body language with raised arms, fists, throwing blankets and pillows. He never accepted that I was in excruciating pain. When I said I had a right to say no, he said, no I didn't, I was his wife, I did not have that right any more.

Sobbing, I just let go; he fucked me, not paying attention to my pain, to the fact that I could hardly breathe through my tears and my pain. He enjoyed it, he was smiling, he got off on my pain. After he was finished he berated me for being a rag doll in bed, then he left to shower and watch TV. I'm not sure how to describe how I felt; totally violated, raped, insignificant, useless, worthless, filled with rage, an impotent rage, helpless, lonely, hopelessly ashamed. I cried all night long. I had to take a codeine pill even with the horrible side effects. Finally as the sun came up, I dozed for an hour or so.

I could tell no one about this. My family was against this marriage. I couldn't tell them. My friends? By this time I had none. He had started to isolate, me and I only had work and him. I knew it would happen again and it did. Even if I needed to wake up at 5:30 A.M. to go work a twelve-hour shift on a heavy surgical ward, he would rant and rave and carry on, screaming, turning on all the lights until, if I didn't give in, I was going to work with no sleep. After I gave in, I couldn't sleep. There were too many tears, too much pain, a lot of emotional agony.

I was diagnosed with cervical cancer that same summer. He didn't want sex then because the discharge of dead cancer cells sloughing off through my vagina really turned him off, but the day after the first treatment, he demanded a blow job. I was twenty-three years old. I had just had a treatment for cancer, not just an abnormal pap smear, and I was worried that it was still there. After all the same bullshit, I just couldn't fight it. I had to do this revolting act. The same thing happened after I needed the laser treatment when the chemotherapy treatment didn't work. At this same time a doctor found some abnormal lumps on my spine, and I was booked for a bone scan. The doctor told me it might be a malignant tumour. At this point I was firmly convinced that I had cancer which had metastasized. I worked with dying cancer patients—I knew that this was it—I was dying. I was not going to live to the age of twenty-five.

I went through various emotional stages and came to an acceptance of my imminent death. I knew that the six to eight months I had just lived through and the next two years were for a purpose. I was to learn something for my next chance on this planet. I needed to suffer these rapes to learn something. I felt this because the cancer and the rapes were occurring at the same time. After six weeks, I received the results of the bone scan, and it was not cancer on my spine. The laser treatment on my cervix was a success. Of course I still needed pap smears four times a year, but I was not going to die.

All through this black period of my life he sexually assaulted me several times a week. I dealt with this by going somewhere else in my mind, by leaving my body. Sometimes I would be with a fantasy man, sometimes I would be flying through the clouds, and sometimes I would be mountain climbing or skydiving. Sometimes, if I was totally exhausted, I would be able to get to that place of nothingness. This was the best place to be. It was peaceful. Accepting. Then sometimes I needed to be experiencing pain in my mind, the injury, the surgical treatments, breaking my arm when I was five years old. And sometimes I was not able to do any of this. I was there being raped by my husband. Crying. He seemed to enjoy these times most of all.

Why didn't I leave then? I don't know. I was young. There was the shame and embarrassment of being in this situation. The isolation. I started to believe all the terrible things he was saying to me. Maybe I really was fat and ugly and stupid and no one would want me. And so on. This treatment continued until the last time I saw him in July 1995. There are many more instances that really stick out in my mind, but they are still very painful for me.

I'm out of this now and will never experience these assaults again, not by him, not by anyone. Writing about all this feels good. I want to know that someone will read it and know. I need to tell people, but not yet the people who are close to me. It's still very painful for me. It's empowering to write it down. It gives me some kind of strength, almost with every word I feel my ball of light, my self, showing through. The darkness is almost gone. Still, I can't helping remembering. There is so much more to my story.

DIANE'S STORY CONTINUES....

I moved to Mexico with my husband and young daughter, realizing immediately that I had made a big mistake, that the situation was intolerable and wasn't going to get better. My husband was in a big legal entanglement which had taken all our money. He forced me to call my father and uncle for money. He threatened me, saying that I didn't love him if I wouldn't do this for him. I felt enraged and trapped, full of hatred for him. I knew I had to get out at the first opportunity, but that it wouldn't be easy. His family acted like my jailer. I had to watch everything I said.

I had told no one, least of all my family, how I felt, because of my horrible shame. When my visa was ready to expire in May, I thought maybe I'd have a chance to escape, to leave with his blessing. But the day before it expired, he insisted on one more trip to the visa office and they granted me my visa. I was heartbroken. I had been up all night packing in anticipation of having to leave (I would have had to leave right from the visa office). He attributed my flat mood to tiredness from having been up all night. I continued to try to make the relationship work, but the next few months were terrible.

I had no money. Christina and I subsisted on beans and tortillas while he remained well fed on fish and beer. When I told him he couldn't treat Christina and me like this, he screamed, threw things, broke things. He insulted me in front of his family and withheld money for food. I had to watch what I said and did or my kid wouldn't eat. He told me I could leave—by myself—but not with Christina.

I was comfortable only with two women friends and their families, but I didn't tell them until three days before I left. I simply wasn't ready to share my story because, I think, I needed a window to see that I could get out first. On July 16, Juan flew to Vancouver on business. I had been encouraging him to leave to make some money. He hugged and kissed his brother good-bye and touched my arm good-bye. I wasn't important. This was the last time I saw him.

After he was gone I had more freedom to see my friends. Visit, swim, go to the beach. I was still pretty restricted with my in-laws around. Juan had tried to stop me from spending time even with them. I had no money and had to beg for food from my brother-in-law. It was the most humiliating experience of my life, having to ask his family for money for groceries. To top it off, his brother was always trying to hit on me. My friends brought me stuff. They sensed what was going on even though I still wasn't ready to talk.

On Wednesday, August 2, my mother-in-law, Madeline, and my niece, Lori, left to go to a village in the mountains where many of the relatives lived. As they were walking to the bus, I told her I was going to miss her, not realizing how true that would be or how definite. I was alone in the house.

I went out with Margie and her daughter Karina that day and then they came over to my place. We had a conversation which began about other people in unhealthy relationships and slowly, after a couple of cups of coffee, I started to disclose some of the things that I had been living through. Margie just listened and encouraged me to continue. After awhile I was silent and Margie looked at me and said that this was a window and I could take it or wait for the next one to happen. The next chance might be a long time coming.

I started to shake at the truth of it. This was my only chance. Juan was in Vancouver and my mother-in-law was in El Chante. I had known it before I ever started talking to her. After she left, I was very frightened but quite sure of myself. I began to take a mental inventory of my belongings, of what I would be able to take with me on a plane. If I took a plane I would be safe in a few hours but have nothing to my name but a suitcase of clothes, nothing to start a new life. If I drove I could sell the car. I called my father in Alberta and he encouraged me to drive, although I had no insurance. He told me I could do it.

By the time Margie came back, I had made up my mind. I knew I had two days to wait as my husband was sending me money. I had to wait for it as I had nothing. I felt as if I had been hit, shocked. Never in this time did I think of seeking out a pastor or priest for help. I didn't grow up in that environment. It didn't even cross my mind.

My friends both came over on Wednesday night and we had a big meeting. Thursday my brother-in-law was there so my friends rescued me and we went to the beach. The books were ready, the closet was organized. Christina sat in the sand playing while we made plans. Margie would drive as far as possible with me. Isabella was buying my TV. I couldn't believe that anyone would help me like this. We'd leave Friday night. By Friday the money from my husband hadn't arrived. I was totally devastated, wondering if I'd have enough to get out of the country, just buying gas and some food. I thought I wouldn't be able to leave. Margie gave me 500 pesos.

I had been shocked and then excited, but by Friday I was calm. The clothes were packed. Anything I could hide was hidden. Nothing was done in the kitchen because my relatives could show up at any moment. It was terrifying. Late in the afternoon, as the sun was going down, I locked the front gate and frantically, quietly began my final packing. I wasn't happy nor was I upset. I was very calm. Margie arrived around ten o'clock to help me load and pack stuff into the car. We had the car pulled up to the back door and were finished packing by midnight. Isabella came with money for the TV and VCR. All through this we had to make like we were having a female get together so my neighbouring relatives wouldn't think it was too strange. When everything was packed, I started losing it.

We wanted to leave around five in the morning, so I decided to try and sleep for a few hours. I lay awake unable to sleep. At five o'clock I gave the house keys to Margie, picked up my sleeping kid, and we left. We stopped at a market in Guadalajara and bought some things, like sandals for me and toys for Christina. We went to a restaurant bar and had a beer and some snacks and read over some road maps. From here on I'd be on my own. We stayed that night at her friend's house. The next day Christina and I drove away at 11:00 A.M. I was scared to death. Always, Juan had done the driving in Mexico. My goal was to get as far as Monterrey the first day. We didn't get that far, and ended up in a city called Zacatecas. By the time I was able to find a reasonably priced motel, it was 8:00 P.M. and very dark. I was exhausted and this was just my first day. At every gas station I had to be very careful not to get ripped off, either with gas or my belongings. The roads were only two-lane with lots of mountains and big trucks that passed on curves going uphill. Along this particular stretch of highway there were many little crosses at the side of the road, each one indicating that someone had died there. It was all enough to make me start to reconsider what I was doing.

The hotel I found did not have security parking so I did not sleep very well because I was worried about having the car stolen. Also the fear of just being alone, blond, in a hotel room in Mexico, obviously a traveller, never left me. We were on the road by 5:00 A.M. I was desperate to be out of the country that day. Near the border people started being more aggressive. There were several incidents, while driving through big cities, where street kids would rush up to the car when I was stopped at a red light. They do this to sell items or wash the windows for a few pesos. But the farther north I got, the bolder these youths became. It was hot, 35° C, impossible to drive with the windows rolled up. I started to run red lights if I could, just for my safety. These brutes would reach into the car and try to touch me, or try to take Christina out of her car seat or try to steal things, or try to open the doors. Being fluent in Spanish did not help me even when the *transitos* (transit police) were looking on. In fact they just smiled when I would yell at them to help me. They would probably get a cut on the take. This occurred not only at signal lights but at gas stations as well. I began to dread the need to stop for gas or food or even to rest for a few minutes. This day was definitely the longest scariest day of my life.

We reached Nuevo Laredo, the border city, at about 3:00 P.M. My fear earlier in the day was nothing compared to how I was feeling now. I was abducting my child out of Mexico, from her Mexican father, and it was close to 40° C. By the time I finally found the place to report that my car was leaving the country, I was a shaking stuttering mess. Fortunately I was able to blame a very cranky hot kid and the heat for this. They believed me. When I crossed the border I had 100 pesos left, plus $40 Canadian and $50 American.

Next I had to cross the U.S. border. I had no insurance, the plates were invalid, and there are international laws about leaving a country with a child without permission from the other parent. I did not even have to get out of the car. I made up a story about my husband having left ahead of me because of his work, and me following with the car and our belongings to join him in Vancouver. Everyone believed it. All the border patrol did was have the dogs sniff out my car. This was no small matter. My husband did drugs. I was frantic. Fortunately they found nothing and I was waved on.

As soon as I hit Laredo, Texas, I went to the first motel I could see. San Antonio was two hours away and it was only 4:30 P.M., but I could not drive any more. I was a basket case. I was exhausted, hot, and sweaty. Christina had had enough for one day too. I was so exhausted. I didn't feel I could make it to Colorado. I had continuing contact with my Dad, calling him about four or five more times. He encouraged me, telling me that I could do it, that I was strong, and that I was a good driver, but he didn't know what was going on. When I called my mother, she told me my husband had called her. I lost it. I thought I wasn't going to make it. He'd have a bulletin at the border. I was a criminal. I was breaking international laws. After calling Margie, I calmed down and started to feel better. Everything was okay until the car ran out of gas.

Christina had been an angel. When she became cranky or had a little tantrum, I still had the energy to deal with it lovingly. I still hadn't cashed a cheque and I was down to a few cents in the ashtray. The feeling of losing control, of helplessness was starting to cover my source of strength. I was almost out of gas and couldn't find a Western Union outlet to cash the cheque. Then Christina began to cry, then scream. I don't know what happened to me. Even now, months later, I still only partially understand what happened. I just started screaming at her. I slapped her. The look she gave me shattered me. There was a period of about 30 seconds when I couldn't think. All I saw was red rage. In that instant, I could almost understand child abuse. When you are so completely stressed out, all it takes is one more irritation and wham, you lose control. There is absolutely no excuse for what I did. I'm a adult and I hit a child. There was a red mark on her cheek for several minutes. I had to pull over, off the freeway, and found myself in a residential area, kind of lost. But I didn't care. I grabbed my child and just started to bawl. Maybe all the tensions of the trip, of leaving Juan, the dangers, no money, just all added up. I don't know, but I just held on to her for a long time and cried and cried.

Finally, I pulled myself together and we found a mall and wandered through it. I found a Western Union outlet. We now had money. Even though we were so close to home, I started to think that I should just stop the car and settle in Denver. I truly felt on this day that I could not continue. After a few collect calls to my parents and a friend, I gathered enough courage to continue.

Then, when I crossed into Montana about breakfast-time one day, the car just stopped. I was about to give up, feeling the tears coming. I told myself enough is enough, no more tears. I was almost home and I was going to make it. I lifted the hood of the car and waited for help. Eventually an older man stopped and offered to drive me to town. Even though I was afraid of what might happen, we hopped into the truck. He took me to a garage where a tow truck went to get my car. I found out that all that had happened was I had run out of gas. They adjusted the carburetor and changed the fuel filter, and that and the tow only cost me $60 US. I was shocked. They could have cheated me, but they didn't.

By this time in the journey, I knew something was protecting me. The universe was on my side. I felt like there was a protective bubble surrounding me. I could feel that it was constructed with love, from my friends, from Margie and Isabella in Mexico, from Alexis and Doreen and Douglas in Edmonton, from Lorraine on Saltspring Island, and maybe even from myself. By this time I knew that I would have to spend at least one more night on the road, but I was so tired, so tired. I made it to a place called Great Falls. The next morning we were driving at 6 A.M. I don't know what time it was when I approached the Canadian border. I think it was mid-morning. My fear was starting to build again. Another border with no documentation. I reeked of fear. I was so close to safety, but I had this one last obstacle. I gave them my same story that I had been telling everyone who wanted to know why I was travelling alone with this child. They believed me.

I was in Canada! I still had some way to go. My mind was very focused. Just be careful, drive, be careful, drive. I couldn't think of much else. At one point I looked down and saw I was driving 140 km per hour. Be careful, almost there, slow down, remember, no valid car registration, or insurance, or plates. Finally, finally, I drove into Red Deer city limits. Suddenly I was at my mom's house. I was safe. I'm safe, We are safe. I am so tired, so tired. My mom hugs me, gives me a beer, but I still feel the road under me. I cannot relax. In fact I'm hyper. Phone calls to everyone. Tears of relief from them. I am a loved woman, and I haven't felt this for years. I'm home. My source of strength is starting to shine through that dark blot in my chest. The eclipse is passing.

Once I was back, safe, my anger surfaced. I was full of rage. I hated him, for putting me in this position, for having to go to the welfare office, for everything that happened to me. I was desperate and humiliated, having to borrow money from my father. After awhile I was able to focus my rage. I could talk to my sisters, to my dad, to a counsellor. I was accepted as a client at Options for Women, a feminist organization for women re-entering the work force. I learned about self-esteem, assertiveness, safety, and abuse through BAS (Beyond Abuse Services) and through the YWCA. I was in group counselling. It was a safe place. I wasn't alone. It was very good being with other women. It helped to know I wasn't alone.

But lately I have experienced rock bottom lows and mixed up feelings about divorce. I guess I'll have to do a lot of the emotional work now. Part of me had been covered, eclipsed. My limit of being a nonperson had been reached. The more I saw of my inner self, the more I believed I could do it. My own power had been smothered by everything else. I do have a will of my own. I have begun to remember accomplishments in my life. I can do this on my own.

The biggest thing about an abusive situation is that you are isolated. You start believing you are alone. You get so fucked up. Isolated, in a downward spiral, you can't talk to anyone. Group counselling has been so good for me. There were nine other women there. It made it possible for me to keep going, possible to get a life.

You have to wait for an abused person to seek help. Otherwise she'll go back again and again. She has lost all control over her life so it has to be her decision to leave. It's a way of getting some control. People can help by listening. Don't judge her for not leaving. She'll get out when she's able. There are so many things to take into consideration before leaving. Money is a big one. Children. Guilt. Breaking up the family. Our society does this to us.

Diane

My Beautiful Golden Bones

Julia

*Julia, is a forty-five year old
woman who has found
Buddhism. She was born in
Edmonton and has two
university degrees.*

atti, atti, atti, my beautiful golden bones ...

Up until I was thirteen, I had a relatively happy balanced childhood. Then everything changed. My grandmother died and my grandfather, lost and grieving, was suddenly very much in our lives. He seemed to like me a lot, made a fuss over me, and I in turn put him on a pedestal. For a long time I had wanted a horse and he suddenly offered to buy me one. The horse was kept at his farm, so whenever I wanted to ride, I had to go out there.

On one of these visits the grandfather I had adored propositioned me. He kept at me all evening with comments like, "Why won't you do it with me? You do it with your boyfriends." This began around six o'clock in the evening and I was stuck in a chair at his house until midnight, with no way of escaping his demands. Before I left he threatened that he would go away if I told anyone. I didn't want to be responsible for further pain to my mother who had her own problems, which included grieving the loss of my grandmother, so when I got home I told no one about what had happened. My whole world had turned upside down.

I went through a period where I was very quiet. I acted normal if my grandfather was around for my mother's sake. He played on this for all it was worth. A couple of years later, when I was about fifteen, I pretended to be a difficult teenager, acting as if I felt that I had outgrown my relatives. When I was seventeen I told my mother. Her response was, "I can't believe it."

Shortly after this I left home and moved to Vancouver. There I experimented with marijuana, LSD, and other drugs. I dabbled in the occult just enough to know there was something scary there. If my parents had known what was going on in my head at that time (for instance, these entities trying to get into my body), they'd have had me committed.

My mother needed to talk about her feelings regarding my grandfather and told our relations what had happened. Our family was castigated by them. I went through hell because they all blamed me. Of course, my grandfather denied everything. Later, my grandfather's new wife accused me of making it all up. She said she would leave him if it was true. I didn't want my family to blame me again, so when she said this I cried and nodded, that yes, I was making it up.

Our family became dysfunctional. One of my sisters was also taken to my grandfather's farm soon after me, and the next week she had a new bike. Sandy became obese. We were raised Catholic, but the whole family left the church when I was nineteen. My grandfather got at my mother by calling us the "family of sluts." It was his way of keeping her quiet. My father was enraged but couldn't stand up for his family because my mother wouldn't let him and because he had never developed a "voice" from childhood. I was angry with him for not standing up for me. He was a wonderful man, but he wasn't there for me.

At that time I could only see the good qualities of someone. I couldn't see them as a whole person. Much later, this included how I saw my husband, oscillating between the good and the bad. My deepest despair occurred when I was a teenager. All that stuff with my grandfather. By the time my husband and I split up in 1993, I was suicidal. I have been in therapy for ten years. I had blocked off so much pain from childhood I had literally forgotten it. There were strategies going on inside me to block, block, block. Therapy destroyed all my illusions. The whole notion of psychotherapy is to get in touch with the original pain and to then release it. You can try to heal with others, but ultimately you have to heal yourself.

Everything I did, the drugs during the 70s, the occasional seance, the occult experimentation, was a way of asking questions about the mind. All of it was a spiritual search. I remember asking for the Holy Ghost in my apartment and fainting in the streets of Vancouver, due to the stress associated with my inner mental and emotional pain. When I met my husband he was in the Rosicrucian Order, a school of mysticism that emphasizes positive thought. He suggested I might find it interesting. I was twenty-five. In my relationship with my husband as a Rosicrucian, I felt like I could not express anger. I went to a group session and then joined the Rosicrucians.

The first night he slept on my living room rug; I covered him with blankets and felt as though I had done this a hundred times. When difficulties in our marriage began to appear, I went back to university to study Eastern religions, mysticism, myth, symbols, and the psyche. I read Carl Jung and Joseph Campbell. I knew that my marriage was beginning to unravel, and I intensified my search for deeper spirituality, for deeper awareness. I knew I had to find strength in order to cope. I went seriously back into therapy. A lot of my search for strength was intellectual. I think now that being intellectual, staying in our heads, is a way to avoid the pain.

I began to explore Buddhism, the opening of the heart. I learned that a person can study spirituality intellectually, but that this is very different from the Buddhist way. I found Buddhism to be a more integrated spiritual path. There had always been an abusive pattern to our marriage relationship. But, as a Buddhist, I was learning to "let things be." I eventually learned to stop taking on the guilt. I began to feel I was starting to get somewhere intellectually and emotionally. I still had low self-esteem, felt hurt easily, locked it deep inside, and got little emotional empathy from my husband, only some intellectual support.

I distanced myself more and more from him as I pursued Buddhism. I was looking for love. I didn't care what I had to do to get it. Buddhism was meaningful for me, especially working for enlightened lamas. My husband couldn't connect emotionally with these wise enlightened teachers. He kept pushing me to pursue my interest in art, but art wasn't the vehicle I wanted. The Tibetan lamas were. I felt the depth of their love, their incredible intelligence, their awakened enlightened minds. Their wholesomeness inspired me. It was like realizing my life work. They are so pure. There is no garbage.

Psychotherapy mirrors everything back to you as do lamas. A person can't be a controller, if they are sincerely willing to see themselves in a mirror. For instance the lamas are so peaceful that being a controller doesn't work. Working with them wears off your rough edges. They have a child-like purity. They are just so awake.

I am the Canadian secretary for a very highly realized Tibetan lama. In 1992, I went to India. Opening the heart is the important thing in Buddhist tradition. It was so easy to feel the love of the lamas, a soft guiding parental love. There is a sweetness and purity about them. It is like bathing in a very sweet love. I had been denying myself love, a discovery for me which had been a breakthrough in therapy because of the grandfather thing. I found the Tibetan experience of chanting to be so primordial. It evokes buried emotional hurt from your depth and it connects you with who you really are. An enlightened mind is simply getting free from all the blocks—the pain and the wounds we are hanging on to inside—that stop us from experiencing our inner divinity and self love. You don't want the experience of being with the lamas to end. But it has to end because you have to reach the depth of yourself by yourself.

In 1991, I co-ordinated a western Canadian fundraising tour for some of the most highly realized lamas. I met all these incredible teachers. It was an eye opener, facilitating the monks in the performance of sacred music, sacred dance, weekend retreats, chanting mantras, and doing visualizations (such as visualizing a deity that is part of yourself). Through this important experience, I felt that I was evolving into a different person. I travelled with the monks, with these incredible lamas who are full of love and compassion. I could see things like the energy surrounding people and that energy being emitted from their crown *chakras* when they were in meditation.

I also went to Hong Kong and then India. I needed to realize me. So I went. It was like going home. I volunteered my time for Buddhist activities because I believed that it was all part of rebuilding myself. I felt an identity with the Tibetan people. I felt at home with them. They give to you. You give to them. There's this lovely dance.

I had been denying myself love everywhere and now I was letting myself be loved while I was in India. I discovered love in a way I had never known before, while I was in India. I had an indescribable need for love at this point and getting it was very powerful. I also experienced a timelessness and a profound peace in India with my Tibetan friends. It was a sharing of their spiritual depth and an opening to mine.

I was fighting for my life in a way. I needed love and recognition. I needed to emotionally feel love, to bathe in it, in the simplest way. I was working for monks who were an embodiment of this incredible love and who are teaching lay people how to allow themselves to experience that love. Even the air around them was somehow pure. I lived what I was looking for in India. After that experience, it was so easy being in the enlightened community of the Tibetans and the monks after that experience because I knew it was possible to live in that gentleness, that softness, that lovingness. I vowed to be in it in my life in our western society. I knew it was right to be a compassionate person.

Buddhism also opens the heart so that you can feel other people's pain. It is so different than the way I have known, which is to put up walls, or to try to help intellectually. I saw and I experienced. I saw beggars. I saw thousands of people sleeping on the streets. When I got home, my husband and I had grown so far apart he seemed not interested in talking about my experiences. I learned from a Tibetan Buddhist abbot who came to my house that physical pain is not the highest pain. Emotional pain is.

The third time I went to India, I knew I was jeopardizing my marriage. I felt confused. When I got home, I saw the dysfunctional patterns of our relationship. After my husband left, the reality of the separation hit me. I felt helpless. I began letting out my anger. I was angry, not only at him, but at men. I was angry at my grandfather, my father, a Tibetan friend in India, and my business partner. I had uncontrolled explosive anger. A friend helped me. Thank god she was there because I wanted to commit suicide. I had opened up, let out all the stops. My physical, mental, emotional, and spiritual makeup is different. I have changed. I loved my husband deeply but I could not live in the relationship we had any more; that had to die for me to become who I discovered I was in India.

I am spiritually awakening. During my depression over my marriage breakup, I did an exercise for ten hours a day, chanting and visualizing a golden light in my bones…

atti, atti, atti, my beautiful golden bones….

After ten days of this, childhood memories began to come up. They were released emotions that had been buried away in my body. My legs felt like they were turning into trees. I started drawing bones. I began to feel like I was nothing but a bag of bones.

I freaked out. I called my Buddhist retreat teacher. She came over, and I told her what I was experiencing. She said I had been carrying around the belief that I was nothing in my body until now, that I had been letting myself and others treat me like I was nothing.

I was suicidal every day for six months and then I began to sort everything out, about my grandfather, my father, my husband, and my life. I did a lot of work with a friend who is a palliative care nurse. I began to heal with an Aboriginal healer and with a Buddhist friend, then with a male friend. I sat on his knee and cried like a three-year-old. He took me through the worst of the shit with my grandfather.

As I continue to heal, I am becoming more objective. I have faced myself. I've done my work. I have value. I am worthwhile. I love and care for myself in a way that I haven't since before I was thirteen. I found myself through Buddhism. Buddhism is a tremendous system of psychology and psychotherapy, and it teaches the most wholesome humanistic values. Its practice includes balance. The Buddhist tradition emphasizes walking the middle path and integration of mind, body, and spirit in all things. It is "living" spirituality.

My journey is far from over. I am still working on some aspects of my rage with my grandfather. What women need to understand is that the willingness to work through their pain and "the spiritual path" are one and the same.

Julia

From Fit to Free

I have felt despair so intense
I thought it would consume me
and I would literally cease to exist.

Danielle

Danielle was born in Canada. As a Catholic, she believes in God and prays to God for deliverance for all women who experience family violence. Danielle discovered her own spirituality through focusing on her physical self and by listening to her body.

For years I lived in an abyss of darkness. My husband was not only physically abusive but psychologically abusive as well. I think the latter was worse. I was never heard. My experience was never validated. I had no truth. Truth was whatever he wanted it to be. It was a commodity that could be created, manipulated, and distributed at will. It took me a while to figure this out. It is really amazing that I ever did, considering I had lost the ability to believe that my own experience was real and valid. This was all part of my eroding self confidence.

He was charming to people on the outside. "How lucky you are!" everyone would say. On the inside I was living my own personal hell. Yet, I thought somehow if I worked on my inadequacies things would change. It has taken me a while to figure out that you cannot ride a teeter-totter by yourself.

One day I started running. I liked it. It was great being outdoors. I kept running. I found that I suddenly had a desire to eat well. I gave up smoking. I pushed myself to run farther and faster. My husband and I had some good times during this period, but every so often he would unleash his temper. Running was a bright spot in the day that I could always count on. My husband liked running with me, but I secretly preferred running alone. It gave me a still, peaceful, safe place to go that I did not have with him.

In an effort to understand and change our problems, I started tracking his violent outbursts. I carried a little card in my wallet. I would write down the date and a few key words to remind me how the fight started. I rationalized that maybe this would help me to be more objective about our problems. Every six to eight weeks something would happen. I silently joked to myself that my husband suffered from a severe case of male PMS. His behaviour never seemed to match the stimulus. It all seemed absurd.

Eventually, I became abusive as well. What a hook that was! He would say, "You lose your temper and I forgive you and want you to stay. Why can't you forgive me?" It always sucked me right back in, another fault to add to the ever growing list. In hindsight, I should have asked myself why our relationship was so intolerable to me while he was quite content to continue just the way we were. Still, every once in a while I would see clearly that an abusive pattern had always been in his life and affected all aspects of it. Maybe they weren't always violent, but he did not and had not had, even one healthy, respectful relationship. Yet, I still did not fully trust myself. If I was the cause of his behaviour, I could fix it. To realize it is not you is to realize what you have to do—leave.

I kept up my running and soon entered a marathon training program. After completing my first marathon, I had more confidence than I'd had in years. Never before had I thought I was strong enough to run one. This experience got me thinking that perhaps I should re-evaluate all the things I believed I couldn't possibly do. You never know your own strength until you really put it to the test. However, I still thought if I worked hard enough on our relationship things would change.

The time frame for the cycle of violence was getting shorter. Even when things seemed good, he had rage barely concealed below the surface. It would erupt in a millisecond. Things were escalating to new levels. I began to fear we were on the verge of something really bad happening. Time was running out for us and for me. I loved my husband, but I didn't think that I was lovable. I didn't want to lose him. I didn't want to be alone.

I was always part of organized religion but did not always have a personal relationship with God. I didn't believe she was answering my prayers, but I prayed anyway. I was desperate. I was frantic. I prayed every day. I believed that if you are earnest and open, your prayers are answered, even though you don't always get the answer you want. Somewhere inside of me I knew I had to leave. The answer and the strength must have always been there within me. When you shatter your own illusion about the life you are living, great sorrow is created, but that sadness is followed by tremendous relief, peace, and strength. It comes from facing the truth.

I will never forget August 28, 1995. It was a Tuesday. It was the day I really left my husband. We were approaching our fifth wedding anniversary. I was dreading the day. Every year, prior to our anniversary, I vowed that the following year was going to be different. How many more years was I going to believe that things would change? We had fought the day before and I had packed my car. My husband was not there to talk me out of leaving. Not yet really believing I was leaving, I drove to my sister's.

She couldn't understand the chasm I was experiencing. My sister never knew what I went through. She phoned a priest. I went to see him. He did not know what to say. Lucky for me, he sensed my desperation and phoned a wonderful counsellor. Somehow, I gathered the strength to leave. Two days later I had an apartment. The road to recovery hasn't always been easy. The line from a Robert Frost poem gives me great comfort,

> The only way out is through.

Every time I went back, I had to relive the pain of leaving. I have had to realize my husband has had choices. He has chosen his path. If he could have fully embraced my experience as an abused woman, I may not have had to leave. When he would beg me to come back, I would quote St. Thomas Logian:

> If you bring forth what is within you,
> what you bring forth will save you.
> If you do not bring forth what is within you,
> what you do not bring forth will destroy you.

Even though, by leaving, I immediately found peace in my life, I still had to fight to stay away. If I found myself wanting to go back, I told myself I should give it one more day or one more week to see if I still felt that way. I finally had to tell friends and family what I had gone through so they could help me in my fight for survival. I had to lean on someone every time I felt vulnerable and wanted to phone him. I had to sever all contact until I was strong enough to really trust my truth because part of me wanted him to say something to make me believe it could be otherwise.

> I hurt for the pain my husband was experiencing. I wanted to help him.
> William Shakespeare speaks directly to me when he writes:
> "Care is no cure but rather corrosive
> to those things which are not to be remedied."

I have had to grieve, grieve for the relationship I wanted, grieve for the children we were supposed to have, grieve for the time I wasted, grieve for the illusion I lived, and grieve for the love I wanted to give.

Now I am now able to love so much more and be so much more than I have been. I like to think I have given birth to myself. I feel as though I have awakened from a deep slumber. My life is going to be good because I am going to make it that way. I alone am responsible for my own happiness. Now at night rather than pray for deliverance I pray that I become all that God wants me to become. I pray the same for all the women who have experienced this particular terror.

Danielle

Women Who Told Their Stories

After collecting the written stories, we realized that we needed a wider representation of women, because, not surprisingly, those who chose to write were predominantly white, Christian, English-speaking women. The next step in collecting the stories in *Lifelines* involved a series of interviews and discussions with women from diverse cultures.

In order to get at this more diversified group we again approached the immigrant serving agencies to help us find volunteers who were willing to talk about their personal experiences. These are the stories of the women we talked to. They further explain what some of the issues are and how these women developed strategies to cope with their situations and to move on in their lives.

Margaret, who came from an abusive family, found herself in one abusive relationship after another. Her experiences with religion were not good ones until she embraced her own Native spirituality. She says that, in her time of trouble, her spirit went far away and that she knew she just had to get it back. When she was running from her husband, Margaret came to Edmonton to die, to kill herself. She ended up at Lurana Women's Shelter. That's where her journey began, a long and difficult journey to self-discovery and self-esteem. Tools she has used to heal herself are writing poetry and taking long walks. For Margaret, spirituality is a sense, a higher power, a way to centre herself. Margaret wants to be a good role model for her children and to be able to help them realize that there are choices in life.

Another, Pushpa, began her quest to centre herself after her cultural and faith community rejected her following her marriage breakup. Pushpa left her abusive husband, and that was not acceptable to her relatives, her neighbours, or her community. She says, "My community despised me." Pushpa's problems began when she immigrated to Canada. She feels that immigration brought many sorrows to her including alienation, loneliness, and ultimately loss of community. Alone and lonely, Pushpa began to rediscover the goddess images of her culture and the value of ritual as she began to search for a sense of self, for peace, and for dignity. Through ritual, Pushpa gathered strength and courage. Discovering her own spirituality enabled her to begin helping and counselling others.

Leila came to Canada through an arranged marriage that turned out very badly. Almost immediately her husband began to batter her psychologically and to humiliate and degrade her. The abuse escalated until it became physical. Leila speaks very little English, has no family here, and was isolated by her husband. She didn't know where to turn for help.* Leila has very little education by

---

* There are a variety of services available to newly arrived immigrant women, often provided by women in their own communities. To find help within your community, contact social and community services, immigrant service agencies, and the local police department.

Canadian standards. She believes that she is a sinner because she left her husband. Leila is very religious. It is her faith in Allah that pulls her through each day. The act of dissolving her marriage has left her feeling shamed and guilty. She still believes that it is the responsibility of the mother to keep the family together. This ideal is a deeply ingrained part of her value system. Now she lives only for her child. Her child is her hope, her mission, her future.

A Métis woman, known as White Swan Woman, after years of abuse, self-abuse, and a destructive relationship, in utter desperation reached out to her Creator. Remarkably her life began to change. She says that without this spiritual strength—a strength she was not even aware of—she would not be alive today. White Swan Woman is studying to be a social worker. She wants to help other Métis who are experiencing abusive relationships. Much of her search for healing came about in trying to answer the question, "How can I change so that I will be able to recognise and avoid abusive people, situations, and relationships?" White Swan Woman thinks that some of the violence that happened in her life was rooted in her expectation that a man would take care of her. Her gradual healing, painful but powerful, has taught her that relationships do not work if they do not have equality in them. White Swan Woman knows, from personal experience, that inequities of power create an environment where the abuse of power is possible.

Loss and Ritual

Educated, privileged—now I am just
another visible minority woman—
I have been deeply lonely and
I have had to struggle alone.

Pushpa

*Pushpa is a Hindu woman who
was born in India sixty years
ago. She has a university degree
and has lived in Canada for
twenty-five years.*

Pushpa's was a love marriage not an arranged one in her home country India. When she arrived in Canada, after waiting two long years for her husband to sponsor his family, the marriage took on a totally different character. Pushpa has been divorced under Canadian law since 1979 but is still hurting from the loss of family and the rejection of her community, the people of her faith.

Pushpa's childhood in India, along with her education at exclusive girls' boarding schools and university, prepared her for a life of privilege. At age twenty-one she had everything—youth, beauty, economic freedom, and a prestigious position. When Pushpa was a young woman, her modern ideas clashed with those of her Hindu in-laws who adhered to ancient tradition and ritual.

When her first child was born she recalls, "They expected me to drink cow's urine but I didn't. I put it on my lips. This ritual takes place after the baby is born, when you come home." At this time in her life, she did not have much time for religion and had not really thought about it much. During one of her pregnancies, Pushpa's mother-in-law asked a Brahmin to come and do a ceremony called "lap filling." She carefully followed instructions and wore the appropriate clothes. Mantras were chanted while she sat on the floor and her lap was filled with money, sweets, and flowers. After this ritual, she was ceremonially purified. This was when she first began to realize that women are powerful. Whether they had careers or not, they ruled the households. And part of their role was the responsibility of passing on these rituals and traditions from one generation to the next.

At the time, Pushpa was taking part in these ceremonies mostly to please her mother-in-law and her own mother. "I did all this because I didn't want them to feel that I was too arrogant to adhere to or to perform these ancient rituals or to defer to their wishes."

In Canada, many things changed for Pushpa. Her degree and experience did not help her with potential employers and she missed her mother and her mother-in-law. "In truth I missed the tyranny of all the mothers." Her husband, unemployed, powerless, and lonely himself, began to exercise power over her. He soon became a stranger to her. This woman, who had been content and rather complacent, with a husband, two children, an involved extended family, and a career with a prestigious women's college in India, says about herself, "Now I am just another visible minority woman, trying to make ends meet with adult children who live with me trying to do the same. I have been deeply lonely and have had to struggle alone."

Are you able to talk about this struggle?
After I left my husband, people in my faith community despised me because I went alone to the temple. I finally stopped going. In Hindu families daughters are told, "You don't leave your husband's house except on the *arthi*." (a stretcher-like carrier on which the body is placed and carried to the funeral pyre for cremation).

So the community became a really hostile place after you left. Why would you even go to your temple after that?

Well, you know, festivals and other events. I used to go with the children but when I divorced it was inhospitable. Actively inhospitable. They sought to destroy my reputation with cruel gossip. The women shunned me because they saw me as someone who might take away their husbands. Actually, it did happen. I have returned them a lot of husbands who came to me. I asked these men, "What did you think when you came to my door like bees to a rose? I will go out with you the day you have the courage to leave your wife that you tell me treats you so badly."

Why would the men assume that you would be interested?

Because I was seen as a bad woman. I thought to myself that maybe I should not be so attractive. I allowed myself to become unattractive so they would stay away.

How did you find the strength to go on? Your experiences with your husband must have been damaging to you in many ways.

Oh yes, very. He compared me to North American women, saying I wasn't at all like them. Suddenly, I was no longer desirable, not at all a desirable woman.

Did he tell you that?

Yes. Then I left him and went to live in the students' residence.

What happened with the kids?

I left them too. One day I wanted to go swimming so I went home to get my swimming suit. My children were sulking in the hallway. I went inside and he had a lace tablecloth on and candles. He made the children sit in the hallway. I went to the bedroom and put the suit in a bag. I told him why I had come and he said, "Why don't you stay and have a scotch." I said, "Thank you, I will," and sat. This woman was there. One thing led to another. Since I had only been in the country for about eight months, I was not familiar with the different sexual mores that operated here. I discovered that this woman was my child's teacher. I said something to her like, "So, in your country, the teacher goes out with the children's father? Is this the usual practice?" I think I insulted her.

What did she say?

She said he told her that he was divorced. I asked her if she believed him. I told her, "You could have called. You could have asked my child." That was very bad. That is the most disgraceful thing that I am guilty of. I told her to leave. She said, "No, I won't leave. If he tells me to leave, then I will leave." I told her that I was just staying in residence because of my studies, and that this was still my home.

What did your husband do?

He winked at her and that just infuriated me. That lace tablecloth—I gave it one good pull—ruining his romantically set table. At that point he really hit me. Hard. This was a very painful thing. Then he had to take me to the university hospital because he thought he had broken my jaw. They kept me under observation for a whole night. But this is worse. In the morning he came to see how I was doing. They discharged me and he took me to back to the residence, and I begged him to take me home. I'll never forget that. I was aware that I was sinking so low. On top of that the bastard demanded that I write a letter of apology to that woman. He threatened that I would never be able to come home again if I didn't. Subsequently, I wrote it. I'll never understand that. I knew that he was capable of physically hurting me and still, I begged him to take me home. But he left me standing there. When my roommates saw my condition, they went to the window and saw him leaving. They called him obscene names. They verbally abused him!

I think at times like that it must be pure turbulence in your mind. You don't think much about praying do you? You clutch at straws.

Mmmm. Now he poisons my children against me. He blames everything on me. I used to tell him, "Why should we go to Canada? It was with great difficulty that we got rid of the British and now we must go and serve them again." I never wanted to come. I should never have joined him.

But through all this where did your strength come from?

It was my mother. It was my mother-in-law. It was Mother India. I became aware that my name is one of the 108 names of Durga, Shakti, Shiva's consort. In my megalomania I thought I represented my country, Mother India, and all the female deities. So all of them, all of these mothers melded into Durga. I was a mother! I had to nurture and support my children.

What about spirituality through all this? When you were rejected by others of your faith, how did your spirit survive?

I just prayed to the Mother Goddess. I have an altar at my home. You know Durga has all the manifestations, from a blood drinking castrating woman to a mother. She is all in one. There has been a resurgence of Devi worship in India, but I did not know this at the time. There comes a time that things happen coincidentally all over the universe and women just pick up on it. Unbeknownst to me, a lot of women were doing this. Being a Hindu I had an advantage. Devi was there. I did not have to create her. There are women of other minorities who are shown Jesus Christ— for god's sake—blond and blue eyed! To a Hindu, Jesus Christ would be accepted as a great holy man, as a guru. Because we believe in gurus, we believe in teachers, but we do not believe that any man is a god. But a woman is supposed to look upon her husband as God. It is a hyperbolic representation in that the husband is the provider, the protector. Also a woman sleeps with him to perform her wifely duties.

Religion did not support me through this. Others of my own faith did not support me. My own quest to centre myself, for a sense of self, for peace, dignity, and courage set me on a path of spirituality.

Was it hard for you financially?
Immigration was the problem. My husband had to establish himself in a new country. He lost his profession and had to deal with it. He just lost himself. He forgot who he was. He was pathetic! It was hard. I had three jobs. Sometimes I worked for $3.75 an hour! And I did a Master's as well. I had come to Canada with a Master's degree, and experience in a prestigious institution, thinking that I would get a teaching job. It was really a nightmare. Now I am in my sixty-first year and I still worry about what is going to happen to me.

Then I go to Delhi and find out what my colleagues have. Some of them are retired now and my god when I see what they have and how well their children are doing it hurts. If terrible things had happened in India, I wouldn't feel so bad. But they didn't. India is booming. I would have been easily working. I went back after eight years. My mother died in 1987. I couldn't bring myself to visit for so long. When I went back, I could not believe it. But it's too late. I can't go back now because I don't have a house there. Besides, I have not lived anywhere other than Canada for a quarter of a century. This is home!

I want to talk about money. My rights, my status, my money, it's all lost. I have losses, losses, losses—inheritance and the cumulative benefits of permanent employment. Whites think we are poor, but many abused women come from landed families. We Hindus believe that we owe people from another life. So it's karma. I must have owed everything to everybody!

Do you think your husband has regrets about the way things turned out?
I don't know. He is constantly exercising and thinking about his physical condition. He has never lived with anyone even though he always has girlfriends. He has never been without one. But he has self-knowledge. I am sure that in a perverse way he is Buddha. In a perverse sense. That is why he has no attachments or sense of responsibility.

My one sorrow is that I am not able to forgive him. I will never be able to forgive him because he has done nothing for our children. Nothing. My children are suffering. His children. When my father sent me to a very expensive college in Delhi, he sacrificed. That is the comparison. He had to send three children to boarding school so he quit his club. Each man is so different from the other. My father was committed to his children. Don't tell me my husband couldn't help because he has been playing tennis and philandering all this time. He could have helped. All the judge told him to pay was $200 per month and he has never even paid that.

I used to cry a lot. If people asked me how I was doing, I would cry. It was a terrible shock that this man, the love of my life, had become a stranger. Now I know. He could have been different. He could have turned things around if he really loved his children. But instead he was constantly trying to prove himself sexually by acquiring younger and younger girlfriends. Isn't that ridiculous? Men look like fools when they do this. But—what I have experienced—has happened to many other immigrant women.

What was it that made you decide to help other abused women in your community?
Well, for one thing, women who are in arranged marriages come here alone. These women are open to all kinds of abuse. At the centre we have found that four out of ten arranged marriages have physical or mental abuse happening in them.

I did not have any information when I came to Canada. Had I known there was social assistance, my marriage might not have broken up. If I had only known about the services. But I was all alone with no one to help me. I might have taken the time to think and to further my education, but we needed groceries. There was just too much stress.

Do the women at the centre ever ask about religious things when they come to you?
Other abused women now come to me saying that the priest tells them *pati parameshwar* (the husband is god). I mention religion because, as you know, our women are not counselling-oriented. Sometimes I talk to them about the deities. I don't suggest that they leave their marriages, but I do suggest that they empower themselves to weigh and choose from options. Auto suggestion helps a lot. Prayer helps. I know. All of these women like the Devi, and a lot of them fast on Friday because that is the Devi's day. Even if they are sick they fast. They also feed some virgins, maybe three-year-olds. Even I used to do this ritual back home with my mother. I talk to these women about the difference between rituals and seeking spirituality through meditation.

So you see I knew about all these things, but I had never thought about them. It is only in Canada that I began to see how my mother-in-law, mother, and Mother India are all within me. I was completely alienated. My alienation and loneliness led to a constant longing for my mother, Mother India, and Shakti in her divine manifestation of the Devi, Mother Goddess. I took to having imaginary conversations with her. I had to save myself.

This separation from your husband and people is still a deep pain for you isn't it? Yes, it is. I think the main reason is that immigration resulted in losses that are irreparable. For example, my children used to do *aarti* (a ritual where one lights a lamp and sings a song to the Divine) asking for both Shakti and Shanti. And they lost all this—my children lost all this. They lost the language, they lost the culture, and they lost the religion. They lost all their cousins and friends and all their connections. They are alone. Those losses hurt. My own losses, particularly the loss of my community, is a terrible thing. But now I have sisterhood!

... from a conversation with Pushpa

Learning to Cry

Margaret

Margaret is a thirty-five year old Aboriginal woman who was born on a reservation in northern Saskatchewan. She is the middle child in a family of ten. Margaret is a single parent with two boys. Her education includes grade twelve and two and a half years of university. Margaret is now working with the Federal Government.

Don't cry, don't cry,
you are holding her spirit back.

We have been talking to people who work in the shelters. We would also like to hear from women who have personally experienced spousal abuse.
I spent some time once at the Lurana Shelter. They were really nice to me. They helped me a lot. I came from an abusive family where I was sexually molested, from age five until eight, by someone close to me. There is abuse through our whole family. There was a lot of violence and my mom was abused by my father. I don't remember much about my childhood. For a long time I felt that I was responsible for being molested as a child. But now I have forgiven myself and my family.

Could you tell us a bit about where you are now?
I'm a single parent with two sons age eleven and nine and I am presently adopting a one-year-old. I have a boyfriend who has also gone through a lot. His mom killed her common-law husband two weeks ago here in Edmonton. He had been beating her for a long time. My boyfriend worries a lot about his mom. But the older women in my culture don't talk about this. They won't admit it, ever, even when all the signs are there. But you know they are being abused.

What are the signs?

Oh you become withdrawn and defensive and very lonely as a result of not wanting anyone to know. When I was being abused, I wouldn't talk. I can laugh about it today, but I couldn't laugh before. I couldn't even cry.

Where did you find the strength to deal with your situation?

I have learned to take care of myself. I have taken Life Skills and had self and group assessment. I couldn't look at people before but now I can. It all started when I went to a healing circle at the University of Saskatchewan. All the women were talking about their experiences. All of a sudden I remembered everything. I remember that I was holding a stone in the circle. I had to go home and my sister was there. I collapsed in a heap on the floor and cried and cried and kept saying he did this to me. Then my sister said, "He did it to me too and I thought I was the only one."

When I was growing up, I used sex. I used people. I didn't care. I was in a Mennonite children's home. At this boarding school we prayed. We got up at 6:00 and prayed, had breakfast and prayed, had dinner and prayed, went to church and prayed. We went to church too much, every day, twice on Sundays. We prayed too much. One Sunday we had a sermon on how the world would end. It was called "The Rapture" and I became a Christian that very night. We all became Christians that night. It was really frightening. I remember thinking I had better become a Christian. I was ten or eleven at the time. There were sixty girls in one dorm and sixty boys in another. We all came from broken homes or dysfunctional families. I came when I was around six, speaking Cree and left at around ten speaking English.

When did you become conscious of your own Native spirituality?

I didn't really find Aboriginal religion until four or five years ago. I used to go to church on skid row. It was at the Bissell Centre on 96 Street. I took the kids there. Sometimes I forget where I came from, how far I've come. I'm thankful. I will never shove religion at my boys. But sometimes when I walk by a church I turn my head or look down. I still feel guilty. I think I should be going to church, but I don't want that feeling anymore.

When you went to the Lurana Shelter, how long had you been in an abusive relationship?

I had been psychologically battered, for a long time, by the father of one of my sons. When my son was two years old, his father started physically abusing both of us. Then I got into another relationship with physical abuse. When my new partner drank he got violent. I used to drink all the time too. We drank together and fought all the time. I was no better than he was. When I told him to stop, he would yell, "Who the hell are you to talk!" I have never been assertive.

Before you went to Lurana, how did you stay sane? How did you cope?
It was my kids. It goes back to the kids. When I came to Edmonton, I was at my lowest. I came here to die. I wanted to die. We left Saskatchewan on a bus with only our clothes because I had to get away, to be alone, and to do it. There was no light at the end of my tunnel. I wanted only to die.

But I knew there was a higher power. Now I sit and listen, but it has been hard. I don't just sit and stare at the wall or the floor anymore. An old man told me that one of hardest things I will do in my lifetime is to sit and listen.

Do you have any people who help you now? How did you learn about these things?
My grandmother taught me a lot. She was an Anglican. My mom doesn't believe in the Indian spiritual way. At the Native Friendship Centre where I am a volunteer, I listen to the old ones, even if they are drinking. They have a lot of knowledge and they have something to say.

My father is there for me. I respect him. He is wise. He has changed a lot. Now he follows the Indian way. My mom and dad have been apart for at least twenty-four years. My dad was always gone when I was a child. He had an alcohol problem and now it's my mom who has an alcohol problem. My mom has only her Christian religion. She is in her fifties. So many women her age are broken.

When my younger sister was murdered four or five years ago, my mother could not cry. I remember my grandmother in her coffin. She was 101 years old when she died. I remember crying and crying. I love my grandmother, but I never told her that. My mother kept saying, "Don't cry, don't cry, you are holding her spirit back." My mother wouldn't cry at my grandmother's funeral. My mother only cries when she is drinking. I try to tell my mom that grieving is okay, but she doesn't listen.

What kind of things helped you to cope with your life?
Walking, I did it by walking. You know, when I came here to Edmonton, I was 280 pounds. I have lost about 80 pounds since then. I used to walk all over the city. I still walk a lot. It makes me feel good. It gives me time to think about things. I have been here for three years now. I am building a support system for myself, and sharing with others has helped me cope.

When you started looking for help where did you find it?
I was still back in Saskatchewan at the university when my class went to a Native healing circle. I wasn't looking for help. It was part of our class in oral communication or something like that. We had to sit and listen and not write anything for four months. Then we had to write about how you get people's attention. We did a video on pow wows in this class. I almost got a university degree, but I quit. I was scared of responsibility so I ran. I went to the Saskatchewan Federated Indian College with students from all over B.C., Alberta, and Saskatchewan.

In talking about your earlier years of education, you mentioned that you were not allowed to speak Cree in the Mennonite children's home. How did you manage to hold on to your Cree language?

I never lost my language, but maybe I misplaced it for a while. I had white foster parents who were very good to me. I have always felt that I was treated differently in the city, but we lived in a small town then. With my foster parents in this town, I never felt left out. After I left I lost contact. I was going through a hate stage. My family all said I was white and white people said I was Indian. After a long time I phoned my foster mother and told her I was drinking and of the kind of life I was living. She said they never taught me that and why was I living that way. I didn't know. It was difficult to go back home. Accepted. Rejected. Accepted. Rejected. Back home I have to live up to other people's standards. Here I feel different.

How was it at Lurana? Do women think about the spiritual when they are going through such a crisis?

I was a heavy person. I had my sons with me and we arrived in a cab. I slept for two days thinking about home. I was crying and telling my kids, "I'm trying for a better life." I felt relief, calm, able to sleep. The staff were so good to me. I still phone them. They support you and let you know what they can do. I didn't find spirituality at Lurana, but I found friends. One woman there had just lost her kids when social services apprehended them. I gave her a hug.

Lurana is Catholic. Did you feel that when you were there?

No. No, they don't shove their religion at you. Not at all. I was there for a month.

Tell us about the development of your own spirituality.

Well, now that I have Aboriginal ways, I know now that there is a Creator. It's different. The church people are always talking about sin. Is there even a word for "sin" in the Cree language? I don't know one. There is no word for "evil" or "sin" or "sinner." When you talk to elders about your life, they talk to you without scaring you. They don't threaten you. They do more to make you feel good. They are kind and loving and explain like you would to a child. I can trust them. They have lived a long time and seen a lot and are wise because of it. One thing I've found is that elders don't tell you "this is right" and "this is wrong." They are wiser and older than I am. I respect that. Their words are more powerful.

In Aboriginal ways, is there a way that a woman is expected to be with her husband?

You have to respect yourself. People make mistakes, but they are not bad people. I don't believe in marriage. It is written how to live with a man, but I can't do it. My boyfriend wants me to marry him, but I will never do that. I tell him that a long time ago Indians were not married. I feel that living in a relationship is more trusting. Now, in my relationship, I can hug, love, cry, and support him. Marriages always break up. I can live without it. I don't believe that I am a sinner.

What does spirituality mean to you?
Spirituality is a sense. For me it is a higher power, a way to centre myself.

We pray in the Christian sense, but how do you pray to the Creator?
I try to pray in my language. You pray like you are talking. When I pray I say, "Help me to help myself." All this Christian stuff is always saying, "give me, give me and please this and please that." You have to help yourself. When I pray to myself, I start in Cree, but it usually trails off into English. I pray every night. I give thanks. I give thanks every morning. If a Native forgets to pray, we pray for him. So you pray for everyone else too, not just yourself.

What about the ceremonies? Do you take part in these?
I have experienced sweetgrass but I have never had my own. I would like to but it is sacred. You don't fool around with it. There are only certain times a woman can use it. You have to know these things.

Once I went to a sweat during one of the lowest times in my life. But I won't do that now. You are not supposed to go to sweat when you have been drinking, doing drugs, or other things. It is not right. One time my friend told me to come to a sweat. "Come on, come on, come to the sweat. You feel really bad. It will make you feel better." I said "no" because I had been drinking the night before but in the end I went anyway. I burned. I burned bad because I had drank. Now I want to go to a sweat to clean myself. I am ready to go again. I feel so clean after a sweat. I feel light again.

I build things up. My boyfriend makes me talk. He is Chippewa but we get along well. Cree and Chippewa didn't get along too well in the past. He lives with me. Well part-time anyway. He is trying for a better life and when he goes to a treatment centre he wants to have Native religion too.

You need to find your spirit to get you to go on. My spirit went far away. I had to get my spirit back. It all came down to one big jump. I let people abuse me. I let it happen. There was nowhere to turn. I just left. I jumped on the bus in Saskatchewan with my kids. I was afraid of everything. I told my family, "I'm leaving tomorrow." But they didn't pay any attention. They didn't believe me. I came here to die. That is the only reason. I wanted to die, but I wanted to get away first. I would come to Edmonton because I didn't know anyone here. Well I knew one girl, but I didn't know where she lived or her phone number.

What did you do then? How did you survive?
When I got here, I looked for her. I went to the Jockey Hotel in north Edmonton. I stayed there for two weeks, until my money ran out. Then I really wanted to

find that girl I knew. I thought how can I find her. I know where she'll be, in a bar. That is where I found her, in a bar. I stayed at her place for two or three days, but I left. I couldn't stay in that place.

Then I went to Social Services but they wouldn't help me until I told them I was running from my husband. Then they sent me to Lurana. I was filled with shame. I couldn't look at anyone. I felt so bad. They were really good to me there. My kids were very relieved. They liked it right away. I just sat at a table crying. My kids enjoyed living there. They liked the two cable TVs. It is a nice place. Lurana has a daycare too.

How did you find strength to get through this? Who helped you?
Within my people, women are powerful. But I was raised in a different way. My boyfriend tells me how strong I am. I can't see it, but people say it is true. People see that I have changed. I have grown since I came here. When I graduated from Slate Training Centre, I was the valedictorian! My father came to my graduation and he cried.

My father talks to me about spiritual things. My father follows the Indian way. He never used to, but he has changed a lot. My sister is very religious. I argue with her. My father tells my sister that if she puts her Christian bible out in the rain it will rot. He says, "My bible is already out there. It's green, it's nature. My bible will never rot out there but yours will." My sister just goes back and goes to church. I want to follow the Indian way. But I still feel guilty when I don't go to church.

You mentioned that you and your boys have been receiving counselling. How is this working out?
My older boy has been very angry. I don't want my boys to think they can do anything they want. I don't want them being abusers. Kids need to understand that life is all about making choices. You make your own choices in life. I try not to bail them out. I raise my kids differently than I was raised. I remember being whipped. I would never do that to my kids. I want the best for my children. I don't have any memories of my mom holding me or hugging me.

My younger boy surprised me recently. He said to his brother, "Hey Bro, you're not spending enough time with me lately." So his brother stayed home with him. I don't remember my own childhood at all. In my whole life I can only remember, maybe once, having a good time. I don't want my boys to live like that. They need inspiration, encouragement, understanding, and most importantly a positive role model which is me. My line of communication is open for them. I did not have that as a child.

... from a conversation with Margaret

The Violation of the Veil

Leila

Leila was born in Lebanon and is a recent immigrant to Canada. At thirty years of age she is a single parent with one child and no income. Leila's education level in Lebanon was roughly the equivalent of primary school and her family back home is poor. Leila speaks very little English. Our discussion took place with the help of a culturally knowledgeable interpreter.

Spiritual belief helped me to cope.
I thank Allah for everything
especially my child.

When I first arrived for the interview, Leila was proudly showing her new driver's license. The sense of accomplishment and the freedom this piece of paper brings to her is beyond the understanding of most Canadians. This young woman is recently divorced. Leila is alone—separated, single—ostracized by her small extended family in Canada and by others in her community. According to Islamic law, a woman is not allowed to ask for divorce. This situation is very traumatic for her because she believes that she cannot go to heaven alone, that she must go hand in hand with her husband. He can ask for divorce, but of course he did not.

Can you tell me what helps you through your darkest times?
"My belief in Allah. I pray. I read the Qur'an. I fast. Each day I pray five times. This verse from the Qur'an helps me through each day." [The verse is written in Farsi and has been roughly translated].

You have to live with Allah and feel him and listen to Allah
Don't think that good things come by force
Don't think about tomorrow but think about Allah
Wealth does not come with power
The bird eats with the eagle
Allah gives the sky for the bird, the sea for the whale
He gives them shelter
He gives life. Even if you live to an old age, you die.

"Everything is written. At our time of birth, our life is predetermined. We have to believe in that. If you have happiness, you still have to die when it has been determined. If you are a good person, you still come from the earth and you return to the earth. Every religion says that. Spiritual belief helped me to cope. I thank Allah for everything especially my child. Every day I pray and read the Qur'an.*"

Did your spiritual leader help you through this crisis?
"I tried to talk to the sheik but he only says, 'Give him a chance, go back to him, he doesn't mean it.' I think it is always the fault of the woman. When things did not get better for me the sheik said, 'Live for a few months alone with your child and see what Allah wants you to do.'"

"The man is in control," says Leila. She explains the circumstances under which a man dissolves the marriage. The man, in front of a colleague, repeats the phrase, "*taleque, taleque, taleque.*" If he later comes home and says he regrets it, that he is sorry, that he did not mean it, then he has to go to the spiritual leader who will absolve him and re-institute the marriage. The sheik will tell him this is not a game and that this is not to be taken lightly and discourage him from doing it again. "But," says Leila, "he will do it again."

Leila says she was terrified about leaving. She knew that husband and wife should stay together. She was so afraid that she could not go out. She felt that Allah was upset with her. But she also knows the Qur'an and her rational self believes that she must obey first Allah, then her husband. But still, she thinks it is her duty to go back to her home.

During the worst of the turmoil, Leila left and went to another city to live with her extended family for forty days. They treated her very badly. Her close relative said, "If you don't go back to your husband, I will never speak to you again." That was two years ago and not a word has been spoken between them

---

* Qur'an, is the term used in this section for the Islamic sacred book. The term Koran has the same meaning, and is referred to in later sections of this book (depending on the preference of the speaker).

since. This relative and his spouse are her only family in Canada. She is desperately lonely. Leila returned to her apartment because she knew someone in this city. But her extended family threatened to call the police who, they said, would return her to her husband.

This must have been very difficult with no financial resources. How did you manage?
"A friend helped. I did not have a job and my English is not good. My friend helped me to get an apartment so I could be with my child. My husband found out and kept calling and giving me a bad time. He is back in the city now."

Leila's husband has been in Canada for a very long time. They met in their country of origin when he went back to find a new bride. His arranged marriage with Leila was his second marriage. He is much older than she is and very controlling. Friends asked her, "Why did you marry someone so much older?" She says it was her fate with Allah. It was determined.

Are you able to talk about your marriage?
Leila now begins to talk freely, relating her agony and constantly fighting back tears. She tells us how she used to spend nights locked out in the apartment hallway when she was married to this man. Leila thinks that if a woman does not obey her husband it means she is not obeying Allah and that the angels will be angry with her "until the sun rises." She tells me that this means that she is a sinner and the shame of this never ends.

Leila's mother taught her the importance of wearing the veil. She is proud of it. She always wears it. It gives her great comfort and it has deep religious and cultural meaning for her. But her husband tells her that he is in control, and if he wants her to wear the *hijab* (the veil), or not to wear it, she must obey. It does not matter what her mother wants or what Leila wants.

He does not want her to wear the veil because he does not want to appear different in this country. He does not want her to stand out. She tells him, "I must obey Allah first and then you." He wants her to cut her hair and to look and dress modern or Western. She refuses, saying, "If you are embarrassed to walk with me, why did you marry me? I have not changed. I am the same person." He threatens to call her closest relative. She withdraws to the bedroom immersing herself in a religious tape. She listens and she cries. Her husband does not want her to look different. He wants her to take off the veil.

One day he locked her out of the house with no veil. He left her for two hours in the sun taunting her from the balcony. He leered at her and made lewd remarks and suggestions to her. She felt naked and exposed. Her feeling of shame was indescribable.

Surely you must feel that Allah understands that you are not a sinner?
"You must believe in Allah and pray, and fast, and read the Qur'an. I watch religious video tapes, and I thank Allah five times a day. If a woman believes in Allah at the most difficult time in her life, then Allah will take care of her. He will take care of the biggest problem, no matter what it is."

With such a strong focus on family, separation must have been very difficult for you.
"Yes, very. Islam gives this freedom to the man but not to the woman." Leila has now been divorced for two years. Her husband went back home and married yet another time. He has since left this newest young wife and wants to divorce her. Even though Leila knows she is divorced according to Canadian law, she hates being separated from Allah's law. "All I have now in life is my child. This child is my life. I live for my child."

Leila tell us that when her father died many years ago, her mother was young. But her mother has never remarried and she never will. She will never have a boyfriend. Her mother feels that she is still married to her husband, and Leila feels the same way. She say she will never remarry and for her, morally, having a boyfriend is absolutely out of the question. She tells me that it cannot and will not happen.

Throughout all this upheaval in your life, have you had support from your mother?
Leila's mother lives across the ocean and cannot write, but they have exchanged audio tapes. She talks to her mother on tape, and once when things were really bad Leila phoned her. Her mother is supportive and tells her she must obey Allah before any man. The loneliness and isolation are unbearable because her family is so far away.

Are there any family members who support you or any friends you can talk to?
"Only my close relative who does not speak to me and a relative of my mother's." The wife of Leila's relative told her, "If you were my relative, I would kill you." Her extended family live nearby, but they shun her and will not respond when she greets them. They scowl at her and turn their faces away. It hurts. She tells me she has lost 30 pounds. She is so frail and so beautiful and so strong.

Is it a religious or a cultural law that says a woman must not leave her marriage?
It is both the culture and the religion. Leila believes that if a woman leaves her husband it is shameful and that it reflects on the rest of the family. She is a bad woman. That is why her family will not speak to her. Her former friend (the wife of her relative) hates her now. They are waiting for her to take her husband back

and give him another chance. It doesn't matter that he doesn't care about her. It doesn't matter that he has remarried and since that he has now left another wife.

Leila feels the shame and that she is the guilty one. She believes it is the responsibility of the mother to keep the family together. She is very conscious of this. It is a deeply ingrained part of her value system, and she feels that this is why the community is against her. She says again, "My life is over now." For a long time she was afraid to go out on the street, afraid of the shame and the rejection.

Is there anyone at your mosque who you can talk to?
The sheik is involved in the case because the husband is once again living here. The husband wants to see his child, and the sheik will be involved in the negotiations. There is a woman helper at the mosque who Leila sometimes talks to. Leila tells me she is embarrassed and humiliated to talk to this woman about sexual matters. For instance, Leila could not go to see the sheik to arrange for her husband to visit her daughter because (while she was menstruating) she cannot go to the mosque.

So her husband came to the apartment. But he wanted only sex. Leila felt that she had no choice and she was afraid. She had to obey her husband. Leila does not know what to do next. She cannot say to her child that there is no father, she cannot say to her husband that he has no child, and she cannot say this to Allah.

He came to her home and he raped her. After, he asked her to say she was sorry, but she refused. Leila believes that if she remains loyal to Allah, then Allah will reward her in the end.

...from an interpreted conversation with Leila

Spiritual Awakening

The sound of the drums and singers
pierced the air and my soul.
You can feel the drums beat right
through your body.

White Swan Woman

*Kim, White Swan Woman, is
thirty-seven years old, the mother
of two children, and about to
graduate with a degree in social
work. She was born and raised
in Canada, her roots are Cree
and French, and she loves music,
singing, and dancing.*

Kim has chosen to be identified by her Native name, White Swan Woman. She agreed to talk with us because she wants to help her people. She has a very calm and peaceful presence, speaking slowly and softly.

Could you tell us how you came out of your own personal suffering. What enabled you to cope and to deal with it all? How did you discover your spiritual strength?
Without strength, in the spiritual sense, I would not be here today. I would not be alive today. Yes, I would like to tell you about who I am, what has happened to me, and how I got to be who I am.

Would you say that spirituality has taken a role in all that?
Yes, I find my strength in everyday life. My family, my work, and striving to follow the spiritual teachings give me courage and strength. My traditions and prayer, the sacred objects such as the eagle feather, sweetgrass, and the ceremonies themselves are very important to me. My spiritual journey began one evening, over ten years ago, when I was in a place of desperation and hopelessness. I was

calling out, in my agony, to a god that I wasn't even sure was there. I was asking for help, not even knowing what help I needed. That's where it all begins.

At that time, my way of life, and all the awful things that had happened in it, did not make sense to me. I was addicted to drugs, and in an abusive relationship. I had a small daughter, and I had run out of hope. Then tragically, my brother died of a drug overdose, and I felt utterly lost and alone. His death forced me to examine my own lifestyle and I realized that I had no idea how to stop what was happening in my life. In this desperate state I was finally willing to do anything, including humble myself to pray and beg for help. Then remarkably, my life began to change. Shortly after I reached out to my Creator, I was filled with a strong sense that something important was about to happen. I was not accustomed to listening to my spirit, my inner voice. I remember talking to a close friend about the fight I'd had with my partner and explaining how I'd received a black eye. She shared a similar story with me, and we were shocked to discover that these two awful events had happened at almost the same time. Then somehow, within our shared strength, we became willing to face the fact that we were being abused. I remember saying to her, "It's strange but I just feel that something important is going to happen in my life and I don't want to miss it." I wasn't accustomed to trying to work with my intuition or to listening to my spirit talking to me. After that conversation I started meeting people who had answers and solutions. These things just happened. I did not seek them out. I felt I was being guided.

What kind of people?
People who were also being guided, I believe. People who understood what I was going through and knew how to make the hurting stop. Much to my surprise, one day I found myself sitting in an Alcoholic's Anonymous meeting. A friend of mine was required to go to AA meetings as a condition of his parole, and so one night I offered to drive him. When we arrived, I realized that he'd need a ride home in an hour, so I decided to wait. He asked me to come in with him. I found myself listening to what these people were saying and I got very excited. I felt like the light was turning on. The Creator was talking to me. That was the beginning of the life I have now, a life in which there is peace.

What was your background? Did you have a Christian upbringing?
I was raised as a Roman Catholic, going to Catholic schools, always attending church. I knew the lessons of Jesus Christ and believed in Jesus Christ. Then somewhere in my teenage years, I lost it. I saw the hypocrisy, became skeptical, and I turned my back on it. I was so idealistic that I felt disappointed in what I was seeing in the church. Of course, my life was a mess. I was drinking and running with the wrong people. I had to become truly desperate before my heart was open to healing.

Did you grow up in your birth family?
I was raised by my mother and her husband. My father was also a part of my life but to a lesser degree. He was, and still is, a powerful teacher for me. He introduced me to Mother Earth in a very sacred way. Yet, still, it seems I have had to learn who I am as an Aboriginal woman on my own.

Did you have a teacher who guided you?
It was a difficult path. There have been so many people who have come into my life that have opened doors for me and allowed me to feel free enough to ask questions. When I was ready, the teacher appeared.

Among the Aboriginal teachers you have encountered, are there any that stick out in your mind? If so, were they male or female?
Actually, I have had both men and women teachers. A very close male friend of mine shared with me some of his knowledge and invited me to participate in my first sweatlodge. Yet, with women I have shared my pain as well as my experiences. One of my teachers was an elder I met in a healing circle. She taught me as much through her presence, kindness, and way of interacting with women as she did through her teachings about the traditional and spiritual ways of our people. It was her "way of being" that was her gift to me.

How did this elder help you and the others in the healing circle?
For a while I attended a healing circle once a week. The elder didn't come often, maybe once a month, but I talked with her regularly. We'd get together for a chat, and then I would work towards some goals. The healing circle allowed us to share our pain, life, and laughter together. Some of my learning and my healing has been in those circles. They can be very powerful.

I was grieving both for a close friend who had just left this world and for the end of a relationship I had been in. It was very painful. I knew I had to find a way to get through it. The elder took such good care of me. She taught me, cared for me, and prayed with me. We shared in the sweatlodge until I finally got through this difficult time. It was one of the most meaningful times of my life. Learning can be motivated through pain and searching. When healing and learning in this way, no one lectures you or tells you the answers. You must go on this search for yourself.

Would you say that your Catholicism more or less receded or is it still there for you?
I do not practice Catholicism today. Still, I'm glad I had that upbringing. I believe Jesus Christ was a great prophet and an example for us. My mother finds something enriching in the church, and I have attended mass with her to support her.

It was a good experience. I can still feel the sacredness of the mass and the church. It works for my mother and I can see that, but it no longer fits for me. I have found my own way.

Can you talk a little about that way, the Native approach to spirituality?
Two events have had a significant impact on me and opened my mind and heart to this way of life. One was the first time I attended a pow wow. I remember parking the car and walking a long way to the pow wow grounds. As I approached, the sound of the drums and singers pierced the air and my soul. You can feel the pow wow drums beat right through your body. The dancers, the costumes, and the drums made for a powerful ceremony. It was a strong emotional and spiritual experience for me. As I got closer the music got louder, and I could see the dancers and the costumes. The familiarity of the whole experience touched me deep inside, and I began to cry. All the teachings of my father came rushing back, and I understood in a personal way what he had so often tried to share with me. I finally embraced my own identity. I was an Aboriginal woman!

The other meaningful experience was participating in my first sweatlodge. Nothing in my life to that point could compare to the spiritual connection that I felt that day. It was so humbling to sit upon Mother Earth in that way, in communal prayer, participating in a sacred ritual of healing and cleansing that our people have practiced for many generations. I left that day a changed woman.

How have these experiences changed you in dealing with abusive situations? Now that you have been on this journey, do you think anyone could give you a black eye again?
That's a very good question! I certainly hope not. That has been what I have been working to change. I'm glad to say that I have not been in an abusive relationship for over ten years. Much of my healing and growing has occurred because I have tried to answer the question, "How can I change so that I will be able to recognize and avoid abusive people, situations, and relationships?" The answers I've discovered are, first, I must be able to recognize what abuse looks like, sounds like, and feels like and then believe that it is never acceptable. Secondly, I need to believe that I am worthy of protection from abuse. And thirdly, I have to make a commitment to protect myself from every form of abuse—every way I can. For instance, I had to become willing to say, "No" when I meant "No," to speak up when I felt mistreated, and to walk away from people who do not respect others. My spiritual life is based on respect and love—the Creator's respect and love for me and all things and mine in return. After experiencing myself as a sacred child of the Creator, I finally recognized that I deserved better than abuse.

I have thought about this a lot, why people are caught in abusive relationships. I find it very distressing, yet interesting as well. I have come to think very differently about relationships. Some of the violence that happened in my life was a result of my expectation that a man was meant to take care of me. He was supposed to be big and strong and able to protect me. Ironically, he's the one I needed protection from. But this expectation, both on the part of the abuser and the abused, can create such a power imbalance between the couple. Inequities of power create an environment where the abuse of power is possible.

Violence is more than a result of drug or alcohol abuse. There is a fairy tale aspect to abusive relationships. You think, "He will protect me, he is big and strong, and I'm small and weak." It stems from the traditional roles that I, and many others, were raised with. These are not traditional Aboriginal gender roles, but traditional European gender roles that place the man at the head of the household and bestow him with more power. I had to let go of the desire to be taken care of, to find a knight in shining armor, and to embrace my own substantial power. Of course, equally important is letting men off the hook and allowing them to be human, vulnerable, and weak at times, and strong and powerful at others. But most important, we need to enter into relationships as equals. This is what my partner and I are practicing and learning about now. It is very fulfilling.

Obviously, your experiences have not hindered your ability to be loving and receiving. Would you say that you have learned some of these ideas about men's strengths and your own strengths through your spirituality?
Yes, I have found that both men and women play important and complementary roles in our spiritual ceremonies and culture. Women are very sacred as the givers of life. Men are taught to respect women and women to respect men. It's so beautiful really. Without each other, our people could not survive. There is a powerful lesson in that. Neither is better than the other. Each must fulfill the role that they are best suited for. Both roles are valuable. It seems we have forgotten that. Do I believe that women are best suited for cooking, cleaning, and caring for children? Hardly! These are all very important jobs but not the exclusive arena of women. Men also have great gifts to share. I am humbled at the depth of love and caring some men express towards their children. They have something unique to offer in caring for their children that is as important as the role women play. As well, women have great gifts to share in leadership roles with men.

I sense that, in spite of your bad experiences, you are capable of loving a man and of giving in a relationship.
Oh yes. I believe in love and I believe in marriage. But I have had to let go of the anger I felt towards men in order to become open and trusting again. At first it was hard to believe that there were men who were not abusive. I looked around and didn't see a lot of sensitive caring men. I felt discouraged. But they do exist.

When I was finally ready to believe they existed, a few good men came into my life to be my teachers. They have taught me about the gentleness of men, their potential for kindness and caring, and the beauty of a man who lives with integrity and trust. Some of those men I have embraced as friends, one I adopted as my brother, another as a grandfather, and one as my partner. I believe that differences in expectations and in power can lead to aggression. But when there is equality, true equality, there is no abuse. This would have to include equality in an economic, cultural, political, and gender sense as well as within a relationship.

Is it the spiritual learning that has brought you your strength?
Yes. Healing can be painful, but it is very powerful, empowering actually. As well, spiritual learning has given me direction, a greater purpose, and courage and hope to keep reaching out for something better, healthier, more beautiful. Through my spiritual learning I met someone who practices traditional healing. Someday he may be a spiritual leader in our community. As I got to know him, he became very human. I found out all his faults and doubts and issues he hasn't yet resolved. At first I was very disappointed, but I am learning about spirituality and humanness at the same time. Now I can accept that this person is just a man. I expected spiritual leaders to be godlike, but they are human. Eventually, I had to stop looking at those people for answers. They are the ones who have the connection with the spirit world, but the answers are within me. I have had to find the strength within myself.

Has your spiritual learning helped you with the question of equality in a relationship?
I'm now in a relationship with a good man. He has gone through some of the same things I have. He has seen the "other side" as an abusive man. Now we are both growing and walking down this path. Interestingly, separately we have both come to the same conclusions. We've had very similar experiences in learning so I think that through his experience he has come to many of the same conclusions that I have. If partners don't have equality and respect for themselves and each other, neither ends up getting what they want. It doesn't work if you don't have equality. The man may have the power, but he is dying inside and he can't touch anyone. That is an empty and lonely place to be. I'm glad my partner has been able to teach me about it from a man's perspective.

That's amazing that he can talk about it.
Yes, it is. But talking about it is what he has had to do to heal and change. It has been good for me because I have had to open my mind, to change my rigid thoughts and to learn. We can change. We do change. It's not easy, but we do.

He must be a very spiritual and emotional person.

Yes, he is, and that is important to me. We share our spiritual beliefs and practices. I believe it is our spiritual connection that has fuelled our quest for healing. And perhaps most importantly, given us the hope and courage to do the things necessary to heal—for me to face my pain—for him to face his shame.

In the Aboriginal way is there an image of what a woman is and what a man is? For instance, in Catholicism the woman is the virgin. According to the Bible, she is the helper of the man. In Western society we have internalized and perfected all these things to the point where it's harmful to women. Do you get a sense or an image of what is intended for you as a woman, what it means to be an Aboriginal woman?

Those are good questions. I cannot answer for all Aboriginal women. But I can tell you what it means to me to be an Aboriginal woman. I have been taught that traditionally Aboriginal women played very important roles, spiritual as well as others. The image of woman is embodied in the concept of complementarity and equality of roles. Aboriginal men were not traditionally oppressive toward women, but they have learned this while walking between two cultures. Traditionally, the woman would walk behind the man. This was not because of subservience but rather for protection as he was bigger, stronger physically, and had the weapons to protect her. This came about because of the dangers of the time. Walking behind a man was considered a position of strength and sacredness. Some elders teach that women are stronger than men. I believe women are amazing. Men's power and spiritual strength has been diminished. They are following women. They are not leading. Women are leading the way for men.

Do you have anything further that you would like to share with us?

Through everything that I have done to get past the pain I was in for so long— the therapy, crying, reading, journalizing, affirmations, positive self talk, work-shops, expressions of anger, writing letters, telling my family the truth and more—through all of it, nothing has created such a profound, substantial and long lasting relief from pain as the healing I have experienced through spiritual practice. This is a source of infinite power and strength that is accessible to everyone. Now I see my path, social work and helping others, is chosen for me. This is where the Creator wants me.

...from a conversation with White Swan Woman

Strength Comes From Within

The themes that run through *Lifelines* are evident in stories women wrote and told. Patriarchy, discrimination, racism, and child abuse are intertwined throughout these stories. Family violence is a social problem that involves isolation, dislocation, and relocation. It involves loss and despair.

But the underlying thread that connects these stories is one of the power of strength from within. The human spirit endures trauma and adversity and rebounds to embrace life and love once again.

Voices of
Women of Faith

Personal Views on the
Diversity of Culture, Religion,
and Background in Canada

3

One of the common threads in *Lifelines* is that spirituality is found within, the result of a life-long search that is nurtured and shaped by participation in a larger community. In this collection of conversations with women from various faith and cultural backgrounds, these women give voice to their personal expressions of faith and of the connections between spirituality, culture, and family violence. These conversations are not intended to represent the official position, or the views of any other individual in a given church or community.

Brenda, also known as Otter Woman is an Ojibway. She speaks of spirituality in the context of her own escape from abuse. She tells the story of participating for the first time in a sweatlodge ceremony and the powerful connection she experienced. She has discovered her Native spirituality and her cultural heritage. Otter Woman talks about having made the choice to search for personal and cultural identity, of the long process of listening to elders and of integrating their messages of spirituality and ceremony into her own life. She illustrates that knowledge gained through personal experience is a valuable tool in providing counsel to others in crisis. First-hand knowledge has provided Otter Woman with the confidence to assure others that, having made the choice to search, they too will find strength within.

Susan Sneath shows how she adopted practices and concepts from Buddhism and translated them into rituals of daily use. For example, she created a sacred place in her own home to practice meditation. As a humourist, she advocates adding a mix of daily lightness by taking short "joy breaks." Other women of faith agree that ritual and contemplation ease the anguish of abuse as well as build inner strength. It helps to bring a sense of calm and enables the mind to think things through, to explore alternatives, and to imagine new ways of being and living.

In conversations with the Reverend Marilyn McClung, Gita Das, Rabbi Lindsey bat Joseph and Dr. Zohra Husaini, we explore some of the ways in which family violence and spirituality are connected to the cultural traditions of faith communities. Marilyn speaks from the position of a recently ordained Anglican priest in the Christian tradition, Gita from the position of a psychologist as well as a member of the Hindu community, Lindsey as the Rabbi of a Reform Synagogue in the Jewish tradition, and Zohra from the position of an educator and member of the Muslim community.

These conversations reveal the complex and nuanced shades of meaning and difference that exist within a particular tradition over time and space, and between families and individuals within a particular community. We come to appreciate that difference itself deserves respect.

Another interesting aspect that came out of our discussions is that the history of patriarchy is variously embedded in the concepts and practices of faith communities, for example, gendered images of the Divine, representations of the good woman, marriage rituals and wedding vows, and methods for dissolving unsuccessful marriages. We learn how sacred texts are interpreted from a male point of view. We learn, understandably, that women caught in abusive relationships may feel abandoned by God and community. However, there are promising signs that traditional teachings and practice are being questioned and changed. We learn of female images of God and of scriptures and sacred texts interpreted from a woman's point of view. We learn of egalitarian influences in marriage ceremonies and vows.

We learn of differences in each culture when dealing with what we often assume to be universal concepts. Behaviours of human beings are culture-bound and are reflected in societal values such as the concept of choice versus the concept of destiny. By closely observing the rich nuances hidden in each woman's words and phrases we can learn much more.

Otter Woman Speaks

Otter Woman

Otter Woman is a thirty-six year old Ojibway, who now considers herself to be a "traditional woman." She went back to school as an adult student and recently earned a master's degree. As the transition year co-ordinator for Native students at a university, Otter Woman helps others in an informal way.

Sometimes you have to hit bottom before you can climb out.

I met with Brenda, whose Aboriginal name is Otter Woman, to hear her story and to understand how women who are or have been abused can find help in the Native community. Otter Woman works with Native Student Services at a university. Many of the students call her "auntie" and seek her out to talk to about their lives. Her own background helps her to listen and understand the problems young Native people face.

Otter Woman's own personal journey includes sexual abuse, drug and alcohol addiction, recovery, and a search for identity. In the past few years she has reunited with her family after years of turbulence and trouble. She tells me, "I was a mean person back then. You would not want to meet me on the street." It was this past life and the futility of her future that led Otter Woman to want to help others and to walk a different path. Going back to school and getting a university degree was the first step. She believes that her own healing is only beginning but that she can help others find their own path.

While attending university Otter Woman met a few Aboriginal students who were also searching for their personal and cultural identity. They helped each other begin to explore their roots. During her first experience in a sweatlodge, she instantly felt a powerful connection and began to believe that Native spirituality was right for her. From that time on she began her personal quest. Otter Woman decided she must find spiritual strength, and found it where she least expected, within herself. This search for peace, truth, and meaning in her life led her to the grey hairs (the elders) and she began the very long process of listening to those who know, slowly trying to integrate the meaning of the messages delivered in stories and ceremony into her own life. She began to learn about "knowing." She sees herself as a fledgling in this life-long quest.

Otter Woman has finally started to heal and this too she sees only as a beginning. She is learning to forgive others, but most of all she is learning to forgive herself, the hardest thing of all. Now that she has discovered the healing power of being grounded, of trying to achieve balance, she will never let go of this new woman, of her own newly developing pride of heritage. And helping others face their own challenges has put new meaning in her life. This caring and compassionate woman, well aware of her own shortcomings, her own inner fears, her own torments, and her own unfulfilled desires, continues on her slow path to healing by being there for others.

In exploring her own destiny, Otter Woman has discovered that, "You are in control." And she tries to impart this important message to the young women and men who seek her counsel. She talks about choices, and they listen because she cares and because they know she has been there. This is a powerful tool. Being an "auntie" to others is an important part of her life and she is beginning to realize that this may be the role the Creator intends for her. But she is willing to wait and see and to change direction bending like the willow to a will much greater than hers.

I asked Otter Woman how she would begin to help a woman who was in an abusive relationship or how her community would begin to help this woman. Otter Woman feels there is now strong support in her community for those who are suffering from abuse. Her first concern would be the woman's immediate safety and well-being. She would ask, "Do you feel safe?" Then she would ask, "Are you really safe?" Getting the woman out of danger is critical. This may involve getting her to a shelter or to safe ground. Then other immediate needs would have to be discussed, the safety of any children involved, getting food, and financial resources. Only after these have been taken care of is it time to explore other needs.

Counselling would be the next step, and she refers people to culturally-appropriate counsellors who can help. These women are in pain and in crisis, and they need someone to talk with, someone who will listen and understand. If the woman is a traditional woman, then she may be ready to seek the counsel of an elder, but during the crisis she will need a different form of help. A talking circle or a healing circle with others who are in pain may be helpful.

The importance of a friend to talk with makes an enormous difference. Knowing that someone is there to walk with you and that you have the support of friends, or family, or community can really help. Otter Woman knows how important these things are, but she also knows that each person must be ready to heal before it can happen and no one else can do it for them. Counselling is always available and Otter Woman is there to help someone connect with the right person for them. But she is able to tell them from personal experience, "You can do it. The strength is there within you. When you are ready you will do it." And each soul in torment must discover this for herself. Otter Woman's parting words were, "Sometimes you have to hit bottom before you can climb out."

Buddhism for Monday,
for Tuesday, for Wednesday...

After enlightenment—laundry—
take time to fill yourself up
along the way.

Susan Sneath

*Susan Sneath is a humourist
who focuses on helping people
through difficult times. She has
been challenged by despair,
addiction, cancer, and personal
tragedy. Susan uses the concepts
she has learned through
Buddhism to live each day and
to begin to help others.*

Can you tell me a little about yourself and how you came to Buddhism?
I discovered Buddhism very much out of personal need. I had been working as an artist, an actress, and found myself approaching (once more) a state of mental exhaustion or what I would call a nervous breakdown. This time a friend suggested I go and listen to Buddhist teacher, Geshe Kaldan speaking on Tibetan Buddhism. At that point I was very exhausted. I remember sitting in a room full of people all listening to Lama Kaldan who was speaking in a thick accent. I did not know anything about Buddhism and didn't comprehend much of what he was saying. Yet, I took away something very valuable from that encounter. He said, "If you sit for five minutes a day, and your mind is concentrating on a positive thought, when you breathe in and out the effects are phenomenal—not quite enlightening, but phenomenal."

Geshe Kaldan says that if you sit and meditate with the right motivation, it could be of benefit to all human beings. But even if you just sit there and breathe in and out, with your mind all over the place, it will still be of benefit. At that time in my life, I couldn't do more than to take my body and put it in a place. That's all that I was capable of. But I found that I didn't have to do more than that. That was my embarking, a perfect entry level for me.

When I met Geshe I wasn't interested in getting dependent on any care giving or counselling, but after hearing him that one night, an extraordinary thing happened. I toddled off to live my life and make sense of the chaos I was living in. I was doing a film when I suddenly started doing it, sitting for five minutes and breathing in and out. I soon began to realize the importance of ritual in our lives. Quite by accident (or was it design?) I started to practice this simple ritual and found a way to get through each day.

When I spoke with you earlier, you mentioned that this tool—your Monday, Tuesday, Wednesday concept—might be of use to women who have experienced family violence. Could you elaborate on that.

I think, when we are in pain, we need something special to help us cope with everyday life. Call it faith, religion, practice, or ritual. But there is no point in seeing a guru, or going to church, or going to a sweetgrass ceremony if you can't take the essence of its meaning with you in your travels through each day. You have to be able to pull out these tools when you encounter the unexpected.

When you have been assaulted with trauma and tragedy, you need something to ground you before you can begin to recover. I don't think you can really begin to heal until you are able to recognise the strength in yourself, that incredible strength within. No one can give it to you. No one can take it from you. Take me, for instance. Just as I was getting steady in my life after abuse, drugs, alcohol, illness, and turmoil, I got cancer. Buddhism helped me explore the unknown, "Was I going to die? How would I deal with a fair amount of intense pain?" Buddhism became a tool for me. Ritual brought out my own spirituality. Buddhism just happened to be there, a coincidence. It could have been something else or it could have been another practice. But Buddhism worked for me, and I began to believe in it. It gave me a sense of comfort, peace, energy, and support.

What about Geshe Kaldan? He must have played a special role in this?

The reason I found Geshe so fascinating is that he is a refugee who has experienced and seen much pain. He has undergone abuse himself and he has seen people he loved tortured and killed. You would think he should be angry, but he's not. Oh yeah, you know, "He has a right! He's had to leave his country and work in a menial job—after twenty years of study!" But Lama Kaldan is not angry. I think that his experiences in life and being a refugee have made him a great teacher and role model.

It is significant to me that Geshe is a refugee because I have always been "on the run" myself, from myself. I can relate to him. He made me realize that there are physical actions I can do to stop running for a few minutes, to centre myself. I can get away from self and situation, leave me behind. I began to realize I can learn how to do this. It made me ask myself, "What do I have that I can take with me in times of crisis?" Geshe Kaldan left so much behind but was able to keep his authenticity of being. What he carries with him has very little to do with material life—it's knowing, knowing about problem solving—it is simply a joy of being.

There is a sense of joy and lightness and delight in Geshe's eyes and in his manner when he is working with people. The depth of his laughter impacts everyone. Children immediately trust him. I have found that children have an incredible instinct in this regard. They are drawn to Geshe. I think that his sense of humour, his playfulness, and his compassion are from deeply working through things.

I understand he returned to Edmonton. It must have been hard when he moved to Toronto.

Not really. It didn't seem to matter because he was so charismatic and so extraordinary that the effect he had on me stayed with me. I had this one little piece from his lecture, and I began to use it. It is *dharma*, the essence of Buddhist teaching, that is most important. I have learned to take a little piece and use it every day, every way. There were times when I said, "I don't think I can take this." But the power of the mantra (a word or phrase repeated or chanted to improve concentration while meditating) is real. And it actually did steady my mind and take me through to another place.

I had no idea where I was going, but my spiritual practice kept me solid. I just took one step at a time. When I looked at my spiritual self, I found two things. The first was something left over from childhood, a god up in the sky that was male. There was no face to it, no guy with a beard. I just sensed an energy, a presence. The second was that one day, while I was in my garden, I found a seed. I remember holding the root of a bleeding heart plant and looking at it at a point in my life where I was burnt out, just fried. I looked at that seed, that root, and I thought, "Okay, if I chop this up and get a microscope and look at it, I will not see anything. I could chop it up into the tiniest pieces, and I will not see anything. But if I plant this little puppy, throw on some water, shove it in some dirt, if I put this dry warped little root into dirt and water it, I know that miracle of life will come." That's something. And that was where I had to go to begin building what for me is the god in all of us. So I planted it.

And through all this I discovered that God—the One who plans everything, who is up in the sky, the Christian thing (I was brought up Anglican), who is loving and forgiving and all those things and knows a lot, was not for me. That's why Tibetan Buddhism attracted me. Buddhism uses very little father imagery, like none, and I've learned so much about being a woman from the Buddhist deities. They're not like gods up in the sky, although at times you will draw their power into you. But it has to be with the understanding that you have them there within you. The deities are in you. And you're only drawing power from outside of you because you don't quite get it yet, and you're not quite open yet, but they are in you. God is in you. That's the point.

Buddhism became a tool for me. First, I stopped being at war with myself. Second, I began to build up my inner powers. Third, I created an alter, a sacred space, in my home. And that was vital for me. I have moved to a period of phenomenal strength where actually I feel very much at peace. I'm still doing a lot of problem solving. Things aren't going easy in my life, but there's a sense of resiliency, a sense of inner strength. There is knowing that all those little positive actions that you do tend to add up.

We talked earlier about the anger loop and its similarity to the cycle of violence that takes place over and over in abusive situations. Can you explain how you would use these examples?

Once you learn the loop you become aware of the beginning stages of aggression so that you have lots of time to react, to move, to change your own energy, or to get out of the way. For instance, Steven Levine, in *Healing Into Life and Death* and *Who Dies?* understands and synthesizes Buddhist philosophy, which is that there's an energy beyond, that things happen in a cycle over and over. Levine's approach is definitely Buddhist, but he also translates it, and I use his guidelines when I do my humour workshops. What faith you follow depends on your individual needs. Think of it like, "What kind of music do you like?" You just need to find one that is authentic for you. You just need to do it—first search out where you're going to look—and then do it.

The graduated path to enlightenment is that you take it slowly. Make small incremental changes. I would say that the changes are permanent. It's not a little thing. Certainly your character changes. When you build and get stronger, it's not a pretend strength. It's not a put-on strength.

What do you see as the most important first step in making small but significant changes?

I would say doing something for yourself, love or self-love. Think of something that would add lightness for you, something that would take care of you, something that would do something nice for you. Eating a good meal could be love. I use "joy breaks," things that I call "playing with a purpose." They take between three and five minutes and they are fun, but what they really do is train the mind, distract the mind. Although you would think these are just little things, if you add them up they have the effect of lightening and lifting.

Generally, we don't start doing things that are really healthy for us until we have a problem. That's the North American way. So in an abusive situation, whether you flee or stay, if you had small things you could carry with you—tiny tools like joy breaks, ritual practice, or sacred space—you could begin to heal. So you focus on these tools and you make them work because they are all you've got.

In times of crisis, even if you're on the run, you still have to have your problem-solving skills. People tend to think this is a time to be serious, but you need the lightness because it will keep you going. If you really see survival as important, then you'd better be in it for the long run. Taking time for lightness and laughter is important. That means take a moment and blow some bubbles with your children. It builds balance. It keeps balance in the face of uncertainty.

Laughter is vital. Ritual is vital. They give form to chaos.

From the Pulpit
A Word or Two on Christianity

Marilyn
McClung

The Reverend Marilyn McClung is an Anglican priest, who is married and has two adult daughters and one grandson. Now in her fifties, Marilyn was born in Edmonton and lives there today.

When they say, "I need to be forgiven,"
do I say, "You are forgiven,"
or do I argue with them saying,
"What have you done that's so wrong
that you need to be forgiven?"

Could you talk about your perceptions regarding family violence and what is going on in the church today. Is there anything about abuse that is hidden, that we don't see?

I think that there's a lot that's hidden that we don't see partly because people are embarrassed to admit to it. Maybe sometimes they don't even recognize it themselves. But more and more people are coming forward and saying that this is a problem that they're having. I think that the Anglican church is probably more open to accepting that it is happening than some churches. Certainly I have people coming to me, both women who are abused and men who are abusers.

How do these people find you or how do they approach you?

Sometimes it's because I've said things in sermons and they sense how I feel about things, or they have heard of my association with women's shelters. People will come to me and sometimes not even tell me what the problem is initially. They'll simple say, "Can I come and see you sometime, or will you come out and see me?" One man who I had never seen before, phoned me saying that his wife had kicked him out, he was desperate, and could he talk to me. As it turned out he was a very controlling abusive kind of person. Another was a man who came to our church services once in a while. He wanted me to come and see his wife and him. They had sepa-rated, and he asked if I could help them get back together. He admitted that he was violent and I said, "No, I can't do that unless I speak with her first." I don't believe that counselling couples together when there's violence works. So I referred the wife to a counsellor and to a support group. I never met with them again and haven't heard from either one of them since. I have heard that she left him. I see my role, not so much in counselling, but maybe helping with spiritual questions later.

Could we discuss that issue a little bit, the difference between counselling and helping them with spiritual issues?
When women are in crisis, we can initially talk about what some of the issues are, but I find that these women are more worried about their safety, the children, or the physical things, so I would likely refer them to a shelter. If the situation does not seem to be at a crisis state, I might refer them to a support group. There are always spiritual questions in people's minds you know, but those are the kinds of things we can talk about when their immediate physical and safety needs have been met.

As far as the teachings of the church go, in trying to do the right thing, trying to recognize abuse or cruelty, do women have a struggle with what they are experiencing? Can they define the problem or know what to do in their situation?
I think that a lot of the women that are abused are very traditional women and so they believe a lot of the traditional teachings. For instance, they believe that the man is the head of the family, that wives are supposed to submit to their husbands, and the idea that marriage is a life-long contract regardless of what happens. Often a woman doesn't recognize that if her husband is abusive, he's already violated that covenant, the contract. I think women struggle a lot with what the church has tradi-tionally taught and what they inherently believe. The more women accept and buy into the traditional role, the more likely they are to stay in the situation regardless of what happens. Until a woman is ready to question these things that is.

Is anyone raising these questions for them? Do you ever hear that they have been forced by circumstance to address this issue?
Not very often. But you know, more and more people are questioning or raising the issue of abuse. I know I do.

Where do they find the strength to remain in a situation like this? This puzzles me. What kind of endurance does one have to stay and endure?
I think it's the opposite. I think it's the battered woman syndrome where you just accept this is happening to you and almost give in to a state of mind where you can't get out of it.

So when women do come to you, and are wanting to leave, what is it that has allowed them to take such a radical step?

Quite often they have already left or else they're seriously thinking about it. What often triggers it is their children and if they are being abused too. They realize that they just can't let that happen. They will somehow accept it for themselves, but if their children are being abused, then they'll start to question things.

However, if they're very traditional in their beliefs, it takes a long time to see things in another way. This is especially true if their family and everybody that is important to them have traditional beliefs as well. The risk is that they could be ostracized if they leave their marriage. There are a lot of factors that are involved in the decision to leave or stay.

So, how do you begin, or how do you approach it from the spiritual point of view?

If they're past the point that they're safe and they're doing okay physically, they'll usually raise questions. "How can I believe in a god that lets this happen to me?" will quite often be the first question that's asked. I usually ask them, "Well is God letting this happen to you or are the people involved letting it happen? I don't believe that God means for you to suffer like this." The suffering that Jesus talks about in the Bible is suffering for a cause that one chooses. That's one kind of suffering. But the kind of suffering where a woman is being abused isn't chosen. That is being inflicted on her, and I don't think any of us are called to that kind of suffering.

Do people want to believe this when you tell them that?

Oh, they sometimes argue with me, but even if it gets them thinking, it's valuable. Sometimes it's the opposite. They have to reject all the teachings of the church. They need somebody to reinforce what they're starting to think and believe. It really varies.

Aside from a pragmatic discussion about safety, how does your conversation proceed at another level, a level that we sometimes call the spiritual?

Only, I think, when the initial stage is past, when the woman is feeling reasonably safe, when it's not a crisis time. At that time she might feel like she can begin to sort it out and discuss what she really believes and is thinking. It might happen in a shelter where and when she is feeling safe.

I know you have been in to see women in the shelters. Do you go in now as a priest?

No, I don't.

Not since you stopped volunteering?
No. That's one of the things that always bothered me when I did volunteer there. There was this general message that they don't want any religious people about, and you're not to raise any religious issues. I think it was more that they were afraid of you preaching at people. In fact in volunteer training that is impressed on you. You are not to preach at people.

And yet, sometimes you'd be driving somebody somewhere and a woman would raise these issues. I would never preach to her, but I was willing to listen to what she was struggling with or what she believed. I really think that there's a need for that, and I came to believe it more and more while I was going to the shelters.

The need to be open to people's many backgrounds is recognized, but their need to discuss spiritual questions is not. I think that we all have a spiritual nature. Our hospitals have recognized it in terms of having pastoral care departments, but shelters are only starting to recognize it. If our objective is to empower women, then there has to be an empowering kind of spirituality too, or we're not going to get anywhere.

And how does one begin to assist a woman, to help her work towards this empowerment?
I guess it just has to go hand in hand with the other aspects of empowering a person, and I'm only beginning to learn how you do that. I guess it's doing things to increase self-esteem and self-confidence, but they've got to do it themselves. It's encouraging them to do it.

Are there certain teachings that one can draw on to help with self-worth or to provide encouragement or reassurance? In other words, from where in your religion can women derive strength for change or for finding peace?
I think you almost have to look underneath the layers because the Christian scriptures are really written from a patriarchal point of view. There are some strong women in the Bible, but even Mary is depicted either as a subservient person (with God telling her she would have this child), or else she's glorified and saint-like. You don't really get a picture of a true woman. Yet she must have been a very courageous person to do all she did, and if she was unmarried, she would have been looked down on by society. I believe Mary was courageous, but nobody ever sees that image. And yet, if you read between the lines, there were lots of strong powerful women around at that time who travelled with Jesus. He treated them as his equals and often he spoke to women when it was taboo to do so; for instance, he spoke to the Samaritan woman at the well. He did a lot of things to indicate that women were equal, but we don't pick up on these because they haven't been emphasized or taught.

So, with traditional women who have been abused, what position are they left in when they have decided they are taking the kids and they're leaving? What are their spiritual needs?

I think a lot of them have a need to feel God's forgiveness, and yet I have trouble with that because I can't see why they need to be forgiven. I am still struggling with that. When they say, "I need to be forgiven," do I say, "You are forgiven," or do I argue with them saying, "What have you done that's so wrong that you need to be forgiven?" Is it the time to tell them or is it the time to simply help them feel better? I struggle with it.

And how do you decide whether this is the person you should challenge or not challenge?

Each case is different, depending on the individual. You can always help them find peace of mind for the moment and come back to it at a later date.

How would you attempt to give someone solace and peace of mind?

I might ask them if they would like to pray. I wouldn't impose it on them. Again, you sort of sense where they're at and what they need. Each person is a little different. Maybe it's just that I know they will be given the strength to deal with the situation and the courage.

When women are past the trauma of it all, do you hear from them? Do they tell you how they dealt with it? Do they relate some small thing—a memory, a sermon—that demonstrates that their faith got them through?

Sometimes they say that they totally lost their faith and that they could no longer believe what they'd been taught. They may have begun to look at things differently. For instance, they may have trouble with things like male images of God and the use of exclusive language. They may have very negative feelings towards maleness. And so part of what they are rejecting is the maleness of the Christian religion. Others will say that they came very close to losing their faith but somehow hung on.

And does that imply they get it back?

Sometimes. Or they may get it back in a totally different way, or have a new way of looking at it.

And does the religion have the tolerance and the flexibility to accommodate this and to allow them to find their place in the church with these changed and transformed views?

It would depend on which church. I think that the Anglican and the United churches are probably more open than a lot of others. My experience with rural churches is that it would be much more difficult for a person there than at the cathedral downtown in a large city. For instance, in large cities, there is a diverse range of people who have all sorts of different beliefs and outlooks, but in rural areas, the people are still pretty traditional. I think it would be more difficult to get together with other women and share what you believe. Finding others who think alike would be tough.

So is this perhaps something that one deals with alone? Is it our culture?
Yes, I think in this culture it is dealt with a lot alone. I don't think it's recognized as a struggle that people have.

Do you ever get called to come to a centre or a place and speak with a woman in crisis?
When I was a volunteer, there were women who were struggling. Most were from fundamentalist churches. I feel that it is something that isn't being dealt with. Occasionally, there are Roman Catholic sisters that come and visit people, but I don't know to what extent they might talk about spiritual issues. I think it's something that could be done if people want it. In our shelters people come from such diverse backgrounds you would have to have somebody who was pretty open to different faiths, to Native spirituality, and to cultural differences.

I am wondering, when a woman has rejected her religion or her spirit has been broken, when she has lost all faith, how does she mend her spirit?
I'm not sure that they always do, but it would take time.

We know there are survivors. Do we know of any whose spirits mend?
I think so, definitely. Many of them have done a lot of reading. They'll go looking for books, whatever they can get on the topic, and just read and read and read to try to find answers for themselves. If one knows of good books to recommend, that sometimes works. Sometimes these are private issues that people have to work through by themselves. And other times talking them through it helps.

It must be difficult to talk about things that are private, things that are hidden away some place. I have always thought that the clergy would be good at helping people talk about difficult things.
Certainly, for one thing clergy are one of the few professional people still going to people's homes. Doctors don't make house calls, but clergy still go and visit people from their congregations and others. The clergy has more opportunity to get a sense of what's going on in people's homes than a lot of other professionals. It's not a very romantic job.

But you must have a way of getting people to open up to you?
Sometimes. It takes time and sometimes it's just a matter of being the kind of person that people trust. If you're visiting somebody or they've come to see you, the first conversation will be pretty superficial. It's only when they get to know that you're not going to judge them that they will begin to trust you. They have to trust you before they'll talk about things that are really private, and they must believe that things are going to be confidential.

What can you do within your congregation to raise the issue of abuse as unacceptable?
I guess you can preach sermons, you can do seminars, and you can leave material on abuse in the racks at the back of the church. During pre-marriage counselling I think it's very important to raise the question, "How do you fight? Do things ever get violent between you?" Abusive behaviour usually shows up before people get married. It's a warning sign. I think it's something that should be talked about with teenagers and youth groups. It can even be part of Sunday School curriculums. There are many opportunities to raise the issue of abuse.

And how are relationships addressed in the church in general?
In the Anglican church the marriage service has really changed. Even in the time since I've been married, it has changed. I talk to couples about the marriage service and what it means, and I refuse to use the old service. Some clergy will still use it if people ask. It is interesting that the origin of the woman walking down the aisle with her father was that she was considered to be a possession of her father and he gave her away as a possession to the husband. The whole thing was based on property and possession.

In our service I encourage both parents to walk with the bride and to give their blessing to the marriage. It's a mutual relationship and that whole idea of property and possession is now gone from the service. The service says that it is a mutual relationship and that both partners are to love and respect each other. The vows used to say the woman promised to love, honour, and obey, and the man promised to love, honour, and cherish. Now they both promise to love, honour, and cherish. When I'm going to marry a couple, we usually go through the service and talk about these words and what they mean. I refuse to marry people in the old way because as far as I'm concerned I'm a part of what's happening there.

When a woman in the church is known to be abused what is her status? What happens to her as the part of the congregation?
Often she won't want others to know and often others don't know. I think people would be very supportive, other women especially. Most of our congregations are very supportive of the shelters. They contribute money and other support. The

woman might disappear if her husband is also a member of the congregation because it isn't easy for both to come if one is being abused. If he's a very prominent member of the congregation, people find it difficult to believe that he would do these kinds of things. So it is possible that she wouldn't be believed.

What happens to the man in the congregation if it is known he is an abuser?
I can't say because I haven't really had that kind of situation. I would imagine he would disappear from the scene. If there's been any kind of conflict in a marriage and there's been a separation or there's been a divorce, it's very seldom that both members will keep coming to that same congregation. And it's very often the man who will go somewhere else.

What do you think the churches have yet to do to respond to spousal abuse? What could they do that they don't do?
An increasing number of people are questioning some of the theology that's taught. I think it's a matter of moving in the direction that we've started to move and live in. The change, even in the last ten or fifteen years, is incredible.

An area that I think really needs to be looked at is the military chaplaincy. Family violence happens in the military. I recently sent a questionnaire to a military chaplain (as well as a number of other clergy) to ask about his experience. He said that he had encountered an endless number of couples where there was violence but he still maintains that the man is the head of the family and that the couples should stay together.

I think there is a great need for education of military chaplains and even hospital chaplains. I was surprised that, in response to my questionnaire, one hospital chaplain said that he didn't encounter this kind of problem and that it didn't really relate to his work. And I thought, "Oh—there must be a lot of abused women who end up in a hospital—what kind of blinders have you got on?" Education is definitely lacking in this area.

You were telling me earlier that many people who don't recognize abuse or don't respond to it take their interpretations from Paul. Tell me the difference between Paul and the Gospel in light of this conversation.
I think that Jesus taught that we were equal, and he preached that there should be justice, but Paul was very influenced by the times. It was a patriarchal culture at that time in history and his writings reflect that patriarchy.

In Ephesians, chapter 5, verse 21, it says,

> Wives, be subject to your husbands as you are to the Lord,
> for the husband is the head of the wife just as Christ is the head
> of the church, the body of which he is the Savior. Just as the
> church is subject to Christ, so also wives ought to be everything
> to their husbands.

But most people don't read the whole of what he said. They just take that part and interpret that to mean that the wife is to be obedient and submissive. That specific passage reflected largely the culture that existed at the time, and the church was influenced by the culture, especially in terms of the way women were treated. In the very beginning of the church, women were followers. They preached and church services were held in their homes. And then the church became patriarchal, and it soon followed that only men could be priests. Women very quickly became subservient.

Peter, which was written even later than Paul, says exactly the same kind of thing.

> Wives in the same way accept the authority of your husbands, so
> that if even some of them do not obey the word, they may be won
> over without a word by their wives' conduct when they see the
> purity and reference of your lives.

Then he goes on to say that women are not to do things like braiding their hair and putting gold ornaments on. So you can see how the culture and attitudes towards women started to get into the scriptures. But Jesus never taught any of those kinds of things. At least nothing that we have recorded shows that he did. He always seemed to treat women as equals.

Some people say that in our culture we tune out. We keep ourselves busy so that we don't attend to the spirit, we don't look after our spiritual being. Can you comment on this?
I think it's probably true, for some more than others obviously. Also, in the last few years there has been a real movement of people searching for the spiritual part of life. People are looking for answers. Modern life hasn't satisfied all their needs. Others will just make themselves busier so they don't have to think about those kinds of things.

I believe that spirituality should be an essential part of almost everybody's life. A lot of people in our society have lost their sense of value for that. Their way is to keep very busy. But it is simple things that heal. Even a walk outside in nature, quietly by yourself, has tremendous value.

When women who are abused speak to you what do they say causes them the most difficulty in trying to change their circumstances (other than the person who's abusing them of course)?
Often, they'll think in terms of their children, helping their children and how they would get help for their children. They will ask, "What do I do? I'm in this terrible situation, or my child's in this terrible situation, and I don't have a clue what to do or where to turn. Should I leave or should I stay?"

Many have a hard time managing. It might even be that they need food from the Food Bank or they don't have any means of supporting their family. So it depends what stage they are at, but I find, at the very beginning, they usually don't have a clue what to do.

I might say to a woman, "If you're not planning to leave, I think you should have a plan so that if the danger increases you know how you're going to leave." I suggest that she have things already packed just in case she has to leave. If women are in those kinds of situations, you sometimes have to tell them what you think they should do because they can't really think for themselves at that point.

I've heard rural areas have fewer resources. But is there anything else that makes the circumstances of abuse different in the rural areas?
Well, the woman might be more isolated if she is on a farm or out in the country. Also you don't have to be in a small town very long to learn that word travels. You say a few things, and everybody in town knows within half an hour. So, if there are family troubles and the woman leaves, people in town find out pretty fast. They also know where she is so her husband can very easily find her. It's much easier to disappear in a big city than in a small town. In a small town everyone knows if somebody comes to talk to me.

I wonder if that prevents some people from coming to talk?
It definitely does.

Do people ever ask you to somehow be involved in keeping their secret or do they find another excuse to talk to you so that no one will guess?
Oh yes, they do that. They might not even admit to themselves that that's why they'd come to see me initially. They'll come with some other issue and then when they figure that they can trust me, they reveal the abuse. Anybody who comes to talk to me knows it will be confidential.

I am constantly amazed how I learn things about people in the congregation via the grapevine. For instance, the whole community will know if a husband is verbally abusive in public. After each incident word travels quickly.

Do you think that the community would then intercede?
No, I don't think they would. One of the communities I work in was offered a social worker to help deal with some of the problems, including abuse. The town council said, "We don't have any problems in this town. We don't need anybody." But I have been with some of the town women when they were staying at a shelter in the city. I helped them get their possessions from their homes so I know there are problems there. But, according to the town council, it does not happen.

I imagine some women need to save face and others think that nobody will believe them, so they don't tell.
Especially if their husband is very prominent in the community.

How does a woman begin to understand the suffering and the cruelty that she endures within the context of the beliefs and values of her religion? How would you explain that. Do you tell them it is just their lot in life?
I wouldn't explain it that way, but that used to be the explanation. Women were taught that we were to suffer for the sake of righteousness. Supposedly, it made us holier if we suffered. Christ suffered on the cross, and we're supposed to do the same sort of thing, especially women for some reason. I just don't believe that.

We need a theology that is centred around resurrection and liberation, not around the cross. Theology should address turning suffering around so that we can be liberated and become free. All that stuff around Jesus dying on the cross for our sins has a lot to do with what's been laid on women. It rationalizes why they're supposed to suffer and why they're supposed to stay in these situations. The rationale is that it makes them holier if they stay and suffer more.

Personally, I think we're meant to be liberated. I think we're meant to get out of those situations, not to stay there and allow those things to happen. I think we have control over that.

Are you encouraged? Do you sense the roots of a theology that is a liberation theology?
Yes, I guess my own theology is very much a liberation theology. Feminist theology is a part of liberation theology.

Does that distress some of your congregation?
Yes. If I preached exactly what I believe I think they'd probably rise up against me. I have to use a bit of discretion. I raise questions. I don't preach everything that I believe, but I don't preach anything I don't believe either. I realize that you can't change people in one day. I have to admit that I'm probably much more radical than my congregation thinks. And it was far easier to preach more radical things at the cathedral in the city than it is in a small community.

Also it is much easier to reach people in small groups where there's discussion back and forth about theology because then people can say, "Hey, that's what I believe too," or they can say, "I don't agree with you." It's a much more reasonable way to do things than simply preaching to people about what you believe. I actually prefer small group sessions because of this.

How do you do this within your congregation?

I might have a Bible study group or a study group at Lent. These would be opportunities to bounce ideas off each other about personal beliefs. I find that much more effective than preaching.

Do you speak about male and female relationships, the position of women in the church?

Yes, at times. I guess it would just come in a natural fashion. We usually preach on the readings for the day. Say we were talking about the readings from Paul. I would discuss the whole thing, the place and time, the historical context. Sometimes readings lead to talk about marriage and I lead a straightforward discussion on the issues. I very much believe that sermons should relate to people's lives and that they should be able to take something home with them to think about.

I generally do a bit of background reading and then try to relate scriptures to something that might make sense in people's lives here and now. There are times when things like marriage come up or it could be the way society looks at women or how we perceive family violence when we are talking about justice. There are many opportunities to bring up these issues.

Is it fair to say that the churches have been tolerant of domestic violence or of wife abuse?

If you go back in history, they actually taught that it was acceptable. I think in recent years they've just acted like it didn't exist. There is a denial that it exists.

What about the question about the good woman and the good man? You were saying to me before the interview something about being stoical.

In the church that I grew up in, the Anglican church, I got the idea that somehow you were a strong and worthy person if you could just bear all this. It was your cross to bear and if you bore it silently without any complaint you were a virtuous person or a good person. This whole idea around it being women's cross to bear grew as patriarchy grew. Women were expected to suffer abuse. Maybe it even came out in the vows "for better or for worse." Who knows. Maybe the "worse" carried that connotation.

For me that cross to bear came from Jesus saying, "Take up your cross and follow me," which I don't think is quite the same thing. I think the latter is more meaningful. Simply put, if you're going to follow the way of Christ, then there's going to be some suffering along the way. If you feel very strongly about an issue and you choose to fight for that issue, you may well suffer along the way. For example, Martin Luther King fought for civil rights and died for them.

But there is no issue involved in wife abuse. It is strictly involuntary suffering. You haven't chosen anything. This idea of abuse being "your cross to bear" isn't really what Christ was teaching at all.

Where does the idea of choice come from?

I think that's all through scriptures. We all have free will and we can choose how we're going to live our lives. Certainly we can choose to live a spiritual life. We can choose to live a materialistic life. And we can choose whether we're going to live in an abusive situation or whether we are going to leave it. We all have those choices.

What is the purpose of suffering in life?

I personally think it's just life. We're all going to suffer in some way. I don't think God imposes suffering on us. I don't think that if a husband is abusing his wife it is because that is what God wishes or God inflicts on her. It's not because of something she did or did not do. I just think that we all suffer in some way.

When people are oppressed and they see no hope of changing their situation, then there's usually a strong emphasis on the cross and on death. That's true with abused women too. If they can't see themselves ever getting out, they'll come to believe that it is their cross to bear, that's what they have to put up with, and the more they suffer the more virtuous they are. They may tell themselves they are going to be rewarded in the future. If they get out of it, more immediate hope begins to break through.

Perhaps their hope may be in having other people walk with them, giving them support and encouragement and to know that other people are with them and that God is with them also. I believe that if somebody is in a situation and it doesn't look like there's anybody who cares or anybody who's going to help them out, then they must be utterly without hope. You can only find hope in knowing that there's somebody else, some other presence there, to walk with you.

That is what the whole Christian faith is supposed to be about. It's supposed to be about hope.

One of the ways of looking at God that's come through feminist theology is that traditionally God was always pictured as up there, transcendent, not reachable. The feminist way of looking at God is that God is in us, around us, part of us, and is acting in us. God isn't up there zapping us. I think God is a part of that transforming because God is in us.

And is there a change in the way the mother is seen? I am not fully familiar with the symbolism, but I do know that God is a boy, the father side of the Trinity. And the mother isn't even there.

One time, when I was talking to the children about baptizing, I said, "Then we baptize the baby in the name of the Father, the Son, and the Holy Spirit"—and a little seven-year-old girl looked at me and she said— "How come God can never be a mommy?"

But there are feminine images of God. In the Bible Jesus talks about God as being like a mother hen with all the little chicks. I'm sure people have feminine images of God in their minds if they think about it. But we've been taught this image that God is the Father and that can be big trouble too if a woman has a negative image of her own father and negative pictures of men in general.

There are women's churches who are groups of (mainly) women that get together and worship, study, and talk in terms of inclusiveness and female images of God. There are a lot of feminist theologians, both male and female.

What do congregations think about such a direction?
It varies. To the congregations I'm involved with, except for a few women, a lot of this is quite new. Even using inclusive language is new to them. You introduce things slowly and subtly. But there are some people who have left the organized church and formed their own separate churches to embrace this new direction.

How would you relate all this to the process of healing?
Usually we think of healing as healing of physical illnesses, but I try to think of healing in the holistic way. It means returning to total wellness. This includes the emotional, mental, spiritual, and physical aspects. When people are sick in the hospital, it is how they feel about things, their mental state, and their spiritual state that often dictates whether they get well.

A woman's spiritual state when being abused probably has quite an influence on whether she can deal effectively with the situation and become well again. I try to view most things in a holistic way.

Is that imagery meaningful in the context of abuse? Is what must occur to overcome abuse appropriately called healing?
I'm not sure. I suppose you could say that this situation needs healing, but yet I'm not always sure that it can be healed. There hasn't been too much success in changing men who are abusive. Often the answer is for the couple to separate and lead separate lives. I suppose in time the woman could be well again so I guess it is a kind of healing. I'm not convinced.

I look on forgiveness as a long process rather than something that can just happen instantly. In some of these situations maybe women can never forgive spouses. I don't know if there's a relationship between forgiveness and healing. I hadn't thought of it in terms of healing. I have tended to think of healing in terms of physical or mental illness.

I wonder whether when somebody's a victim if they need healing. I have more of a sense that it's the abuser that needs healing. I don't know.

Yes, I get your point because if you need to be healed, then...
Then, there might be something wrong with you. I heard one fellow talk once who was working in the North. He'd gone in on some kind of a mission and he

was praying with some native women, saying that they would be healed and that they should go back and forgive their husbands. I was angry! At the time I thought, "No, these women don't need to be healed, to go back and forgive their husbands." Those husbands need to have something happen to them. I'm not totally sure that, for the woman who is the victim, healing is the thing that's needed. Empowering maybe but…again, I don't know.

But then what do we say to the woman who says "this cruelty is intolerable and it must change but I must save my marriage"?
You have to talk about the meaning of marriage. I believe that the husband by being violent has broken the marriage contract, and there's no need to save that marriage. I believe that marriage is finished unless he can show that he's totally changed his ways. He's violated what he's promised to cherish, so I would not encourage many to save the marriage. There are times when marriages are meant to end.

How does one help a person resolve the notion that marriage is forever and that there might be implications in the next life if one chooses to end it, or maybe Christianity doesn't have that notion?
Not so much, no, no. But there is the idea definitely that marriage is for life.

Till death do us part.
That's right, and divorce was not acceptable. It's only been in the last twenty years that the Anglican church would remarry anybody who was divorced. Sometimes you have to say this marriage didn't work. You don't perpetuate something that's already broken.

Not a decision to be taken lightly.
No, no, no, I mean, you don't just walk out of the marriage at the first little thing. But when somebody has already broken one-half of the covenant or contract, then maybe there are things that are more important than the marriage vows, like a woman's safety and the children's safety and all those kinds of things.

And when a man beats his wife, what in the contract is broken by that act?
The vow to love, honour, and cherish.

So those words have a certain meaning don't they?
I think so.

Can you explain the difference between the phrase "to love and to honour and to cherish" and the phrase "to love, to honour, and to obey?"

Well, "obey" says that one person has control or power, doesn't it? And you know it's the wife who is to obey. I think "love, honour, and cherish" has a certain mutuality that you both care for each other in the same way. It doesn't involve abusing each other in any way. Women, as well as men, can be verbally abusive and emotionally abusive. People should be able to believe in those vows, in a mutual agreement.

Now I can see the importance of what you said earlier about the change in the vows. This change is a symbolic move towards a more liberal theology. It's a more equal notion of partnership.

Definitely. I'll read you what the marriage service currently says,

> Marriage is a gift of God in which man and woman become one flesh and they give themselves to each other in love that they can grow together and be united in that love. The union of man and woman in heart, body, and mind is intended for their mutual comfort and health.

So it is to care for each other. It's not about the bad times or not caring. The vows are definitely to love and to cherish for the rest of their lives. He promises to love her, comfort her, honour her, and protect her, and she promises the same thing, to love him, comfort him, honour him, and protect him.

Abusing someone isn't protecting her. The mutuality throughout the service spells out equality to me.

Views of a Hindu Woman

Gita Das

Gita Das, a Hindu, was born in the Orissa region on the coast of the Bay of Bengal in India over sixty years ago and has lived in Canada since 1968. She is a mother, grandmother, and a chartered psychologist.

There is a dichotomy here, a great split— between mother as "sacred goddess"— and woman as "pleasure giver."

What is your perspective on family violence? Is it influenced by an individual's cultural background or religious beliefs?

Of the nine hundred million people in India, the majority are Hindu, with roughly twelve percent Muslim and three percent Christian. With this great diversity it is obvious that culture is the key, not religion itself. Hindus are diverse in their religious beliefs and practices with many sects and sub-sects. They are separated from each other by caste, class, and region. In addition to this diversity, the women's movement within various communities is bringing rapid change in gender and role relationships. I think this demonstrates how impossible it is to generalize, in any religion. And if we refrain from generalizing, we lessen the risk of stereotyping others.

People can be socialized by a religious culture. No religion sanctions violence against women. In India, a woman's vulnerability depends on social status because this determines whether she is powerful or powerless. Similarly, if a woman is classified as a "bad" or a "good" woman, she can either become a victim or escape victimization. People are always looking for external sources that contribute to the problem. We need to explore the inner causes as well. For instance, if we want to know what made a certain individual a "victim," rather than looking at religious beliefs, we need to look at the "inner barriers" and at the culture itself.

The desire to stay married, even to an abusive and violent husband, is common in women from India. It does not matter whether she is Hindu, Muslim, Sikh, or Christian. Many traditional women will put up with a husband's beatings, interpreting them as "chastisement," while expressing contempt for weak men who try to please their women. Traditional men also have similar perspectives. For example, a friend of ours once said, "People criticized me for slapping my wife occasionally. Well, I slapped her so that she would improve herself. I was concerned about her well-being. She is my responsibility. I did not beat other people's wives." In this case, both parties accepted verbal abuse and physical punishment as long as it remained within certain bounds. This is one example of the inner barriers I mentioned previously. Traditional men do not feel they need to change their behaviour because a husband is expected to dominate the wife to control her and to be punitive if the situation demands it.

Women used to accept this. But educated and economically empowered women are challenging the status quo. In particular, when they immigrate to Canada and see that a husband-wife relationship can be egalitarian and need not be hierarchical, they no longer wish to put up with it. They begin to believe in "zero tolerance" for violence against women. However, the men often do not see their own behaviour as abusive or violent.

Many ex-husbands who are now remarried to other women keep strong control over their former wives and continue to dictate what they can or cannot do. An ex-wife accepts such control because, in a new country, her former husband is often the only person she knows well. She is often dependent on him for child support and other help. In addition, the woman has come from a society where women are always protected, sheltered, and guided by others. She is not used to making even minor decisions without first seeking somebody's approval. These women, especially in a new country, are afraid to live with the consequences of their decisions, always worrying that it may turn out to be the wrong decision. This is another example of the internalized barriers we need to be aware of.

In the case of the Muslim faith (in India), a man can divorce his wife simply by repeating three times, "I divorce thee." Males have always had this right under Islamic religious law. Today, many leave the community to get an education or a position in another country. After becoming wealthy some go back home, divorce their wives, and marry a younger woman. Yet the ex-wife usually thinks of herself as still being her husband's "wife" and of necessity, remains under his control. The legal relationship may end, but the emotional bondage stays. The women feel humiliation, shame, and anger, and blame destiny for treating them so unfairly. Nonetheless, many women still cling to their former husbands.

Is there anything in religious texts that could be interpreted as condoning abuse of women?

No. There are clear instructions to honour and respect women. The human mother is a symbol of cosmic mother. A wife is especially honoured because she keeps the family line continuing and it is said that, without her, no one will have children or grandchildren. A daughter is sheltered and protected, and it is one of the great obligations of a father and brothers to make sure she marries well. As a woman does not inherit the paternal property, her share of the family's resources is given as a dowry. Thus the infamous dowry system started.

Religious texts are not seen by the masses, so the majority of people are guided by the norms and traditions of their society and sub-culture. Also, the religion is interpreted differently for men than for women. The often quoted dictum that says, "Women have no independence," never mentions the context. It is said that in childhood the father will shelter his daughter and provide for her. The husband will do the same during her youth. In old age the son takes over the role of father and husband. But the common interpretation is that during her entire life cycle a woman will be under the control of one or the other of these three male relatives.

In Kerala, male domination among Hindus is a recent happening because, until the nineteenth century, Kerala non-Brahmin Hindus lived under a matrilineal system (descent is traced through females only and property is transferred from mother to daughter). Northern India has had a long history of being invaded by outsiders; consequently, a patrilineal system replaced the ancient matrilineal one. This history of military invasion and warfare paved the way for lessening the worth of women. As women could not be warriors, battle brought with it the abduction and rape of women. Women were seen as a burden. Female infanticide provided one way out. Another was that many women chose to die in fire to escape rape and dishonour. Their actions were glorified and idealized and were adopted as the ideal for all women. Similarly, some women died in the fire by choosing to climb onto the funeral pyre of their husbands rather than lead the tormented life of widowhood. They, too, became deified in popular imagination. So it is not what religion preaches but what religious leaders idealize and condone that guides the behaviour of ordinary people.

Could you explain a little bit about the relationship between husband and wife?

Husband and wife relationships among Hindus can be understood by examining their family roles as well as their interpersonal relationship.

Hindu family structure is hierarchical. The husband has higher status, power, and authority. But he knows he has to have his wife's goodwill, co-operation, and active support to have harmony in the family. So, in many cases, a husband tries to establish a positive relationship with his wife by treating her with affection, consideration, and respect, showing his willingness to forgive her imperfections. He sees himself and his wife as two parts of one unit, not equal but totally inter-dependent on each other.

On the other hand, there are husbands who wish their wives to remain subservient so that their power will remain unquestioned. They tend to start the relationship with intimidation and control. In such a fear dominated negative relationship, the woman's lesser rank, lack of power, and dependent status (combined with a desire to keep abuse secret to avoid social humiliation) can create a high risk situation where abuse can occur easily and can continue indefinitely. Absence of checks and balances and the power imbalance in the husband-wife relationship make it very difficult for wives to seek outside help such as mediation or counselling. So the wives stay, imprisoned by the situation.

Is there anything in the culture or the religion that would condone abuse?
The Mother Goddess taboo against treating women poorly is a deterrent to abuse. Women are believed to be the image of the Goddess; therefore, they must be treated with respect. However, aside from the Mother Goddess image there are not many deterrents against abusing women. Though it is legitimate to divorce, there is social stigma when a Hindu woman remarries even though it is legal to do so. In 1955, the law was reformed in India; monogamy was instituted and divorce for women was recognized. However, it takes a long time for society to change its ways of thinking, and there is still social stigma when women divorce or separate. It is acceptable but the degree of acceptance would depend on her economic and social status. Traditional Indian men do not want to marry divorced women or highly educated women with equality on their minds. So, you see, even though it is legal there is a barrier of mind, created by social convention. Consequently educated economically independent wives put up with abuse. Often they do not see any dignified way out of an abusive situation.

It is very difficult for a woman to remarry. For one thing, there is the expectation that a woman be a virgin to be marriageable. For another, there is the bond which is formed between man and wife once there are children. In addition, unlike a Christian marriage, the Hindu marriage bond does not dissolve at death. This is a cultural practice and edict, not a religious one. People who changed Hindu religious laws carefully examined the religious texts to determine what religion truly says about remarriage of women or for that matter about widows getting married. Though widow marriage has been legalized for over a hundred years, very few widows remarry. Such are the powers of convention. Unless women are willing to examine the difference between sinful behaviour and unconventional behaviour, they will remain trapped by customs and conventions.

Is there a double standard in your culture regarding sexual relationships?
Sexual relationships outside of marriage are widely accepted for Indian men (though it is frowned upon). So a good man will remain discreet. He respects his wife, does not do anything to humiliate or hurt her, and is not uncaring. It is acceptable for him to be unfaithful, but he is expected to be kind and considerate. Women are held to much more strict standards of behaviour. However, these expectations are now changing. Educated women are demanding a different attitude and the end of the double standard in moral code of behaviour.

Now that Hindu wives are in Canada, do they look differently on marriage?
Not all Hindu wives are alike. Modern women think and live differently than tradition-bound women. So let us talk about traditional women in arranged marriages. When a woman is married through an arranged marriage, she often does not know her spouse beforchand. So she marries a stranger, comes with him to a new country to live with his family members who can, in many cases, be unsympathetic strangers. But these women have been socialized to believe that a Hindu marriage cannot be dissolved. They firmly believe that if they leave their marriage, they will no longer be accepted by family, friends, or community. In their eyes such reactions are sinful. The concept of virtue and sin guides the life of tradition-bound women. No traditional woman wishes to think of herself as unchaste or committing an act of sin.

Bad marriages are viewed as misfortunes that one has to bear stoically without complaint. Only among educated and modernized families can widows and divorcees contemplate second marriages. In Hindu belief death ends marriage for men but not for women.

When a woman considers divorce, it is her status in the community that will affect her most. How will others label her? There are also problems with housing, income, support, and advice. A woman who leaves is usually labelled as a "home wrecker" who lacks loyalty, commitment, adherence to duty, and the honour that distinguishes Hindu wives. If she has children, she is portrayed as a selfish mother who is putting her own self-interest ahead of the children's economic security, family honour, and future well-being.

Many abused women have labelled other women with these epitaphs until they themselves have been victimized. So they assume others will view them as "bad" women because they are not conforming to societal conventions. Very few women confront abuse with defiance and ask for justice. The majority swing between self-pity and self-hatred. They also feel bewilderment, fear, anger, and betrayal because they feel they have done all the right things. Why must they suffer? Why has the protective family abandoned them? Why are they being vilified? Why are they not being rewarded for being good and virtuous? And what have their children done to deserve such misfortune? Many devout women also feel abandoned by their deity and feel profound despair about losing their personal link to their god.

Then what is it that finally drives a Hindu woman to leave her husband and family?
There is only one reason generally and that is danger to her children. For instance, if a son or daughter is being brutally beaten, or is sexually approached, the woman will do anything to protect her children. Her motherliness overcomes her diffident femininity.

Could you elaborate on the good woman versus the bad woman?
I would like to answer this from the husband's and his family's perspective. Hindu laws say clearly that good women must be treated with adoration, appreciation, love, consideration, and respect. The bad women will be punished, rejected, abandoned, or ostracized. Folklore, fairy tales, theatre, movies, and popular literature usually strengthen such strict categorical labelling of women.

In a sexual context a good woman is a virgin until marriage. After marriage she will practise strict fidelity, not talking to or touching unrelated adult males. She will remain celibate when her husband is absent or dead. She is expected to forgive her husband's sexual transgressions whether it happens to be occasional or frequent. Since 1955, Hindu law has not permitted bigamy or polygamy, but there are common-law relationships that men may form with other women. A good woman will be kind and friendly to a husband's paramour.

The other important sphere is money. A good woman will let her husband manage her money and property. She will give him her entire paycheque. A good woman shares her wealth with her husband's family. If she needs to help her own parents or siblings, she will ask her husband for monetary help. If a husband says "no" she will accept it without resentment. On the other hand, she will be asked to go to her parents to get better gifts, money, and other things. One of the causes of bride-burning is pressuring the new bride to get more money or expensive consumer goods from her family. The girls who refuse are called "bad" and sometimes are driven to commit suicide. They are considered bad women because they still think of their natal family as their own family and give their husband's family less importance by not siding with them.

In the sphere of power, most mothers-in-law dread the easy access daughters-in-law get by sharing the son's bed. As the son now spends more intimate time with his wife, the wife can influence him more than the mother. So a good woman shares the power generously with her in-laws. A bad woman asks more for herself and her children and influences the husband to distance himself from his natal family. In many cases it is family infighting that starts the abuse of the wife as she is seen as a threat to her in-laws.

What is the relationship between the son and the mother?
A son is very close to his mother. It is a bond that is somewhat like that of an only love. In an arranged marriage it is a very strong emotional bond. This is why a mother sometimes cannot share her son with his wife. So you see, the family structure is against the young woman when it comes to family violence because first, there is the husband to contend with and second, the mother-in-law could also be an abuser. To understand these relationships, one must go beyond the religion and culture and look at the life cycle. It is all interconnected. A woman's power increases or lessens depending whether she has sons, daughters, or is infertile.

How does the life cycle affect women's power and probability of being abused?
Once a woman has children, and particularly a son, she gains power and status. As she approaches adult life and as she gets older, she has even more power in the extended family through her son's status. Ultimately, she establishes a power base in her husband's family. There are three distinct status changes in a woman's life cycle. She goes from a young bride, to mother and mistress of the household, and to an old woman where she becomes the mother-in-law, the pinnacle of her life. But many middle aged daughters-in-law abuse their elderly dependent mothers-in-law in the same way that they were abused as young low-power wives. So examining the power relationships within relationships will tell who is at risk. A woman's well-being will largely depend on whether she is a good woman or a bad woman, as defined by other family members. For example, men's promiscuity is tolerated by his family and is frowned upon by his wife's family whereas, women who are perceived to be unchaste will be severely reprimanded by both families. Virginity for the unmarried, chastity for wives, and celibacy for widows is the norm for good women.

How does a Hindu woman, who chooses to stay in the relationship, deal with the situation?
Some go through it stoically, accepting it as a part of women's lives. Others protest and seek legal help. Victims of abuse in Indian and Indo-Canadian culture are not so concerned about their legal status as they are about their emotional well-being, social status, and security because they can live in separate households without breaking the marriage.

Why are women seen to be weak?
When a woman's spirit has been broken from childhood, her personality has been shaped by emotional and verbal abuse. Therefore, she will also accept physical abuse. It is like a stone rubbed and rubbed with a rough instrument until, eventually, it cracks. Then the spirit is truly crushed. This is a process which slowly evolves until it erupts in a crisis that results in suicide, emotional disorder, or self

hatred. Such self-destructive behaviour or mental ill health has nothing to do with strength or weakness in an individual as we understand it. It is simply too many negative things happening to the woman from birth onwards. If she is cared for, the woman will wish to live and will start to heal and recover. Education and economic status are extremely important. It is the educated and wage earning women who are protesting and organizing themselves to bring changes in the areas of bride-burning, female infanticide, abortion of female fetuses, and other violence against females. Such practices in the home-country indicate the status of women in the eyes of men who come to Canada. So women need to encourage other women to seek the protection of Canadian law.

How does one's spirituality fit in here?
First, let's look at the terms "religion" versus "spirituality." Religion is a boundary. Spirituality is a development. By the time a person is talking about spirituality they have already developed a spiritual identity. Spirituality means to "be good" not "to feel good." So inner tranquillity is very important. The concept of the "mind, body, and spirit" is different in the Eastern versus the Western context. For example, in Eastern thought spirituality is not associated with organized religion but rather with inner tranquillity, calmness, and goodness. It addresses mortality versus immortality as related to the body and the spirit. In the name of religion there has been hatred, bigotry, and intolerance—the license to put others to the sword and rape their women. Bosnia is an example of religious warfare. Kill the enemy at all costs. Spiritual practices focus on restraining our destructive negative behaviour and transcending the fear, hatred, anger, and despair that darken the spirit.

Interpretation of sacred writings is an interesting exercise. People are like cherry pickers. They pick and choose, believing what they like and doing what they want to. Spirituality has more to do with a social and cultural tradition that aspires to experience connectedness between the sacred and all created beings. A truly spiritual person embraces this thought, including everything and everyone. We are all one—all human beings—not separate pockets of various organized religions. Hindus think of the body as a container, a sacred vessel. It is a sacred space for the spirit within. The body, the container, is limited whereas the spirit is truly boundless. It has no limit. It is with our mind and spirit that we connect with others. Narrow, limited, self interested people find it difficult to reach out to other people. They are very involved in their own pain and are blind to other's pain and suffering. Spiritual people think of others first and they empathize with others. That is why they do not abuse, exploit, or destroy. Spirituality is, of course, the base of all religions. It encompasses compassion, wisdom, and selflessness. If a woman is tied down with her own pain, she cannot be validated. There is egotism, even in suffering. The ego says, "My pain is greatest. Your pain is nothing in comparison to mine." There is a great difference between experiencing and owning one's pain and suffering, and harbouring and clinging to it forever. Spirituality makes us aware of our self-centredness and inspires us to help ourselves by helping other sufferers. Women can't get better until they start to give to others.

How does one deal with her own life situation then?
As a victim of family abuse she must learn to empower herself. This would mean that the woman would try to develop her skills, improve her economic situation, and concentrate on her spirituality. The more she feels the pain, the more immobilized she becomes. It is important to deal with pain, with self-hatred, but one has to untangle oneself and move on. Instead of accepting others' evaluation of herself as an unworthy person, she must affirm her humanness, the essence that transcends her gender and social role.

In Buddhist and Hindu practice, the concept of becoming "non-attached" is important. This does not mean the woman doesn't acknowledge pain or suffering. It is more a concept of "letting go." It is a process that leads to transformation of self and rebuilding of life in a spiritual plane. Spirituality is the core of human existence. Without focusing on our essence, we cannot renew ourselves.

When does the turning point come for the abused woman?
It comes when she does something life affirming. One example, in the Written Stories in *Lifelines*, is Danielle's story. She began by running and by treating her body with care and respect.

The difference between Eastern and Western philosophy is essentially that Westerners see everything as "choices" as decisions to be made. Their concepts are solution-oriented. The Eastern mind has learned to live with the concept of "destiny" and tries to work around it. In Eastern thought, a person who has been abused may think of it as bad karma and she will use her spiritual power to break the karmic cycle or the wheel of destiny.

With the current rise of fundamentalism, the spiritual side of religion is becoming eclipsed. Often conforming to religious laws and following religious dictums are considered the most important religious practices. We need to be reminded that spirituality emphasizes development of the human self that will make an individual wise, loving, and giving. Christianity preaches the "gospel of love." Buddhism talks about "compassion." Hinduism speculates about "oneness of life," looking at nature and all created beings with reverence and respect. Anger, hatred, and violence can be overcome if we continue our spiritual journey. Similarly, pain and suffering can be overcome in time, but only if the abuse and violence stops. There are many parables in Hindu and Buddhist literature that tell about recovery from pain and suffering as well as about starting a spiritual life after removing oneself from violence and domination.

So that caregivers can better understand where women are coming from, their world views, their understanding of relationships, and their beliefs about healing and recovery, could you tell me a little about the Hindu religion?

Hinduism is one of the world's oldest religions. It evolved from the rites and practices of the Indo-Aryan and Indo-European civilizations and incorporates such germinal faiths as the worship of the Mother Goddess. Archeological discoveries date back at least 25,000 years in the human experience. Hinduism has its own mythologies, philosophies, religious laws, and procedures for the concept of the Divine.

Like followers of Christianity, Islam, and Judaism, Hindus too believe in one almighty God. However, Hinduism differs from the faiths of Semitic* origin in its assertion that the immensity of God cannot be grasped within the limits of the human experience. God is an all encompassing and all-pervading presence who is manifested in the phenomenal world in many different forms. The worship of these aspects, called polytheism in the western tradition, evolved so that the human mind (which cannot envision God entire) may come near to understanding the nature and character of the Divine by experiencing the One from a myriad of perspectives. Thus, the various manifested gods and goddesses are in fact many different facets of the One Divinity.

Hindu mythology describes the origin of gods and goddesses and their great deeds. Their relationship with one another and with the human world is told in story form. Most of these mythological stories are carved in the walls of temples. These are found most notably in the ancient temples of the Indian sub-continent, the Indonesian archipelago, and the parts of Southeast Asia once known as Indochina. The stories have been narrated by storytellers and inscribed by scholars in hand-written manuscripts. They also survive in the traditional dance forms of south and southeast Asia, particularly the story of the Hindu epic *Ramayana*.

Through stories and dance, religious ideas and beliefs remain vivid from generation to generation. The *Ramayana* is one of two great epics, the other being the *Mahabharata*. *Ramayana* tells the story of Rama, an ideal king who established a utopia, a golden age of benign and altruistic monarchy, and a society based on moral principles. It portrays Rama the Divine against a demonic king Ravana, who abducts Rama's wife Sita and provokes a ferocious war wherein Good wins over Evil and Darkness.

The *Mahabharata* is the story of a civil war between two related clans. The epic war between the Pandavas and Kauravas engulfed all of India. At its heart is the principle that a society must be based on justice and on moral and ethical codes so that none can be denied their legitimate rights. At the core of the

---

*   Semitic: relating to Semites, particularly the Jews.

Mahabharata is the Bhagavat Gita in which God, manifest as Krishna, explains to Prince Arjuna that the essence of life is fidelity to dharma, the rightful universal order that underlies God's creation.

What sets Hindu women apart?

- Arranged Marriage—A majority of marriages are arranged by parents or other family members. Usually bride and groom are not know to each other, and in some cases they first see each other on the day of the marriage.

- Dissolution of Marriage—Hindu legal code (revised in 1955) allows divorce and remarriage. In reality widows or divorced women rarely get remarried. But widowers and divorced men often remarry. In this case tradition works against legal rights.

- Family Living Arrangements—Often three generations live under one roof. Living in an extended family is the norm not the exception. Family structure is hierarchical with women having less rights and less power. They defer to the father, husband, and sons.

- Belief in Destiny—Within the belief system is the concept of destiny. Many Hindus believe life's happiness and sufferings are pre-ordained. However, powerful people will try to change their destiny whereas those with less power often meekly accept destiny.

A Woman as Rabbi

A Message of Hope

There are all kinds of doors
out there waiting to be opened
and there are people who can help you
through those doors and over
the bumpy roads and around the corners.
Don't be afraid to ask for help.
There is hope and if I were to say
anything it would be to hang on.
Don't ever give up on yourself.

Lindsey bat Joseph

Rabbi Lindsey bat Joseph is presently the only woman rabbi in Western Canada. She is a thirty-six year old single parent, the mother of two. Lindsey went back to school to start a new life, after being involved in an abusive marriage.

I am delighted to have this chance to speak with you, particularly since you have experienced spousal abuse yourself. It has been difficult finding someone from the Jewish community who was willing to speak out on the issue of spousal abuse. Several people told me that they had never personally come across this situation and did not know anyone else who had.

I'm not surprised. It's funny because I was having lunch with a woman this morning and I mentioned to her the difficulty that you had and she said, "Well, I know for a fact that there are women within our community that are abused." These women may even be in the congregations of the people you contacted. My friend was quite sure that the rabbis of those congregations would be aware of them. But yes, it's not something that they like to talk about, and the reason is that we are a faith community that puts a great deal of stress on family values. It's our central focus. It's not just the 1990s political-speak with us. The family really is central to the Jewish way of life.

Because our faith is very family oriented, family violence obviously disrupts that centre. And it's something that is absolutely abhorrent to us. We are brought up and taught to be good Jews. The first thing about being a good Jew is to be a decent human being. A decent human being is not going to beat up on his wife and children or on her husband and children (spousal abuse works both ways). And so when you're confronted with the reality that there are people in your community who could very well be going to *schul* every day of their lives, praying along with the best of them, and keeping the most kosher homes, it is difficult to accept that they may have another side to their personality—a dark side—that they may be abusing their loved ones. I think it's something that none of us likes to admit exists.

We would all like to be able to say that we live in a society where everybody is treated with kindness and respect, and parents don't beat their children, and spouses don't abuse one another, and men and women treat each other with dignity. That's the kind of world we all strive for, and I think within the faith community that's the rule, the ideal. We create these little cocoons for ourselves. We'd like to think that this doesn't happen in our schul and in our church because the people that are here obviously are God-fearing people who believe in their faith tradition. We see them here worshipping every Friday night or every Saturday morning or every Sunday morning, depending on their religion. So I think it's hard for any of us to accept. But obviously, we have to accept it if we're going to help the members in our communities who are suffering. However, knowing this doesn't make it easier. Spousal abuse is a hard thing to accept because it goes so deeply against the grain of everything that we believe in.

I've heard from other faith leaders and cultural communities that there's often a struggle about being different. For instance, newcomers in a new country often face racist attitudes or stereotyping that stigmatizes people who are part of a particular group. When religious or cultural groups experience the effects these attitudes have on them it's understandable that they tend to deny that family abuse happens in their communities.

Yes, and I think even in cases where we do know it's going on, there's a tendency to want to shut the outside world out and to deal with it ourselves. The message seems to be it's our problem, leave us alone and let us handle it. And I think that happens for a number of different reasons. For one, there is obviously a desire to protect the integrity and the reputation of the community. And for another, I think there's also a genuine desire to somehow shield the family that's suffering from being put into the limelight.

Families and communities take care of their own? Is the ideal that their community will help them through this?

Yes, for instance, there's a line in our tradition that says each Jew is responsible for the other. There's that sense of responsibility built right in. We trace our heritage back to the tribes of Jacob, and the sons of Jacob and it produces a sort of tribal mentality. We kind of laugh at ourselves for it, but there is, I think, a certain strength in that mentality. We identify with each other as part of this cosmic family, if you will, that stretches backwards and forwards through time and around the world. There's a sense that we are somehow uniquely connected with one another. That connection is in very many ways like a bloodline connection.

Could it be another way of building strength within your community? You suggested earlier that the Jewish community tends to want to help its own members in its own way? But is family violence a problem in the wider community? In your opinion, does it cross all religious and cultural boundaries?
It absolutely does. There is a poster on family violence downstairs by the front door. It came in the mail to my office last week, and I felt it was too important to be stuck up here on the second floor. I wanted it on the main floor where it would be seen so I mentioned it to the director of the centre. This poster is put out by a group that started a national hot-line in the United States for Jewish women who are being abused. And the poster says, right up front, that spousal abuse does not discriminate. It does cross all boundaries.

So we have placed it in a prominent place in the Jewish Community Centre. Obviously, the 800-number does not work in Canada, so we blanked out that number and wrote in all the local emergency shelter numbers. We also called Jewish Family Services to see if there was a specific number in Canada for Jewish women. There isn't, but there is an emergency number through Jewish Family Services.

Have you been involved in counselling women who have been abused?
As I've only been in this community for six months, I have not had to deal with a specific case of abuse, and I'm certainly hoping that none of my congregates are abusing one another. I'd like to think that they're all decent human beings. But I anticipate, because I am the only woman rabbi in the community, that at some point I will be approached. And that's fine. I mean to say that I would very much want to be that kind of resource for women and families.

I sense that, in your new appointment here as a woman rabbi, you'll be having an open door and a very busy office.
Well, that's fine, and that's part of what you get into this vocation for.

And that leads me to another question. What drew you to this line of work? What made you decide to become involved in your religious community in this way? Obviously you have a special interest in women's issues. What brought that about?
Well, it's interesting, you said, "What made you decide?" I'm never quite sure if the decision was entirely mine or if somebody else had plans for me. I came out of what was a short marriage, an emotionally abusive marriage. I really lost all sense of self in the time that we were together. It's funny. When I was in my teens

I can remember reading stories in magazines about women suddenly picking up and leaving their families and going off to find themselves, and I used to laugh rather derisively at them. I don't any more because I remember very distinctly waking up one morning and not really recognizing the person that was looking back at me in the mirror. I had so completely lost who I was. All I really knew for sure was that I was very unhappy and that I really didn't like the person that I was looking at in the mirror.

At my lowest point I wasn't even sure any more why I was still here and was seriously debating whether or not I wanted to be. There were a couple of times when I seriously considered suicide. And I know now what got me through those times. I can remember one occasion when I had more than a few bottles of pills in my hand, and I was quite intent on swallowing them all. What pulled me away from it was that I had two small daughters, one of whom was a newborn. I believe now that my initial decision to live was not so much to live for myself but to live long enough to be able to raise them. And so that got me through each crisis and then when the marriage finally crumbled completely—three months after my second daughter was born—we split.

I immediately went to a counsellor because I was deathly afraid that somehow, by being a single parent, my kids would automatically end up being juvenile delinquents or whatever. I mean, you buy into all these stigmas, and these stigmas are out there, this perception that somehow single mothers damage their kids, that we can't be good parents. And so I went to see a counsellor, I guess to allay my paranoia about that but also to start putting myself back together. And one of the places that I went back to—to heal—was the synagogue. My youngest daughter had recently had her naming ceremony at the temple in Calgary. So I felt I had some sort of connection with that place because I had both my daughters named there, and I had infrequently attended services there. But I went back basically to heal.

There was a lovely lady who was working as the temple administrator at the time. When I went to talk to her about attending services and what have you, she said, "Well you know, when you were here before, when your first daughter was born, you joined tentatively, but you didn't really get involved. Now that you're here again and there's just the three of you, we want you to get involved, to stick around this time because we think we can help you." I went to a Saturday morning service, and at that time Calgary did not have a full-time rabbi. We had student rabbis that came in on weekends. The rabbi who had done Elizabeth's naming in October asked me how things were going. The last time I had seen him was in December at Hanukkah and my husband and I had split up shortly after that. It was January when I saw this rabbi again.

When he asked me how things were going, I told him that we had separated. He said he was sorry to hear that and asked if the kids and I were okay. I told him that we were fine and that we were staying with my parents. I had barely walked in the door after returning from the synagogue, and he was on the phone. He wanted to make sure that I was safe, that the children and I had enough, that we had food, clothing, shelter, the whole bit. And within the next couple of weeks there were a number of people from the synagogue that called to make sure that we were doing all right.

So you had instant support?
It was instant support. And these were people that I didn't really know very well at that point. In the coming months and years, they gradually became my secondary family. Because they created a safe place for me to be, I was able to heal there. I used to jokingly refer to Friday night *Shabbat* services as my weekly mental health break. Maybe it was not so much mental health as it was spiritual health. That was really the place where I began to rediscover my Jewish roots, and it was a place where I could shut the outside world out for a while. It was just me and God. And I was with these other caring people that I shared a common heritage with. It was a couple of hours each week where all I had to do was to sing and pray. I just had "to be" and I didn't have "to do." That was the beginning of my healing.

As I got more and more involved with the synagogue and with the Jewish community in general, I came to know that this is where I wanted to spend my life, that this is where I wanted to be. I started going back to school when my youngest daughter was around a year old. I went back to school right away and that was also another safe place for me to be. I'd been a good student as a kid, not straight A's, but I'd been a good student, and I always liked school. So I went back. I figured, if nothing else, I wasn't going to be on welfare and having more education would help me find a good job. At that point I really didn't know where I was going to go or what I was going to do. I just sensed that school was a good place to start.

I actually started out in an accounting program at Mount Royal College. I had this ridiculous idea that I would graduate in two years with a good paying job. Except, I had forgotten that me and accounting—like oil and water—just don't mix. I still can't balance my chequebook to this day. I think one of my daughters is just going to have to become an accountant just so she can manage my affairs.

How old are your daughters now?
They're now thirteen and a half and eleven. I've been a single parent for a long time. It works well for me. I'm at the point now where I'm happy to perform marriages for other people, but it's just not what I want for myself. When I see myself standing under the *chupah* (marriage canopy), it's as the rabbi doing the ceremony and not as the bride. And I don't know if that will ever change. Maybe

when I hit my sixties I'll feel like I want a companion for the rest of my life because I'll have an empty nest then. But right now I have, thank God, two beautiful healthy daughters that I absolutely adore. I feel really privileged to have these kids as my daughters. It's absolutely wonderful.

And I have two Siamese cats that think they're human beings too, and they are pretty much. I now have a congregation of eighty-some families and I have wonderful friends who are an important part of our lives. It's like I have a full plate, and I don't feel that I need more than I have right now. Everything I could want I already have.

I have a place to pray where I can continue to grow spiritually and where I can nurture others spiritually. At least I hope that I am able to do that for them. I have a creative outlet for teaching and educational programs because it's a Reform congregation and we're not so stringent about liturgy and other things. I have a place to explore and play with the liturgy and be creative when I want to be. And there are people that I can pray with when I want something that's a little more formal, a little more traditional. So for me life is really good, and I'm really glad that I didn't swallow all those pills. I am probably happier to be alive now than I have been at any point in my life.

How long have you been a rabbi?
Seven months and about two or three weeks. Yes, seven months and three weeks. I was ordained June 1st.

And you've been a mom for at least 13 years and probably married a year or two before that.
Yes, I was married for a year before my eldest daughter was born, but the emotional and psychological abuse in my marriage began right away.

Did the abuse ever become physical?
It was getting that way at the end. It got to the point where I really felt that the physical was coming next and I thought, "I'm not sticking around and waiting to get hit." It sounds like being strong, but it's not really strength. It's fear.

Were you hesitant to leave? Were you afraid of the possibility of poverty?
Oh yes. This year, right now, is the first year in my children's lives that we are not living below the poverty line.

What a wonderful feeling that must be, knowing you're going to come out of this somehow.
You know, it's funny. I was reading an article a couple of weeks ago in the newspaper. They were looking at families in the city in terms of comparing different

income levels and looking at poverty lines. I was reminded that you get into this mind set, of thinking of yourself as a low income family, and I looked at it and I thought, "We're not a low income family any more!" That was the first time that it really hit home. I'm really not in that bracket any more. Seven months ago we were living below the poverty line. My daughters and I were living in Cincinnati where I was going to school. I was supporting the three of us on the equivalent of about $1,200 a month Canadian, but I was buying everything in American dollars. It was incredibly tight for us.

And you managed together, though, you and your girls.
That was survival and it was tough. But this was our thing that we did together as a family, and we are all incredibly proud of it. Jessica was talking with a classmate on the phone last night, and I overheard her conversation. She's thirteen so she's always on the phone. I guess the question was something along the lines of, "Is she like a rabbi?" And Jessica said, "She's not *like* a rabbi, she actually is a rabbi. She does everything a rabbi does—and no—she doesn't just pray for a living!" Jessica was adamant about this.

I remember Jessica five years ago in Israel when she was only eight years old. When Israelis argued with her and told her that women couldn't be rabbis, Jessica's answer to them was, "Well, we're Reform Jews. We can do anything!" That was her line. My youngest daughter Elizabeth has always been a little quieter about it. But she came home from school a couple of months ago, shortly after she had started at Laurier, and said, "You know, my friends at school think it's really cool that you're a rabbi." And I said "Why is that?" Elizabeth replied, "Because it's just so different. Nobody's mother is that! We've got mothers in the class that are brain surgeons and lawyers but anybody can do that. But I'm the only one whose mother is a rabbi." So I'm sort of a novelty item I guess.

That's quite a nice feeling, though, isn't it? Even though we're in a new age, it must be a wonderful feeling as a woman.
Yes, and if nothing else, I hope that I've set a good example for my daughters. I think I've grounded them in our tradition in such a way that I can say now, with confidence, that I will have Jewish grandchildren. I think that my kids feel connected enough with their tradition and their heritage and that it's important to them. I don't know a lot of women my age who have eleven- or twelve-year-olds that would feel confident saying that. I think that most of them would say that they hope to have Jewish grandchildren one day. I know a lot of them whose children are in their twenties are saying that they simply hope to "at some point." But I really feel confident that in my family it will be so.

It sounds like you are confident that you have been the role model that you would like to have been. Do you think this has anything to do with having been a single parent?

I think so. I think that's a major contributing factor. I think the one thing about being a single parent is that although parenting is a tough job, it's even tougher to be a co-parent. The advantage of having the other spouse there is that you've got each other to lean on. It's sort of team defense when the kids get older. But it doesn't always work that way and sometimes you are at cross purposes. Of course, sometimes being a single parent is ten times harder, and you don't realize how difficult it is until you're doing it. Yet, most times it's so much easier. I never have to argue with anybody about parenting. Yes, I bear all the burdens and all the responsibilities, and if something doesn't go right, I have only myself to blame. And if I really screw up and my kids end up messed up, it's my head on the chopping block because I'm the one that screwed up. But at the same time I have complete latitude. I'm the one that calls the shots. There's no one else that I have to answer to. There's a certain sense of freedom in that.

I think I've been able to explore parenting in a way that not all parents get a chance to. In some ways, when they were younger, I probably tended to be more strict than a lot of other parents. But now that they're older, I give them a lot of latitude. I think they have a lot more freedom than even I did when I was their age. And they handle it very well. My kids are certainly very independent and mature for their ages. They've learned to be responsible and to take on responsibility for themselves for certain things, and I think that that's important. It doesn't mean that the cat litter box gets scooped out or the dishes get done on time every day; but at the same time, if something comes up, I can call my kids and say, "I'm going to be a couple of hours late," knowing that they'll be able to go ahead and cook supper for themselves, that their homework will get done, that the doors will be locked, that the answering machine will be left on, and above all, that they are going to be fine.

That must be a great feeling. And how about the rest of your family through this healing period? Have you had support from your extended family?

Oh, absolutely, and now that I'm back in Alberta, it's wonderful because my brother and his wife and their two kids are in Red Deer, my parents and my sister and my niece are in Calgary, so we're just up and down the highway from each other now. It's wonderful. In fact my girls went down to Calgary during the December break, over the holidays. I was still recovering from surgery and I wasn't really all that mobile so this was great. I put them on the bus and they went down and visited. And a couple of weeks ago, I was out of town for a weekend and my one daughter stayed here in Edmonton with a family in the congregation that we've become friends with and the other one got on the bus and went to Red

Deer and spent the weekend with her cousins in Red Deer. So, yes, the family support is really terrific.

So, it's not a worry for you then when you have other obligations to meet.
No, and for the years that I was a rabbinical student they went everywhere with me. I schlepped them all over as we say, "all over hell's half acre." We went all over the United States together.

Well, it sounds like you've really got an exciting few years ahead in a new and very challenging job. I'd like to hear a little bit more about the Reform congregation and how it differs from the other congregations locally and world wide. Maybe you can tell me a little bit about the Jewish faith in general and its position in society.
According to the top ten list that I was reading a couple of weeks ago when I was in Regina (I also serve a congregation there on a part-time basis and one of my congregants there showed me this list), we're the sixth largest religion in the world. We're definitely a minority group, particularly in western Canada where there are very few Jews. Our traditions essentially come out of the Bible, but there are some traditions that developed later, post biblically. Hanukkah is one of them.

The story of Hanukkah is not in the Bible at all, but it's a part of Jewish history and so it's become one of our holiday celebrations. And within this century we've also added modern holidays such as Israeli Independence Day and a memorial day for victims of the Holocaust. Aside from these three, all the other holidays pretty much come out of biblical times or out of the Bible traditions or as a result of biblical events. For instance, we have a fast day, *Tisha B'Av*, which usually occurs sometime in August or late July which marks the destruction of the Temple. So, while the fast day isn't in the Bible, the event that prompted that fast day certainly is.

There are three main branches of Judaism and there's a lot of variation within those branches. Broadly speaking, they are Orthodox, Conservative, and Reform Judaism.

Do these branches have good relationships with each other?
It all depends on the community and where you are in the world. Internationally, the Reform and Conservative movements are linked as part of what is known as The World Union for Progressive Judaism. The Conservative movement actually started off as a branch of the Reform movement. Initially there was Orthodoxy and then there was Reform later, and then Conservatism has branched out of Reform. From the Conservative movement there has been a recent offshoot called Reconstructionist Judaism. And there are humanistic movements within Judaism. Within the Orthodox community there are many different ranges as well. You'll

hear some people describe themselves as modern Orthodox. There are Hasidic Orthodox Jews, there are non-Hasidic Orthodox Jews, and there are the Satmars. There is a great variety.

It is strange because the political/religious right-wing element in Israel keeps claiming that they've got the one true definition of Judaism and that everybody has to be the same. It's a fallacy because we've never been the same. There's always been variety, right from biblical times. There have always been Jews that were adamant about following every single law that was written in the Torah and adamant about performing every ritual exactly as it was written and exactly as it was supposed to be. And there have been Jews for whom that wasn't important at all. They paid their annual Temple tithe and they went about their way, and that was their connection to the community. And then there are always those that fall somewhere in between. A plurality has always existed. Whether it existed officially or not, the fact is it's always been there.

The Reform movement, in terms of what's become the Reform movement, got its start back in the eighteenth and nineteenth centuries in Germany and in western Europe. It was a move initially to try and pull Judaism out of the ghettos and to allow Jews access to modern society. It was a way of preserving Jewish tradition and at the same time being able to interact with the modern world. But within our movement there have also been polarities. There have always been some who have wanted to stick closer to the tradition and there have always been those who have been more concerned with being able to assimilate into modern society. It's kind of like a pendulum. It swings back and forth.

I tend to liken the growth of our movement to being pretty much like the life-time of a child. When Reform was in its infancy, it stuck very close to Orthodoxy, and after it gained ground, it hit the rebellious teen years where we literally threw everything into the junk pile. And so we got away from wearing prayer shawls, we got away from wearing a *kippah*, dietary laws were thrown out, and a lot of other traditions were as well. Certain prayers and things were pushed to the side and liturgy was very compacted. Whether or not Israel was an important thing for Jews was a subject of debate. There were people for whom it definitely wasn't important and there were those who maintained that it was. Another question was how much Hebrew should be in the service. There were those that wanted the services entirely in English, not wanting to bother with Hebrew at all. So it really ran the gamut.

The analogy is that by the time this Reform child hit its adult years, she looked around and realized that she had thrown out everything of value. Now we know who we are. The movement is a hundred years old. Obviously it's not going to die out or go away overnight. So we're at this wonderful stage now where we're rediscovering and re-incorporating traditions that our grandparents, sometimes our great-grandparents, threw out.

Now we're seeing an increasing number of Reform Jews that are observing some level of the dietary laws. I keep a kosher home. My parents don't. My mother comes to visit and my kitchen just confuses her to no end. She says she is always very nervous about going into my kitchen because she's not sure which dishes she should be using. It's funny because to my kids and to me it's second nature. There are the dairy dishes and there are the meat dishes. For my daughters, it's nothing unusual. This is what they've grown up with. This is normal for them.

So your parents are Reform as well?
Yes and they've seen quite a change. My father has a prayer shawl and a kippah that he's worn on special occasions. It's not something that he uses all the time. The first time that I decided I wanted to wear a prayer shawl for the Yom Kippur services, I had to borrow my father's because I didn't have one of my own. Now I own two of them. In fact last year, just before my ordination service, as a combined birthday and Father's Day gift, my sister and I went together and bought my dad a new prayer shawl.

My dad is actually someone who converted to Judaism. He was not raised as a Jew. He's still shaking his head about this one. He says, "When I adopted this religion the last thing that I expected was that I would raise any of my children, especially my daughter, to become a rabbi! If it had been your brother, it would have been a surprise all right but a normal surprise. But for my daughter to go to rabbinical school? This is really not what I expected." But that's Judaism. You always get more than you bargained for. That's just the way it is.

Let's look at marriage vows for a moment. For instance, in certain Christian ceremonies not so long ago the woman promised to "love, honour, and obey" her husband where the husband promised to "love, honour, and cherish" his wife. Now both man and woman say "cherish." Another example of change is the custom of father walking his daughter down the aisle. It is becoming more common for both parents to do this. Is there a parallel in the Jewish marriage ceremony?
In Jewish tradition, if we're going to talk about strict legalities of it, a man does acquire the wife. I mean, historically that was it. And she was very much acquired as property. Now the caveat to this is that the woman is given the ketubah which is the marriage contract and it's not a certificate. If anything the *ketubah* is a precursor to the pre-nuptial agreement because what the ketubah spells out is what she is going to get from him in terms of settlement if the marriage is dissolved.

Now, strictly halakhically speaking (according to Jewish Law), the husband is the one who has the power to dissolve the marriage, not the wife. This is an ongoing problem because there are some women in Israel who have left husbands who have been incredibly abusive, or who have had husbands who have abandoned them, but they can't get a Jewish divorce. These women are referred to as being *chained women*, still legally bound to their husbands because a woman can't initiate a divorce.

Outside of Israel we have this marvelous thing called civil divorce, but again there may still be problems, specifically in the case of Orthodox women. An Orthodox woman in Canada could get a civil divorce, but she is still somewhat dependent upon her rabbi to try to compel her husband to agree to the Jewish divorce because, technically speaking, she can't get married in the synagogue again without one.

So, she may be legally divorced, but the reality is she is still considered to be married to this man.
Until she's given the Jewish divorce. But in Canada, I am told, the divorce laws are such that a spouse can't prevent the religious annulment anymore. The law makes it binding so it's certainly less of an issue in this part of the world, but it's still a problem in Israel because divorce law is according to Jewish tradition. So, the ketubah, which protects women, really is an enlightened document.

Is it like a covenant? Is it a promise to uphold certain ethics?
The modern ketubah certainly is. Within the Reform and to a large extent in the Conservative movement, we've seen a move towards what's being referred to as an egalitarian ketubah. It addresses shared values and the spiritual, moral, and psychological, if you will, responsibilities of the spouses to one another. But in its strictest sense, for instance in an Orthodox traditional ketubah, it really is very much like a pre-nuptial agreement. It spells out what the financial settlement is going to be if the marriage doesn't succeed. That's because historically marriages were contracted for economic reasons as much as emotional ones. That's a historical reality. But in terms of the Jewish wedding ceremony a woman cannot be forced to sign a ketubah. So a woman can refuse a marriage.

In terms of the wedding ceremony itself, the ketubah is signed by both bride and groom. They both agree to the terms. It is witnessed by people who are not related to them. It has to be, traditionally speaking, witnessed by two men because only men can serve as witnesses. However, within Reform and Conservative movements, depending on the bent of the particular rabbi, most will accept a woman as a witness also, but she has to be Jewish and not related. The idea is that they can't have a personal or financial stake in the marriage. It's tradition for both parents to walk down the aisle. The groom is brought under the *chupah* (marriage canopy) first by his parents, and then the bride is walked down by her parents.

Are there still arranged marriages?
Oh, sure there are. There are communities that still arrange marriages. We don't do them in our community, but you will still see that.

In your own case, did you have your husband's permission to obtain the divorce?
No, because we had not had a Jewish ceremony when we got married, I just went through a civil divorce. It was strongly protested, very much over his objections.

Does that mean that the Jewish faith does not consider you as ever having been married?
No, I'm not married. I don't know how it would be defined technically, but it was, from a Jewish perspective, not a halakhically valid marriage because it was not a Jewish ceremony, and so it was as if it had never happened.

In your opinion, is the Jewish religion a little more egalitarian in recognizing the relationship between man and woman compared to some of the other major religions?
I don't know that I would say it was egalitarian. I think what Jewish marriages have done since the beginning is acknowledge that there are two human beings involved in the marriage. Both have certain rights and responsibilities, and even though one of those partners (traditionally speaking) is subject to the other, she nevertheless has certain rights, certain things that she's entitled too. Historically and today the husband would be subject to pressure by the community if he did not fulfill his obligations.

Is the husband in a traditional Jewish marriage the voice of authority in the family? Is he the head of the family?
Certainly in older times, yes. I don't know that it would be the case today. I think that because we now grow up in a modern society where men and women do play equal roles, marriages tend to be more egalitarian anyway.

I presume you are referring to Canada. What about other countries that are less modernized?
I think societal values impact on this sort of thing. In a society where women traditionally hold very different roles from men, and those are still the prevalent values of the day, then Jewish families are also going to reflect that to a certain extent. But then again, the Jewish rabbinical tradition calls for ketubah that guarantees certain rights for the wife and protection for her and the children. It is a form of guarantee that ensures that the husband fulfills his responsibilities.

Would you say that Jewish women are a little more protected than other women on the breakup of a marriage because of ketubah?
Historically that probably is true. If a man decided he was going to run off with his secretary, he had to pay out the ketubah. That was his responsibility, like in a pre-nuptial agreement. The wife could say, "Okay, now you may want to dissolve

the marriage but I have this agreement here that says I'm supposed to get 'x' dollars a month from you for support. This is what you've agreed to."

So it really does take care of the wife and the children?
It does. And it protects her from being left penniless. So in terms of these agreements existing way back in biblical times, it was very progressive in terms of the way it protected women. I don't know that that's so much the case now.

I think a lot of contemporary women might find the language of the traditional ketubah insulting because it's still very much a case of the husband acquiring the wife. He acquires her by the gold ring. It is a sort of bridal price that he's paying. Nevertheless, there still are things worked into the marriage ceremony itself that do, to some extent, level the playing field a little.

For instance, marriage is definitely looked on as something that is sacred and special, something that should be sanctified and entered into in all seriousness. It is understood that these unions are in a sense creating a new family and that is a God given gift. It's not something that just happens. Animals don't create families, they find mates, and most animals don't mate for a life time. There are some exceptions, but the majority don't. Humans are unique in that we create families, raise our children from infancy to adulthood, and then enjoy grandchildren. There is an understanding that there is something sacred about marriage.

From a communal perspective every time two Jews come together and create a new family it's considered a blessing for all of Israel, that we have strengthened the Jewish people as a whole. So this isn't just a moment of rejoicing for the bride and groom or for the immediate family. This is another sign of Jewish survival, and it's something that really is to be celebrated. I remember reading an essay written by a woman who is a Holocaust survivor and she says, "Every time that a Jewish boy becomes a bar mitzvah, every time that two Jews come together in marriage, every time that there is a circumcision or a baby naming, it's like another nail in Hitler's coffin." It's another way of grounding in the ashes and of saying, "We're here. You did not destroy us. You know that we are here and that we're vital and that we're going to continue." A Jewish marriage is an affirmation of life for the entire community.

And it isn't just regional obviously.
No, it's global. It's not just something for the couple. Interestingly enough there isn't this whole "love, honour, obey." The translation of the traditional wedding vow, what the groom says when he gives the ring to the bride, and now in modern times with the advent of double ring ceremonies, what she also says to him, is literally, "Behold, you are consecrated to me according to the laws of Moses and the Jewish people." A couple is sanctifying themselves to one another. What the wedding ceremony basically does is to say that you are separating yourself from other men, and you are connecting yourself with this man, and that the man is

separating himself from other women, and connecting with this woman—and there isn't going to be anybody else. The man and woman consecrate themselves to one another and are united that way.

The notion of women being submissive to men or playing the lesser role in the marriage has more to do with the dynamics of the household. Traditionally the man is the one who goes out to *Yeshiva* and studies or goes out to work and earns a living whereas the wife is the one who's responsible for the domestic domain.

On the other hand, in a lot of traditional Jewish communities, the women were the ones that went out and worked because their husbands would go to Yeshiva. They'd go to houses of study. They are at school, essentially, during the day. They are studying Torah and Talmud, which is considered to be very important. This study is highly valued and respected. Education has always been a very important value in our community. To be able to devote your life to studying scripture, without even having to become a rabbi, just to be able to become a scholar, is a wonderful thing. What happened in a lot of families is that while men were busy studying and becoming scholars, the wives were the ones running shops and doing other jobs because they brought in the income that supported the family.

And traditionally the wife did not have the privilege of studying, did she?
No.

How modern is this?
Well, we say that it's modern, but there have always been exceptions. There have always been women throughout history that have been particularly learned.

So they were not barred from the scriptures, or were they?
Well, in some communities yes. They are to this day. There are some extremely Orthodox males that will say that women shouldn't be studying scripture and shouldn't be studying Talmud.

But is that their own interpretation of the scriptures, a male interpretation?
I don't know that it's a male interpretation. I think it's just the way that society has evolved. Certainly if you're looking at the Jewish world at the turn of the common era, before the Temple was completely destroyed, the *Sanhedrin* (the great rabbinic court) still existed. In all the rabbinic academies and schools of the day, it was the men who went to study. Women didn't.

But that doesn't mean that women didn't learn. They were certainly exposed to Torah although they didn't study the text first hand. They didn't have the opportunity to read and interpret the texts or study the grammar. That was very much a male endeavour. But there are stories of biblical scholars who had daughters that did learn from them. Probably the most famous would be Rashi, in eleventh century France, who was one of the great scholars and biblical commentators. Rashi did not have sons. He had sons-in-law who also became great scholars, but the story goes that his daughters also studied from him.

On the other hand, you will also find passages in Jewish tradition that say it's better to burn the Torah than to allow women to study it. So, you see the latitude of one side to the next. I think the turning point, to some extent, happened when we started coming into the New World. America and Canada were these big wide open lands of opportunity. Certainly in the United States there was public school education that was available to boys and girls equally. Universities were open to men and women. But even with all that, there were certain fields that women just didn't go into. How long did it take before women started becoming doctors and lawyers?

I think there's been less of a concern about limiting study in the Jewish faith since the Holocaust. The historical reality is that there are fewer of us around now than there were before the Second World War. Hitler didn't wipe us out, but he sure put a dent in the head count. If we're going to cut off Jewish education and only allow our men to study Torah and only allow our men to be leaders in the community, then certainly we are facing extinction. If you live in a community where half the population is automatically cut off from everything, then, realistically, how long can that community survive?

So the community is driven by historical events as well as modern pressures?
I think to some extent we are driven by historical reality. We need rabbis, we need educators, we need cantors, and we need community leaders. At this point in our history the debate over whether they are wearing pants or skirts for many of us is immaterial. I realize that for some segments of the population that will always be an issue. Male leadership for them is the ideal, and I fully respect that. That's fine. If that's what they choose for their particular corner of the world and for their particular community, I think it's perfectly valid. I don't think that anybody should be pressuring them to change.

But by the same token, I think it's also important for them to recognize that for the majority of us that model no longer works. Most men now expect that their wives and mothers and sisters and daughters will be their partners. I think it's an expectation that men and society have of us now. It's not just a case of us wanting to be their partners. I think we've reached a point now where men are so used to women being in these other roles now that they expect us to be there.

What about your own spiritual community here in Alberta? Do you feel widely accepted as a religious leader?
The Edmonton Jewish community as a whole has been wonderful to me. They really have been very embracing. I've had people from the Orthodox synagogue come and introduce themselves to me. They have made a point of it.

As a religious leader and a woman do you ever feel threatened by the sacred texts?

There's this wonderful fluidity to the text that we can still learn things from. We can still see ourselves in it. I think that's one of the strengths of the Torah. That's what makes it timeless. But I think it's also its weakness, in a sense, because a text that is that fluid can be twisted around and misinterpreted and used misguidedly. It can be interpreted in a way that can cause harm.

And do you think it is at times?

I think it is at times. We, in the Reform movement, have certainly experienced that in the last couple of years with the extreme right wing Orthodox groups in Israel that are seeking to change the Law of Return and are seeking to change the definition of who qualifies as a Jew. They would really like to disenfranchise not just Reform but all progressive Jewish movements, including Conservative Jews. One of the ways that they do this is to try and twist around the text, twist around the words of the Torah.

Would you call them fundamentalists?

No, I don't think I would because when you think about what the word fundamental means—basic beliefs—then no self respecting truly religious Jew would arbitrarily seek to cut off other Jews. It's a very un-Jewish way of behaving if you think about it.

Can you think of any examples where religious text has been used to control women?

Nothing really pops into my head. There are some laws within the text of the Torah that deal specifically with sexual mores and sexual relationships, ones that are forbidden and ones that are accepted and considered acceptable in Jewish tradition. There is a whole passage that deals with the *captive woman* and how she is supposed to be treated. When you look at the text closely and the way it's written, the obvious intent of it is that this woman is given time to adjust to the fact that she's become a captive. She is given time to mourn the fact that she's not with her family and her own society any more. That mourning period comes before any sort of relationship can exist between her and the person that is her captor. So, on the one hand it's sort of enlightened when you think about it because it emphasizes that raping and pillaging is not the way to go. The message is that you may take women as captives, but you've got to wait a while before you can take them into your household.

But at the same time the whole idea that men could take women as captives and force them to become their brides, even after waiting a certain amount of time, is still essentially forcing them to be submissive to their captors. That is a notion that really is an affront to twentieth century sensibilities. I believe that passages like that and passages that deal with women's rights within a marriage and male responsibilities to women within marriages are open for further interpretation.

It goes beyond interpretation to application. I think the classic example is the one that I mentioned earlier of the chained wife. The Torah says, "When a man gives his wife a writ of divorce," some interpret this by saying it means that the woman can't give the man the writ of divorce. But if you think about it, maybe that is not the intent at all. It could simply be an example. For example, if this is going to be done, this is what is expected. Further, there's nothing in the Torah that specifically says that a woman can't divorce her husband. But we've always operated on the assumption that because the Torah says a man can divorce his wife and it doesn't say that a woman can divorce her husband, that she by default cannot.

Yes, like gender sensitive language. It is no longer acceptable to say "mankind." We now substitute "humankind. "Could the term "man" in the sacred text mean humankind (previously mankind)? Perhaps we should consider its historical and linguistic context because we know that words change over time and their meaning changes over time. Are you ever able to talk to your congregations about these interpretations and suggest alternative interpretations?
Absolutely. There have been a number of rabbis, including a couple of Orthodox rabbis, that have tried to address this whole issue and tried to find a way within the *halakhah* (Jewish law), not to abrogate the text, but to find a way of reworking and re-understanding the text so that, for instance, women could be issued a writ of divorce, so that they aren't chained women.

But, the problem is the argument then comes back from the legal authorities that there is no Sanhedrin in session. But there hasn't been one now for centuries. So until there is a Sanhedrin in session, as far as they're concerned, we can't change the law. We cannot interpret it in a new way. The law has been this way for centuries.

But, in reality, they are re-interpreting aren't they?
Well, Orthodox authorities are not going to re-interpret it. Certainly I think, for the vast majority of rabbis in Conservative communities and Reform communities, yes it could be. But in a Reform synagogue you would not normally end up with the situation of a chained woman, of a woman not being able to be given a Jewish divorce. It seldom happens in Orthodox communities.

These women really are the exception, an extreme exception. Because usually what happens when a man starts to be obstinate (and this happened historically also), the rabbi and the leaders of the community would go to this man. They really would lean on him and try to encourage him to be reasonable. There were cases a couple of centuries ago where a few stubborn husbands were beaten by members of the community. It was their way of encouraging a man to give his wife a divorce.

There was a recent case in Israel where a guy died in jail after having been put there in an attempt to convince him to give his wife a divorce. He died there. He must have rotted in jail for a good fifty years. His wife is now legally single. She can marry whomever she wants. And she's inherited all the husband's property as well because she is his widow. So, really, what did he accomplish by being stubborn?

Persuasion is the usual approach. Even most Orthodox rabbis would say, "Look, it's obviously not working. You're not going to get her to come back and live with you. Give your wife the divorce. You can go on with your life and she can go on with hers and let's have a little peace in the household." Divorce has never been looked upon as a sin in Judaism. It's been an accepted part of the society and its culture since the earliest days. So is remarriage after death.

But divorce is still looked upon as something that's not desirable. The ideal in any perfect world is that you have a stable loving relationship that sustains you throughout your lives and that you're able to, God willing, bring children into the world and raise them to be stable adults also, who also go on and have good marriages. That's how civilizations get built. That's how a community is maintained, and that's how the world functions best. The sad reality, though, is that humans are frail and we're flawed and we mess up. We marry the wrong people sometimes and we pay a terrible price for it. But we do it.

Before we end this conversation, is there a message of hope that you can pass on to women who have suffered abuse?

Absolutely. There is a message of hope. The message is that this is not the end of the world; that living in a place where you are not validated as a human being, where you are hurting—emotionally, spiritually, physically—is not where God wants you to be or intended you to be. If that were the case, we'd all be born in that kind of state. And we're not. The majority of us are born into loving supportive families. The reason we are is because, and I really believe, that is what God intended and what God wants.

So, it's okay to leave it behind you. Leave it behind. A life has come to an end. But your life hasn't. The reality is that your life is just beginning. There are all kinds of doors out there waiting to be opened and there are people who can help you through those doors and over the bumpy roads and around the corners. Don't be afraid to ask for help. There is hope and if I were to say anything it would be to hang on. Don't ever give up on yourself.

I want to share one more thing with you. In my rabbinical thesis, dedicated to my parents and to my daughters, I wrote:

> To my parents who never stopped believing in me
> Even when I couldn't find the strength to believe in myself.

There were times when I literally did not have the strength to believe in myself, but I was very fortunate that there were other people around who did. I think for me the turning point was when I suddenly realized that, while I was busy not believing in me, I still believed in God. And it dawned on me that if I could maintain my faith in God, then God could in turn believe in me (that somehow it had to be a two-way street). And if God could believe in me then I could too. That was my turning point.

God is always there. I firmly believe that we go through points where we may stop believing, but God doesn't. I think that God is always there waiting for us, and we just have to decide that we want to open the door.

I guess the only other thing I would say is that my door is one of the doors that is open, that if there are women who feel that they would like someone to talk to, I am here—for those of *any* faith.

Rabbi Lindsey bat Joseph can be contacted at Temple Beth Ora located in the Jewish Community Centre in Edmonton, Alberta, Canada.

A Voice from the Muslim Community

A woman has to believe that
her God is compassionate
and beneficent and is
watching over her.

Zohra Husaini

*Dr. Zohra Husaini was born in
India. She received her masters
degree at Cambridge and her
PH.D. at the University of
Alberta. She works with the
Faculty of Education at the
University of Alberta on
educational policy and is the
president of the World Interfaith
Education Association.*

In the Muslim communities, generally, is spousal abuse a problem?
We all know spousal abuse exists. I don't know the extent of it, but it exists, and
it exists across all educational categories and socio-economic classes. I have known
it primarily through others who tell me about women who suffer abuse as opposed
to working directly with abused women. Without knowing names, I have come
to hear about it. Also, I am a member of a couple of organizations that help
women, and through these organizations I'm aware of wife abuse. Although I have
met some abused women, I learned of their struggles primarily though others.

What kind of abuse do you think might be common?
Beating or hitting is common. There are cases, among Muslim communities,
where husbands have turned the wife out, though not for good, at least for a
period of time. And intimidation—verbal intimidation, verbal abuse, criticism—
that is there all the time. In some cases I know of, members of the community
(elders, so to speak) have come to help women. Sometimes they take those women
to the homes of other people.

Sometimes some friends help. But it's not a real help because the families (into
which they go to stay for a while) can't keep them for long. And they certainly
can't help them with some of the legal or medical issues.

The issues are complex?

Oh yes, the issues are complex. Some women I know have gone on welfare. There are several women that I know who were beaten by their husbands so badly that they ended up in the hospital. There are others that, because they have children, feel they have to cope with it somehow, no matter what their own feelings are. It's not uncommon. I am not able to tell you the extent of it, but there are many I have met. It's terrible when the person you are talking to has suffered all that.

Who is the first source of help that a Muslim woman might turn to? Would it be an elder in the faith community?

I suppose the first one would be a friend, a woman friend. There is a woman whose husband did not allow her to even pick up the phone, so when she met someone who learned about it, then that friend used to phone her and through a third person they would communicate. There is an organization called Islamic Family Services Association. There are some women I know who are active in it, and they may be able to answer this question better than I can. Also there is the Indo Canadian Women's Association. They help all women, including Muslim women. They may be able to answer that question.

Is abuse something that is kept secret?

Oh yes, there is a lot of shame attached to it, a sense of failure, a sense of being the laughing stock of the family. A woman has to be abused quite a number of times before she begins to talk or before others suspect and they talk about it. The general feeling is that the husband, brother, or father (whoever is the abuser) seems to be saying, "It is your fault, you asked for it, you are wrong, and that's why you are suffering." So both guilt and shame are part of it. And it's kept secret, until I suppose, it becomes unbearable.

I'm now wondering about any of the myths that might exist in the community—myths that might support this notion of shame or that might help to keep the secrecy. Are you aware of myths that reinforce women blaming themselves?

I am more familiar with the women from India, Pakistan, Bangladesh, and Sri Lanka because this is the culture that I understand and that I come from. The main myth, and I repeat myth, for Muslim women, is that your husband is next to God for you, and your purpose in life should be to obey and please him, and if you do not then there is something wrong with you. There is a myth among the uneducated Muslim women (I'm not talking about those who are educated) that your pathway to heaven or the gate to heaven will open if your husband is happy with you. But if he is not happy with you when either of you die, then it doesn't happen.

I heard a woman who was lecturing other women say, "Every night see to it that your husband is happy because if he dies and he is unhappy then the gates to heaven will not be open for you." So, in keeping a marriage happy and working, the onus seems to be on the woman. And if that marriage is not working, then it is considered to be the woman's fault. I have heard, again and again, that young girls are advised with words such as, "Now that you are going to get married, it is your responsibility to see that your husband is happy. You are like a field which your husband will till as and when he wants to." So the idea of the supremacy and dominance of the husband is ingrained in the minds of the young women, particularly those who have not had an education or have not learned to think for themselves. And that's why they keep taking this abuse thinking, "It's my fault," and that leads to a sense of shame and guilt. And peer pressure is there, "My friends are happy so what is wrong with me, only me."

Is there anything in the culture of the family itself that also is supporting or that acts to limit the possibility of abuse?
Not all, of course not. Not all women are abused. The majority of Muslim families are happy. There are many families where there is mutual respect and understanding or at least tolerance and smooth living. These husbands and wives freely share their feelings with each other. But there are different situations. For instance, if a man comes from a childhood in an abused family, then there is one of two reactions (I'm generalizing but roughly speaking). Either he'll never show any violence to his wife and children or he'll perpetuate it. Then, among uneducated Muslims, there are some areas where the culture is a macho culture, a culture of dominance, a culture of considering that wives or women in general are inferior. There are all kinds of myths attributed to religion that reinforce the concept that women are inferior.

What I am saying is that such myths, not religious teaching or essence of religion, are a male interpretation of the religion. This interpretation reinforces the concept of inferiority. In Judaic-Christian tradition, there is a belief that Eve was created out of the rib of Adam. Am I right? Now, when Islam arose, with its beginnings in Arabia, these ideas were prevalent in the culture. But the religious scripture of the Muslims, the Koran, never mentions the issue of Eve being created out of Adam's rib. The actual text says, "Obey thy Lord who has, out of the same self (or being) and from the same self (or being), created man and woman and from them created innumerable pairs of men and women." So, for one thing, it's not spoken of in gender terms. It's not that he is created and then she was created. It's that "the mate" is created. "Created out of the same soul or self" (it is sometimes translated as soul or self) and from that essence, a number of beings were created. But among Muslims, not only is the Adam's rib myth prevalent but any Muslim man or woman will tell you that Eve was created out of Adam's rib and add another insult by saying "created out of Adam's twisted rib." That's why a woman is twisted, and you have to straighten her by whatever means, even physical force or beating. This is the kind of myth that exists. There is no basis for it in the primary source, the spiritual or religious texts. Many women do not realize that, spiritually and theologically, their creation is exactly on par with men. So this is an example of the myths of women's inferiority that exist and are perpetuated today.

There are many other passages among the Koranic text that highlight the egalitarian relation between men and women.

Could you elaborate on this?
Well, in terms of marriage and husbands and wives and family, what the Koran says is that husbands and wives are "vestments" or garments to each other. Why garments? Because garments are seen as protectors. Garments protect your body, they comfort you, they are close to you. So, the simile has been used to bring out the sense of protectiveness and closeness and comfort that husband and wife provide for each other. It's not said that the wife will provide comfort for the husband or only the husband will provide, but it is said that they will provide for each other. I think this is significant because it brings out mutuality of relationships and reciprocity of relationships. But most Muslim women continue to believe male interpretation (especially those who have not thought about or read the religious texts). They believe that they are supposed to take care of their husbands and please them, but not that it is a reciprocal relationship.

There is another passage in the Koran that talks about the reward of good deeds, and there is no difference between men and women in that. That is again spoken in purely egalitarian terms. For example, it is said:

> The man who believes, the woman who believes
> The man who is righteous, the woman who is righteous
> The man who gives charity, the woman who gives charity
> The man who shows generosity, the woman who shows generosity ...
> [*there are about eleven categories*]
> ...Shall receive great rewards.

So, from the spiritual point of view, there does not seem to be any distinction in the spirituality, or belief, or goodness of a man or a woman. Both may be equally rewarded in terms of the spiritual. The problem is the social-economic inequality that exists within any creed. And that is another issue.

So, if we can imagine a woman who is suffering from mistreatment, and she accepts the myth, is there a ray of hope for her? How does she find a way out of the beatings?
Very difficult. It's a complex thing. I will just try to identify two things that are not sufficient in themselves, but they are necessary. An abused woman should get financial, medical, and legal help. This has to be a two-way process. It has to come

from the woman herself and from outside; she has to seek it and they have to offer it. That's one. The other important thing is that these women lose their self-esteem. They begin to doubt their own capabilities and competencies. So the other equally important step is to build that self-esteem.

I think some of these religious passages and sayings can be used to make her believe in herself. You see, if she is a believing woman, she begins to say, "This is my destiny. This is what God willed for women." This is what most women are made to believe because they do not know the true teachings of their religion. A woman has to learn that she is not an inferior being. She has to learn that she can find support in her religious scriptures (since that is what we are talking about, faith and faith communities). From her own faith have come passages that help her see herself as a worthy being, as created out of the same spirit or soul of which all human beings are created. For if she is worthy, doing good deeds and living a good life, then great reward awaits her. These are spiritual things. They bring some kind of strength to her as a believing woman. There are innumerable passages about justice, about compassion, about mercy in the Koran. The Koran has over a thousand different passages each beginning with words which mean, "begin in the name of God who is compassionate and merciful." This is the thrust of the Koran. A woman has to believe that her God is compassionate and benefi-cent and is watching over her.

But unfortunately, most Muslim people (the community, the traditional men) look upon the punishing aspects of the Book. God is wrath. God is anger. And continually the message is bombarded into the minds of women, "If you do this, God will punish you. If you do that, God will be angry. If you do not please your husband, God will not be pleased." So the concept of a punishing God is some-thing that is always in the back of women's minds and thoughts. They tend to live with this concept instead of believing that it is a compassionate God, a merciful God, a God that rewards. They don't know. They study the scriptures but only in the Arabic script. Many of them do not know the language, and I suppose that many of those who do probably do not reflect on the meaning of what is given.

In the Koran it is openly asked, "Do you not think? Do you not reflect?" So you see, the teachings of the scriptures and the practice in Muslim culture are two different things. And all that combines to put so much pressure on women that they lose their sense of worth and self-respect and they accept the abuse. I believe this pressure results from the culture, patriarchal culture. I suppose the way out is to educate people, women and men, spiritually and otherwise.

Is it an easy thing for women to find the interpretation of the Koran that is more favourable to the equality of women?
It's not easy. No, I do not think it is easy but I can tell you effort is being made in the Middle East, in Asian countries, in the United States, and in Canada. There are Muslim women who are trying to read and understand the religious scriptures.

They are reading it from the viewpoint of women, not from the viewpoint of men. But their works are not known. Another general myth in the Muslim culture is that God has given man the right to divorce his wife when and if he wants to. That myth is like a sword of Damocles that hangs over the heads of women and forces them to take the abuse. But if divorce is allowed—for instance, no-fault divorce—both men and women have the right to it. This is something that many Muslim women don't know. Now there are women scholars, Muslim women scholars and theologians, who are trying to interpret these religious texts in a fair and egalitarian manner. They try to interpret the Koran in the light of the weight of evidence, the weight and thrust and spirit of the Koran.

You see, it's the Book that came to create unity among people and to help the oppressed and the downtrodden. From that point of view women were among the most oppressed and downtrodden. That is why Islam arose. The prophet of Islam (I will say this and not many people will write about these things) hit at the structure of patriarchy by giving women rights at a time when women were like chattels. They were property of the men folk. If a man died and there were many wives, all the wives were the property of the son who could sell them, marry them off, marry them himself, or enslave them in the household. Female infanticide was practiced in those days. The Prophet gave women the right to consent at marriage, inheritance rights, right to expect respect, right to divorce, right to property, and the right to be employed in gainful activities. He would listen respectfully to women when they came to him with their problems or with their grievances. What was expected of a woman was to be chaste and modest.

But today Muslim women, unfortunately, have been put in exclusion and seclusion. They are excluded from many aspects of religion, politics, social, and cultural life. And I am not talking about the veil (that is an entirely separate issue). But, I am talking about the way in which women do not participate in equal measure in the affairs of state or religion or culture in their original societies. In Canada, they do not practice that kind of seclusion, but they carry that kind of psychological and historical memory with them which continues to affect them. And so, the woman is down there in the hierarchy, her place is home and her task is service. Added to it is that if men are angry, or if they are violent in their temperament, they keep women down by taking it out on them.

To top it off, things that happen in other communities happen in Muslim communities too. Anytime there is economic crisis, women bear the brunt of it. When there is family crisis, women suffer and some of the religious and cultural myths reinforce men's beliefs. One way out is to try to fight these myths by educating people in various ways. An effective approach is to have the *Imam* (who is like a priest) include some of these issues in his sermons each week. People have thought and talked about it.

I think that one reason men do not consider women their equals is that many Muslim women don't get a chance to show in any way their competence or their abilities in public life because, as I said previously, there is a culture of exclusion of women from the (I don't like the word but I'll use it) power structure of society. Today, of course, some Muslim women are getting education in law, medicine, engineering, science, and the arts. They are becoming professors and doctors and members of parliament, but it is a very small percentage compared to the total Muslim population. There are half a billion Muslim women around the world. It is a very small proportion that are able to take advantage of these positions.

As a result of the culture of exclusion, what are they good for? They are good for cooking and cleaning. That's how they are perceived. How can women talk about important matters of state or politics, or religion? They don't know, they don't understand, they are not equipped to do it. And added to it is the perception that their brains are inferior to men's. Women are not considered to be fully rational. All these existing myths add to the sense of inferiority and inadequacy that has been ingrained in women. So of course, as inferior beings, they should be put in their place through family violence and violence in other ways and other contexts.

So, this is one of the things that added to the present situation of Muslim women, the perpetual exclusion of women. And I am not talking about the Middle East, I am not talking about the Asian countries, I am talking about Canada in the 1990s.

Do you see any progress being made in the way men and women congregate in religious or quasi-religious services? Has there been any progress we might point to?
You mean where men and women congregate together? Unfortunately, right now there is a wave of orthodoxy that has enveloped many Canadian Muslim communities where there is more separation than being together. But one ray of hope, in terms of women finding self-respect, self-esteem, and their place in society, is in the young women who are getting educated in Canadian schools and universities. There they meet all kinds of people on an equal basis, and I am hoping and have faith that they will grow up having real self-respect and self-esteem and will claim their rightful place in all the institutions of society and in their community. Many of them are religious, many of them observe religious symbols including, for example, the veil. I have heard these young women talk about respect and self-respect as well as modesty, morality, and equality. I have heard them talk about the kind of things that their mothers and aunts would never even dream of talking about. So, I think that, in terms of progress, there is some hope.

The fear is that there are many mores of life in Canada, the United States, and the West that Muslim families do not approve of, particularly sexual mores. They are afraid that their daughters will be influenced by these mores. They are worried that there is no respect for family or for elders, that there is a lack of modesty, and they are worried about dating. These are some of the things that Muslim families are concerned about. So, young Muslim women have a challenge before them to find a balance between their Islamic values of modesty, of caring for others, of sharing and of respect for family members, and the Western values of individuality, freedom of thought, freedom of speech, and self-respect, the values of the Enlightenment. Generally, young Muslim women believe in the importance of family and community.

In the strictly social activities, not the religious or semi-religious ones, the more community oriented ones, is there a place for women to show their competence and their worth?
In some families they do, particularly those who are educated and have adopted some of the more progressive ideas, for example, in weddings. But weddings are more an affair of women than of men. In other community matters there are some celebrations, for example, EID festival. At the end of thirty days of fasting each year, there is a day of celebration for having performed the religious duty of fasting for a month. In Canada, both men and women now participate. That is an example of mixing, of some kind of change. But then again, men organize the activities while women organize the cooking. That hierarchy of service still exists for women. But there are examples of Muslim women here who have moved forward and done things on their own in organizing socio-cultural artistic functions. There is a woman in our community who organizes it, and I am always happy to assist her. She also includes members of other communities and makes it is a multicultural activity. There is the Canadian Council of Muslim Women that aims at educating Muslim women in equality and participation in their society and community. And there are others where Muslim women are active.

Are there any strategies we can use to deal with the issue of family violence?
Reinhild Boehm and I were involved in a conference to find ways and means and strategies to combat family violence. We thought it might be worthwhile to invite the imams and ask them what they can do about it and gently, through a kind of autosuggestion, suggest to them that through their sermons and in their counselling sessions they should spread the idea that family violence is wrong, that it is un-Islamic. We thought that may be one way and it just might be.

I know of one young couple who were married about one and a half years ago. There are all kinds of problems, and I know the mother of the girl has had several counselling sessions with the priest who married them. She has tried to encourage him to talk to the young man and his family to determine the source of the problem. So, this is one case I know of where the priest is involved in conveying to the man what is wrong. In Canada, there is a chance for this kind of strategy to be effective.

Are the priests eager to do this?

Well, the priests may themselves have a problem not only because they are men, and as I said earlier they carry the historical memory of patriarchy, but also in the kind of clientele they have. I'm not sure how it would be taken if they tried to impress on their congregations what people should do and what they should not do regarding family violence. But, there is no other way out of this. I think we have to encourage it and make them honour-bound to do it. I know that they can, and in terms of some individual cases they do.

There is one special person here, Mr. Saleem Ganam, who has worked with the Muslims all his life. He performed a marriage ceremony that I attended that was a very good example of how it can be done. He talked to both the young man and the young woman.

Mr. Ganam had the two young people stand together in front of the microphone and the whole audience and asked them to repeat the marriage vows. He then explained to them what was expected of them, how they are to honour and cherish each other. It was very much like and very close to the Christian wedding. So you see, some little things are happening here and there. Still, we have a lot of work to do for the majority of our people.

I am not too familiar with the traditional wedding ceremony. Please tell me a little more about it. The bride is with the women, the groom is with the men, and the ceremony takes place among the men?

That's right, because traditionally it is a male priest who will recite the verses of the Koran and will pronounce the couple husband and wife, without the woman's physical presence. Certainly in Southeast Asia and the Middle East it is like that. Here it is different. Here they do come out and sit together in front of the gathering. That is changing.

Which is some small sign of equality?

Yes, I would say that is true.

Do you think there is a message of hope for Muslim women who have experienced abuse?

Purely, in terms of faith, you can tell a woman, "What has happened is not your fault. You are not worthless. It is the way society is structured." Women must realize that it is not their destiny, and it is not what God willed for them. It happened for other reasons. The other thing that one can tell women who have suffered abuse is, "God holds you dear because you are a worthy being." And in terms of hope for the future many among our young women and even our young men are becoming conscious of the socio-economic and cultural roots of the abuse. They realize that it involves a perception of women as inferior and of a lack of respect.

People have to have role models that they can respect. There are large numbers of Muslims, young men and women studying together in schools and universities. Many of the professors are women. So here are these young men seeing women who have achieved something—knowledge—in positions they respect. So, they have a role model. But if all they see is their mothers being abused, why would they not do it to their own wives thinking that is the natural thing? So I suppose there is hope. And the other thing is for Muslims, women and men, to search for true understanding of the sacred texts, their religious message, and the spirit of this message as it is relevant today.

I'm thinking now of someone who might work in a transition house or might work as a counsellor and go into someone's home. Is there some message that we might give to such workers who have contact with Muslim women and families? Something that might give assurance?

In these cases, many times a woman's faith in God is shaken, and it will help a believing woman if that faith is somehow restored along with all the other measures such as financial, social, legal, and medical issues where immediate assistance and crisis intervention is needed. Some of the ways I have suggested may be helpful.

I hope I have been of some help in addressing some of the questions. I am hopeful that others will gain further insight into the issue of spousal abuse having heard the perspective of someone from the Muslim community.

Women of Faith

A common thread in our conversations with women of faith was the belief that spirituality is found within. It is the result of a life-long search that is nurtured and shaped by our participation in a larger community. Our lives are influenced by family, friends, and community. Our worldview is a result of our personal experiences, our cultural roots, our religious beliefs, and our level of education. In every culture, society (the larger community), establishes norms of behaviour, codes of conduct, and rules and laws. Each of these influences contributes to the attitudes, beliefs, and perspective that make up our own spiritual being.

Conversations with Front-line Workers

The Issue of Family Violence as Seen by Individuals Who Work for Community Service Providers

4

The experiences and opinions in this chapter were gathered from the front line workers who see and try to help families in crisis. These caregivers represent mainstream agencies, immigrant service groups, women's shelters, and cultural communities as social workers, psychologists, police officers, counsellors, helpers, and friends. The views expressed are those of each individual. Their experiences do not necessarily represent or reflect the opinions of their departments, organizations, groups, or their broader communities. These front-line workers come from a variety of cultural and religious backgrounds. Their collective viewpoints reflect their own cultural and religious backgrounds as well as the influence of family, friends, and community.

In *Lifelines* we have focused on women who are or were involved in hetero-sexual relationships. We have learned that family violence is a community issue and that the women we have represented here are not the only victims. It is a problem in gay and lesbian communities, in older populations, and for the men who experience abuse. Our hope is that our communities recognize abusive relationships in their many and varied forms and take steps to ensure that all victims of family violence have "lifelines." Lifelines enable survivors to get through crisis, to make changes, and to begin to heal.

People from diverse communities and cultures who have experience in dealing with spousal abuse, are telling us that a common thread in the healing process is spirituality. Yet, when we asked service providers, community leaders, shelter workers, and the women themselves if women's cultural and spiritual needs were being met during the time of crisis the answer was, "No."

Many women told of their spiritual anguish in the midst of family violence. But ultimately, their strength came from within and their healing was, for each of them, a personal journey. Anna Maria Fantino, a psychologist, believes that spirituality is a human quality that allows us to see beyond narrow concepts. A person's spiritual dimension connects the individual with more holistic experiences, ideas, and ideals. Many people fulfill the need for connectedness and belonging in the notion and the experience of a transcendent being, a god. Others find it in other ways, for instance in communing with nature, in identifying with human-itarian causes, or in community work.* Human beings have an incredible inner strength that comes from each individual's spiritual self. It is this inner strength that enables survivors of spousal abuse to change their lives and their futures, whether they choose to leave or to stay.

---

* See "Catholic Social Services," pp. 167-70.

Marie MacDonald, a partner in the Spousal Abuse Follow-Up Team, believes that the contributors to family violence are global, the socio-economic situation, inequalities in the social system, the legacy of our patriarchal societies. As members of the community, we must recognise that family violence is a social problem. It is not a problem of culture. It is not a problem of religion. It is a perceptual problem centred around the issue of equality.

Perceptions are formed by the ideas, beliefs, values, and traditions that communities, families, and individuals collect over a lifetime. Cultural background, education level, and family beliefs influence the behaviour of each individual. Whether they are the abuser or the abused, whether they are the children caught in the middle or the extended family on the sidelines, whether they are professionals who help or members of the community—all are influenced by their own worldview. This is one of the big challenges for those who help and care— for the counsellors, the service providers—and the policy makers.

And despite the isolation that surrounds the abused, there is a support system out there. There are organizations and agencies who help survivors of trauma and abuse to gather strength and gain hope and begin to plan for the future. According to Johanna Bukczynska, a counsellor and therapist at the Centre for Survivors of Torture and Trauma, there are four important guidelines in helping abused and traumatized people.*

Vida Naji, of Changing Together: A Centre for Immigrant Women, believes that a counsellor can help a woman discover the skills to cope with the situation, but a counsellor cannot give her the skills. Women do have choices, if they know their rights. Organizations such as Changing Together play a critical role during and after crisis. Counsellors and workers in these agencies and departments help

---

* See "Mennonite Centre for Newcomers: Centre for Survivors of Torture and Trauma," pp. 171-73.

to get women to safe ground (safe places such as a women's shelter or a friend's home) before addressing their other needs. A good counsellor listens and does not judge. She must be able to recognise and identify the real problem underlying the situation. Those who are effective counsellors and helpers look at each individual's need.

Heather Roberts, executive director of Safe Place Women's Shelter, recognises the diverse needs of abused women. She is the first to admit that the helping community has not been meeting the needs of all women. But Heather believes that positive change is now underway. Even small changes, those that do not result in increased costs, can make a difference. For instance, creating a sacred space, a place for reflection, a quiet room within each shelter, would begin to address the spiritual needs of women from any culture.*

The time to act is now.

---

* See "Safe Place Women's Shelter," pp. 190-94.

Views of
a Chinese-Canadian Counsellor

I feel that I am blended.
With my cultural beliefs and
a Christian background I think that
I can relate to both worlds.

Diana Yiu

*Diana is a clinical social worker
and family counsellor special-
izing in mental health. She was
born in Hong Kong and has
lived in Canada since 1989.
Diana works with the Chinese
community, Community
Cultures Institute, and
Catholic Social Services, and
describes her faith as Christian.*

*As a counsellor, do you have any idea as to what some of the causes of spousal
abuse are within your cultural community?*

Beliefs, values, and tradition instilled over a lifetime are part of the problem for
Chinese women who are caught in a cycle of family violence. A strong belief in
"family ties" and the value of "loyalty" binds a woman to an abusive situation.
In addition, the established hierarchy within the culture can work against her.

As do women of every culture, Chinese women have fears, fears for their
future, worries about children, and financial uncertainty. Traditional expectation
can bind them to an abusive husband or family. These "bindings" often work to
depower Chinese women. For instance, within the traditional family, the family
and societal hierarchy can limit the support a woman receives. Emphasis on strong
family ties, on loyalty, and on respect for elders is sometimes a problem for women
in these situations.

Although most of the abuse in Chinese families is not physical, the results of
emotional and psychological abuse are just as destructive. For example, a woman
of Chinese origin who came to us from a small town in British Columbia had
married a Caucasian. She had been tolerating an extremely abusive situation in
the hopes that it would get better. However, this was not possible because the
husband had serious emotional and mental problems.

When she finally sought counselling she explained that she had been using an approach of "patience." Her reasoning was that, if she could just tolerate the situation a little longer, maybe he would change. This fit in with her perceived role of being a submissive and dutiful wife. During the counselling process the woman began to see that her traditional values of loyalty, submissiveness, and patience were working against her.

Is spirituality a factor in the family abuse cases that you see?
Values such as loyalty, patience, and submissiveness, although not tied specifically to a particular religion, are part of the spiritual aspect of this woman. Her traditional values, morality, and nature have been ingrained in her since she was a small child. They are her spiritual way of coping with her world. In this particular case, the qualities of her "being" acted to depower rather than empower her.

Would you say that there is a cultural aspect to the "depowering?"
Certainly. Culture conflict is a problem for all first generation immigrants, but it is a particular problem for women in their forties and fifties who are not financially self-sufficient.

For instance, younger Chinese women from Hong Kong who are somewhat Westernized, with a higher level of education and a good command of the English language, tend to see themselves with more options. But women from countries like mainland China, Vietnam, and Thailand, who may not have had the same opportunities, experience a conflict between traditional and Western ways.

When women, who are going through this culture conflict, approach you for help do they openly identify family abuse as their concern?
There is usually some other issue that brings them to us. The abuse aspect often comes out later in the process. For instance, one of our clients is a female factory worker who came to Canada twenty years ago. She brought her daughter to us for counselling. After talking to the mother and daughter it was obvious that it was the mother who needed help.

After coming to Canada, she had married a Chinese man who had been a compulsive gambler for many years. The psychological abuse, which began with demands for money, had become so extreme that their young daughter was frequently running away. The situation could not be discussed with the family because of the woman's need to keep this shameful secret to herself. Fortunately, the mother and daughter sought counselling together.

The tendency to avoid exploring the real reason for the problem is strong. In this case the mother felt that her daughter was the problem and that talking with a counsellor might straighten her out. Many parents send the children for help in the hopes that someone can fix the situation.

With such strong family ties, could the abused woman find help and support within her extended family?

Over half of my clients feel that the extended family can't or won't help. For example, a distraught wife came to counselling after trying to talk to her in-laws about her problem. Her abusive husband was having an affair but her in-laws did not want to hear about it. This woman, from a lower socio-economic background, worked in a restaurant with her husband. They had been experiencing trouble with their teen-aged child. Again, it was the relationship with the child that initially brought the woman to us. Information about the real issue, the affair, came out slowly.

This is an example of traditional hierarchy working against the woman. As she was not self-sufficient financially and her mother-in-law was the matriarch of the family, she felt she had no recourse for the humiliation she suffered.

How does your own cultural background and spirituality affect the way you counsel women?

I feel that I am blended. With my cultural beliefs and a Christian background I think that I can relate to both worlds. Although I do not consider myself to be submissive, I do value the bonds of family and believe in respect for one's elders. However, my Western experience has also given me an appreciation and respect for the individual.

These blended values definitely affect my approach to clients. Personal beliefs are very much a part of my working tools. As a counsellor, you use yourself. I share my values.

Do you have any Christian sayings or cultural parables that you use to help people?

Yes, I use the Bible occasionally, with discretion, and if I think it will help. Usually, it happens when the subject of religion comes up or if the person refers to their spiritual beliefs in some way. Of course, this would not necessarily be in a Christian context. Sometimes guilt can be addressed through religious text.

Recently, a Catholic teen, who had been sexually molested at the age of six, came to us for help. This young girl had begun to feel an overpowering guilt at around age twelve. She was unable to concentrate and was having difficulties at home and at school. A verse from the Bible was used in a discussion with her to help free her from binding. I used this verse to help tell the young girl that the truth should set one free. "'God is faithful if we confess our sin,'" I tell women, "this is not your sin but 'God can cleanse all our sins.'" (1 John Chapter 1 Verse 9)

In the case of ongoing abuse, I might use a Chinese parable. The concept is that if you act patiently, then you will have a lump of gold. The more you tolerate the more gold you will have. I think that I am able to see beyond the sharing of common beliefs and sayings such as this so I am able to help the troubled woman see the larger picture. At first this teen was anxious and very nervous, but over six to ten sessions a trust grew and she began to heal. In the process the girl introduced a troubled cousin, with a similar background, who was suicidal and who in turn was able to get and accept help.

You must have a wide variety of techniques to draw from.
I use several different techniques during therapy, drawn from many resources, including sharing my own feelings about spirituality. It is important to keep in mind that when we counsel we have to come to the client's level.

For instance, a woman from a Jehovah's Witness background came to me. She was no longer of that faith. However, while she was a Witness she would rather have died than submit to a blood transfusion. I have trouble with this concept myself, but I had to accept her position.

Even though this woman had left the Jehovah's Witness church, she still holds the values from this religion. She feels restricted. This woman is not able to deny her husband because her family would not accept her. She exhibits excessive-compulsive behaviour and is on medication for it. She is compelled to steal. The process of healing involves helping her to gradually diffuse these compulsions. Hopefully, she will become more open, be able to trust, and to reject the abuse.

Do you think religious doctrine or passages from sacred texts are ever used to control women?
Sometimes there is manipulation of religious doctrine. It is not explicit but subtle. For example, a Christian Caucasian couple came to the centre. They had being receiving pastoral counselling because the husband was abusing the wife and basing it on a passage in the Bible.

> Wives, submit yourselves unto your own husbands, as unto the Lord (Ephesians Chapter 5 Verse 22).

Using the Bible, in turn, one could point out that the passage goes further and that people should note that it also says,

> Submitting yourselves one to another in the fear of God (Ephesians Chapter 5 Verse 21).

It is human nature to hear only what we want to hear or read something into a text that may alter its meaning somewhat. In this case, the counsellor advised the couple to read further.

> Husbands, love your wives, even as Christ also loved the Church, and gave himself for it (Ephesians Chapter 5 Verse 25).

So ought men to love their wives as their own bodies. He that
loveth his wife loveth himself (Ephesians Chapter 5 Verse 25).

There is another verse in Ephesians that can be used to help people—Chinese, Western, or any other culture—who are afraid of anger. They have seen disruptive and destructive anger and have a fear of it, but they need to become aware and in touch with anger, their own and that of others. They need to be able to deal with it or to express it. One can tell them that it is okay to show anger, but assertively rather than aggressively. The verse I use to illustrate this point is,

Be ye angry, and sin not: let not the sun go down upon your wrath
(Ephesians Chapter 4 Verse 26).

What is the relationship between your centre and the clergy?
If a person expresses a need to talk to a priest, we make the connection. But sometimes people feel they cannot confide in their own religious leader but need to discuss the matter with a stranger. There is often the fear that the community will hear of one's personal problems.

For instance, a Polish Catholic woman needed to talk but did not want to discuss the situation with her Polish priest. In this case, we were able to get her some spiritual counselling outside of her own community.

Do people ever tell you that they have had either a good or a bad experience in seeking help for family violence with a spiritual leader?
Yes, there are stories on both sides and in about half the cases the experience is not a positive one. We always hope that the pastor or religious leader, if helping in these times, might not do too much harm and that perhaps he or she can remedy the situation to some extent. However, religious leaders are not usually trained in this type of intervention. Sometimes the spiritual leaders recognise this themselves and will refer the couple to agencies like ours.

Do you find the nature of abuse different in Chinese couples versus Western born couples?
With Caucasians, there seems to be more physical violence because there is alcohol and drugs. So the connection could be a cultural one. The Chinese believe that one should not ever hit a woman. On the other hand, Western men are also taught not to hit a woman, so how can one be sure the connection is cultural. However, as a recent court case illustrates, some people, including a judge, believe that being drunk is a valid excuse for this behaviour.

Many Chinese women, although they do not experience physical abuse, experience severe emotional and psychological abuse. But to these women, who are generally caught between generations, the abuse is simply not an issue. It is referred to as "rebuke." And rebuke is often an accepted fact of life for these women. So there is a problem here. The worker needs to address the woman's own experience. Perhaps she might ask her, "Do you think you and your husband have equal rights?" Then the counsellor explains that, in Canada, husband and wife do have equal rights. Sometimes there is a scripture to quote from in this regard and sometimes there is a need to refer to the Charter of Human Rights. I try to point out to both that rebuke may be accepted in their own country but that humiliating and degrading another person is not accepted in this country and is indeed considered abusive.

Changing Together
A Centre for Immigrant Women I

We cannot stereotype a culture.
I have to know the situation
to be able to help. Knowing about
different cultural backgrounds
is a tool for a counsellor.

Vida Naji

*Vida is a program co-ordinator.
She was born in Iran and lived
in Iran, England, and Pakistan,
before coming to Canada in
1988. Vida is the mother of
three and is of the Muslim faith.*

What influenced you to do this kind of work with immigrant women?
I was educated as a teacher with a Bachelor of Science degree at Tehran University in Iran. While in university I married and soon went with my husband to his city. A close friend of our family who was highly placed in government encouraged me to teach there. I decided to try it and became a biology teacher at age twenty-two. I had gone through high school and university early, and some of the students were older than I was! But I enjoyed it and was very happy. I loved my job and my new profession, and I taught there for nine years.

Our next move was to England so that my husband could pursue his career as a specialist physician. When we returned to Iran, I became the director of a women's college, Markuz Sepahe Danesh. It was very satisfying work and a real challenge. The girls came from many different areas and trained for six months as teachers. It was a very progressive program, all paid for by the government. The girls wore the uniform of the army and always greeted me by saluting. I was very comfortable with this as my father was a general. It was a very exciting and wonderful time in my life.

Then things began to change in Iran, and we decided to leave the country. One of the reasons we left was that our sons would have been conscripted into the army to fight. It was easy for us to leave because we travelled out of the country frequently and had valid passports. The whole family left for Pakistan. Then we went our separate ways.

I was alone with the children for eight long years while my husband went back to Iran. I stayed in Pakistan for eight months getting medical clearance and papers. Then we immigrated to Canada. We chose Edmonton because I had friends there.

Were you worried about your husband's safety during this time? It must have been very difficult to be on your own.

I knew my husband was safe. Because they needed doctors in Iran, he was well cared for and they were glad to have him. He worked to send money to support us in Canada as it was many months before I was able to get a job.

It was hard. Basically we left with our suitcases. We left everything, all our friends and family. We left all our belongings, all our precious things. It's not so hard to immigrate when you are young because you have not yet accumulated material things, and you still have your full life ahead of you. But when you are established and your children are in their teens, it is very hard. During that time I felt like I was dying, and it was terrible having the family torn apart. Eight years is a long time! But friends and other people were so good to us. I don't know how I could have done it without them.

I came to Edmonton about eight years ago and began a new life here by helping other women. Employment opportunities were abundant then, but now it is getting harder all the time for new immigrants. It is so hard to find a job now. I was very fortunate. When I arrived I was able to volunteer right away and to find work soon after. But it is very hard now, especially for immigrant women. I was fortunate also that I did not have to deal with the language barrier that most immigrant women face. As soon as I came here, I asked where I could go to find out about Canada. Someone gave me a phone number, and I went to EISA (Edmonton Immigrant Services Association) to find out what services were available to me. I needed to find out about Canada, my rights and responsibilities. They had a wonderful consulate who was very helpful to me. Right away she told me they needed me as a volunteer to help another group of immigrants who were expected. Therefore, I took the training myself so that I could begin to help.

How did you finally come to be the New Friends Co-ordinator at Changing Together?

After a year and a half there was an opportunity for a paying position at Changing Together. Although I had planned on going back to university to get more education, I preferred to have a job. That is how I came to Changing Together. I wanted to help other women overcome the isolation and the language barrier. Our program here gives people more time to settle in and to learn all the many things about their new lives in Canada. This help is so important.

For the women who visit your centre is spousal abuse a problem?

In the immigrant population women are often the ones who suffer the most. However, I think that the mainstream population faces the same thing, increased family violence. And most of the time it is directed against women, seldom against men.

The immigrant population is vulnerable because so many things are happening so quickly in their lives. First of all, differences in cultural values change their role in the family. For example, when they first arrive sometimes the man cannot find a job and the woman is the one who has to work. This is a burden for a traditional woman because she is expected to prepare the food and take care of the children and household. But, in Canadian society, she is also expected to take on a job outside the home. This new dual role is too much of a load on her shoulders. In addition, the husband may be asked or expected to help with the household. He may feel this will lessen respect for him. The family has difficulty adapting, and it sometimes ends in family violence.

The language barrier is also a significant problem. Finding family counselling is difficult. Most immigrants are not familiar with counselling services. Most of them had their own social and health networks, family, friends, or people in the mosque they could trust and talk to. But here, in a new country, they often do not have those informal support systems for counselling. Being counselled by a stranger is very new for them. They don't know these problem solving services are available to them. Women who are in abusive relationships don't know where to turn. Aside from the lack of knowledge about services and help available, there is a tremendous lack of self–confidence because of abuse. This really hinders a woman from even trying to find help. She is often blaming herself.

Abuse is not always physical of course. In my culture it is the husband's right to control the finances. For instance, once a woman marries she is considered to be of her husband's household and does not have the means to help her own father and mother or her siblings without the generosity of her husband. If they were in need of help, she would have to approach him and explain the situation. If he were kind and generous and had the means to help he might.

One lady, who I was helping, had a husband who was very fond of money and he didn't want to give extra money to his wife (even though she was working). In Canada, this is a form of financial abuse, but in our community, this is not abuse. Women accept it and simply say, "Okay, my husband is a little greedy or doesn't like to give me money." This couple I am talking about had so many arguments and fights, but these were not considered by either of them to be family violence.

We do see women who are clearly victims of violence. Sometimes they come to the centre with bruises after the police have been called. Once I met a woman who was lonely for her family and wanted to call them back home. But her husband said, "Don't call your mom, don't call her. It is too expensive." At first the wife thought because he didn't have any close family he could not understand.

But things got worse after the husband said, "Don't call your family. Even twice a month is too much." So this woman became very upset and worried. They started to fight and gradually this very small matter ended in family violence. People from the community intervened, and the couple is now getting counselling together. Emotional or mental battering is not seen as abusive behaviour in my culture. We accept it as the husband's attitude or personality.

Sexual abuse is also a controversial issue. I saw it in my own country, and I see it here when counselling women. In many cases husbands force wives to have sex when they don't want it. These men claim it is their right as a husband and become very angry. They will put their wives down, yelling and degrading them. But again, in many countries this would not be seen as being abusive. Neither husband or wife would consider it to be abuse. They don't recognize it. They have trouble believing it's a crime in Canada.

Is it about control and power then?
Yes, in many immigrant families the husband has the authority to control the behaviour of his family, but it is not the only reason.

Do you think that the strains of immigration have something to do with this? For instance, when the man can't get a job or things are very different, does he feel more threatened?
Yes, spousal abuse may happen when resettlement threatens the husband's control of his family. Immigration causes many problems. Status and the whole family and social structure changes. That's why adjusting to Canada is not just knowing the transportation system, the legal issues, parenting practices, or the health care system but adjusting emotionally also. To be in another environment with new rules, a new language, and no job is very different and very difficult for newcomers.

How do you think your faith community reacts to women in such a situation? If a woman went to her priest or minister, how would he or she react?
It is hard to say this, but it is a reality. Although, in most cases the leader of the faith or faith community would side with the man, you can find a few that don't. They are the ones who are very balanced and they recognize women's and men's rights and will help them. But the majority of them would not empathize with the woman. Why? Because some of these rights and freedoms might be very new ideas for them. Or they are so attached to the religious studies that they don't have time to read other studies. They search in the holy books for their answers, but some rules are very old. They do not apply to the world of today, and society is constantly changing.

I have just come across a new brochure here about court challenges. The government in Canada is encouraging organizations to fight laws that don't uphold human rights. They want to encourage all Canadians to stand up against these laws. So they want you to fight that law. In Canadian society we may change our laws because society changes so quickly. But some of our traditional faith leaders are so emotionally and spiritually attached to the world of their religion and its messengers and prophets that they don't want to hear or read about injustice and change. They are often not aware of the human or women's rights that have been recently recognized. So even though they think they are progressive, they often are far from being that way. People who are very traditional often don't take into account what is happening in the twenty-first century.

As a result, some of the faith leaders seem to be working against the laws of modern society. That's why young people cannot go to the Mosque or very educated people cannot accept some of the old ideas.

How does your own cultural background affect the way you counsel others?
Within any culture families and individuals react differently. For instance, we may both be Muslim, but maybe my family has a very fundamental attitude so it's completely different from her family. We cannot stereotype a culture. I have to know the situation to be able to help. Knowing about different cultural backgrounds is a tool for a counsellor. For example, if you don't know about the Vietnamese culture, it is essential to find out about it before doing any counselling. You can talk with a few Vietnamese to gain this knowledge.

I try to find out about each individual person. What they believe about their rights is very important to me as a counsellor. I am also concerned about how their culture and family view rights and responsibilities regarding specific issues. The whole picture is valuable, but most of all what I need to know is how the woman herself views the problem.

Changing cultures does not come overnight. I try to find common things that will ease the person first, and then address those things that need to be changed. Then I would consider the rights and responsibilities of her culture as compared with those of Canada. What are the laws, responsibilities, and rights? At that point I can find some common ground at least. Then slowly I help the person to modify her ways in a way that is acceptable to her and hopefully her family. Finding out the issue she is involved in, the cultural context, relating it to the larger society, her family's viewpoint, and the woman's own perception is important. We cannot stereotype how all Muslims or all Iranians think. Every family has different attitudes and beliefs and every person has too. People are so different.

Do you think religious passages or sacred texts are ever used to control women?
In some situations it is true. They sometimes are used to control women. Every leader seems to interpret the holy book differently because they are influenced by their own ideas. There is an attempt to control our freedom. For example, in

some Muslim countries women cannot leave the country without the permission of a man—husband, father, brother, or even her son. But sometimes this depends on the current political situation of the country. For example, our religion was very moderate in my mother's time. We did not have those restrictions. We could leave any time to have *Haji* [religious observance at Mecca], as long as we covered our bodies and our hair, like other moderate Islamic countries.

So you wonder what the source of these regulations is. Is it the Qur'an? Other countries, like Saudi Arabia, have the same rules. Is it control when they have to give me permission to go on a trip alone? It is control. It is not written, but I still have to have permission to leave the country. But there are exceptions of course. If a woman wants to go to Haji, to make a trip to Mecca [the holy city in Saudi Arabia where the prophet Mohammed is buried], she can go even if the husband says she cannot. It is very important to all Muslims to be able to pray there, at the site of the first mosque.

Are you of the Muslim faith yourself?
Yes, I am Shia. Islam has two branches. One is Shia. The other one is Sunni. Most of the Islamic countries follow Sunni Islam. Iran is the only country in the world where Shia is the official faith of Islam.

Presently, in Iran the extreme Islamic activities are reinforced on TV and the radio. You hear it over and over. If you are a good Muslim, faithful to God, and a good woman, you don't travel without your husband's permission, you don't sell your property without his permission, and you don't go out of the house without covering your face with the *hejjab* (the veil), then you are a good woman.

Do you have any quotation from the Muslim faith that would be helpful, that would give a woman strength?
We have a quotation that can give comfort and pride to women. It is a beautiful sentiment. The prophet Mohammed said that "Heaven is under mother's feet." This means that women are respected in society. And our religious leaders say it in the same way. I interpret it that way. It is a compliment for all women. Women are special, God loves them, Heaven is under their feet, welcoming them.

But it can have other implications. For one thing, it refers to mothers, not women. And if you are a not a mother, it doesn't apply. So it can be used to weaken women. It can be harmful to give that idea to women. If they are young, vulnerable, and easily influenced someone could say, "Don't go to school. Just learn to be a good mother. That is enough because Mohammed said, 'Heaven is under mother's feet.' Get married very young, have many children, take care of them, and be a good wife, a submissive wife, and do what your husband says. That is the role of woman that God and the Prophet defined."

Some faith leaders might use it in a misleading manner. It sounds like such a beautiful thing, but it can make more women illiterate. It can isolate women in society and make them powerless. On the other hand, many women find comfort from this passage, knowing that they are special in God's eyes.

And what if a woman marries but is not able to have children? Does she have a special status or is she different?
The ideal is to have children and be a mother. "Heaven is under mother's feet." So if you want to be a good woman, get married, have children, and think only of taking care of them, nothing else.

Isn't it discriminating against women who don't have a child?
In some passages equality and discrimination and women's rights and freedom are ignored. Some faith leaders take advantage of this to empower men over women.

What if you never married?
Faith leaders always encourage girls to get married.

Then what about virginity before marriage? Is it expected?
Virginity is mandatory in Islam. A woman must be a virgin before getting married.

Then, a woman could not remarry if divorced?
She can remarry as a married woman, if her husband approves.

Can a man get a divorce simply by saying the words?
If they are traditional Muslims, the man can say three times, "I divorce you," and then they are considered to be divorced. It is different in the more modern marriage and modern Islamic societies. For instance, my culture doesn't accept the words alone. It must be a written statement. This could happen to a woman, who still loves her husband and was not wanting to divorce.

If the woman wanted to divorce her husband, could she?
In some modern Islamic countries it is different. There are family laws that decide about divorce or encourage the couple to go to marriage counselling. According to the Islamic laws a woman cannot divorce her husband but he, at any time without her agreement, can divorce her.

So are we talking about the difference between fundamentalism and modern society?
Yes, and the distinction is very important. That is why it differs so much even from family to family. Fundamentalist ideas are very different from modernist ideas.

And if your son were to marry a Muslim girl and things did not work out, how would you feel about them divorcing?
Why should the couple have to suffer? It affects the kids also when parents don't want to live together. However, we would not rush to separate them but would try to find out the main issue, if it is possible to solve. But if it does not work, sometimes it is better to divorce.

What about adultery? Is it condoned for the male but not for the female?
Men can practice some extramarital sexual activity, but women cannot. Virginity is not a matter for men, but it is for women. It is important in both the religion and the culture at the present time.

What happens to a woman who does have adulterous relationships? How would she be viewed in the community?
It depends on the family. If they are educated they might understand; however, they're not comfortable with it. They don't condone it, but they face it when it happens. However, the gossip would upset the family. They would be under pressure because the community would not accept it.

But here in Canada, families or parents are more relaxed. Society accepts it. When you choose the country, you have to choose the culture too. I cannot push my kids or make a special world for them. I cannot keep them in a prison. It doesn't work that way. If we are here, we have to accept the societal values, otherwise we would be in trouble all the time.

It doesn't sound like a woman would enter into an adulterous relationship lightly.
Women in the Muslim community cannot enter into an adulterous relationship at all. Without marriage it is a big sin. According to the Islamic law, if a married woman has an adulterous relationship, she should be stoned to death. Her feet are buried up to her knees in sand so she cannot move or run. Muslims would throw stones at her from a distance until she dies. This is Islamic punishment under the law and some countries still enforce this law.

Do you have a message of hope for women who have suffered abuse, whether they choose to stay in their marriage and deal with it or whether they decide to leave?
We can empower people with what they don't know. For example, if they don't know their own rights, their self-confidence is so low that they cannot even have hope because hope comes from one's self-confidence. And knowledge is power.

The question is, how can you build self confidence in a woman who is having a bad time with her husband? One of the first things I say is, "Do you know what your rights are? Are you aware as a woman in Canada that, no matter what has happened, you have rights and there are community services available for you? You have so many supports around you. Now, you have to choose which one you need most."

Next, I would tell the woman, "Believe in yourself." If we believe in ourselves we have hope. She has to know her rights and responsibilities. The problem will not go away overnight. I would tell her, "Here are some small steps you can take":

1) talk to a counsellor;
2) build your knowledge;
3) attend support groups;
4) choose some friends;
5) build a new support system;
6) know your rights;
7) fight for your rights;
8) make choices.

I tell women, "There are many support systems out there to help you. Make the effort to find out about them. Although talking to a counsellor may not be a part of your culture, it can work in Canada. By going to focus groups, you might be able to say, 'Oh, that is against law,' or 'that behaviour is not accepted in this country.' You can find out what your own position is by talking with other women."

"Fight for your rights. They do not come as a gift. Tell yourself, 'I am not alone, I do not have to be miserable.' Slowly you can rebuild your confidence. There is hope for the future. You can find happiness here. And remember you do have choices. If you know your rights. Gather strength and hope and begin to plan for the future."

Vida, do you have anything else to add?
As an immigrant, wife, mother, and educator, my opinion is that there are beliefs that trap women in abusive relationships. These are personal perceptions about family, society, and religion, especially about the role of women. Women are economically disadvantaged in many communities. In addition, they lack knowledge of their rights and the means to seek help.

They need support by individuals and organizations outside of their families. Counsellors can help, giving them all the information they need and educating and informing them about the progress of women's rights throughout the world.

This is my personal opinion as a woman and a professional, and I want to pass these messages on to women who have suffered abuse. They do have choices. They can choose to leave their marriage or choose to stay. I will support them either way.

Changing Together
A Centre for Immigrant Women II

Helen Soliman

Helen spoke as a social worker for Changing Together: A Centre for Immigrant Women. Helen is an Egyptian-Canadian from Cairo who came to Canada twenty years ago. She is a social worker who counsels immigrant women. Helen is of the Coptic Orthodox Christian faith.

When I was a new immigrant
my spirituality got me through
a very touchy period.
Spirituality overcame the isolation
I felt. It helped me feel empowered,
that I was not alone.

How does your own spirituality affect you as a woman, and how do you use it to help others?
My spirituality helps me to cope. If I pray, I can achieve peace and healing. When I was a new immigrant my spirituality got me through a very touchy period. Spirituality overcame the isolation I felt. It helped me feel empowered, that I was not alone. I believe that through spirituality comes hope, strength, calmness, and peace.

What drew you to this line of work?
Since I was young I liked helping others. When I got to university I chose a social work program and today, as a social worker, I still enjoy helping others. When I first came to Canada in the late 1970s, there were not enough resources to help immigrant women. But now it's really rewarding for me to be able to help women through the centre's Family Violence Prevention Program. Today I feel that all the experience I have gained through helping other immigrants, I owe to these women.

What do you think makes an effective counsellor?

First of all, listening to my client's needs. I respect them and try to be non-judgmental. Second, is to be able to recognize and identify the real problem. From this point on the healing process starts. I think that a counsellor must always keep in mind the client's spiritual beliefs and be culturally sensitive. This is how I build trust with my clients. It keeps the counselling on a positive level. To me being a good counsellor means listening. You must be a good listener. You can help a woman to discover the skills to cope with her situation but you cannot give her these skills.

Does your centre have a good relationship with the spiritual leaders?

Some of the women who come to our centre have already exhausted the possibilities of receiving help or achieving any change in their lives through their own spiritual leaders, while other women choose not to seek help from their own spiritual leaders because of fear of being told that this is the way it is. Sometimes women come here because they don't want to go to their own community or their own spiritual leaders. There is male dominance in the institution of religion and in the world. The answer to the spiritual question is to empower the woman.

There are many things upon which a woman must reflect in order to make the decision to stay or to leave an abusive situation. Some of the influences in making these decision are spirituality, inner strength, and one's own beliefs. You cannot fight these.

For example, one of my cases involves a woman from India who contracted a sexually transmitted disease from her abusive husband. She speaks English, has a job, and has no children, but she cannot leave. Her belief, as a Sikh, is that the woman should stay with her husband. So, in this case, I try to help her find belief in herself.

Is the patriarchy in religious organizations a problem?

In different faiths women have their role and their role is respected. However, some women report that because spiritual leaders are men, they tend to lean toward supporting the husband. This would negate any benefit from spiritual counselling from the woman's point of view. It is not religion that is at fault but individual interpretation of the doctrines.

If you know the priest and if you respect him, you might refer a woman to him. But there is a lot of denial in the immigrant community. Many believe that abuse does not exist in their community, whether it is spousal abuse, child abuse, or elder abuse. It is often denied. Some men take this issue personally and feel that everyone is against them.

Faith leaders must become more aware of the issues. More cultural awareness is needed and we must all try to understand the roots of abuse because abuse is a societal problem not a religious one. The approach is to help women to focus on themselves.

How do you help women? What if they decide to stay in an abusive situation?
As a counsellor, one can only listen and help that woman find her own inner strength. The woman must decide whether to stay or leave and the counsellor must support her in her decision. There are many things upon which a woman must reflect in order to make the decision to stay or to leave an abusive situation. You must respect her decision. Some of the influences in making these decisions are a woman's individual beliefs, her family background, and her cultural origins. If she chooses to stay, I am still here to support her.

Do you find that religious doctrine is sometimes used against a woman?
Yes, some women prefer to discuss their problems with counsellors instead of their spiritual leaders because, with the counsellors, they feel that all obstacles imposed upon them by their culture are removed. In that way they feel that they are discussing their problem while standing on a level playing field.

Catholic Social Services

You must be aware
of your own worldview.
You cannot suppress it.
So be aware of it and be proud of it.

Anna Maria Fantino

Anna Maria Fantino, MA, MEd, is a chartered psychologist who was born in Argentina. She has been in Canada for over twenty years. Anna Maria describes herself as Christian by nature but not a part of organized religion.

Could you tell me a little about your experiences in counselling women who have experienced spousal abuse?

Catholic Social Services immigration and settlement programs assist immigrants and refugees. Generally the clients have limited English skills and are experiencing individual and family difficulties in adapting to the new society. Many of the families that we see come from very stressful situations of war, persecution, and hardship. After arrival in Canada they have to overcome a number of obstacles like learning a new language and finding adequate employment. Migration and the struggles of integration into a new society add increased stress on the family, often leading to crisis situations.

There are some cases in which family violence occurs. Stopping the violence and securing the safety of the people involved is our first priority. It is important for us to offer continued support to the family in a way that is sensitive to gender, language, and culture. Our guiding principle is respect for the dignity and integrity of those involved. We also make every effort to facilitate access to appropriate services and support groups and to provide opportunities for friendship in the community.

What drew you to this field of work?

I believe my professional background in psychology, with a family and group oriented approach, had an influence. In addition, I had the experience of living in different cultures.

What is the relationship between your agency and various spiritual leaders?

Catholic Social Services recognizes the importance of spirituality in peoples lives, making it an integral part of its service delivery. Through our programs we minister to the spiritual needs of people respecting their particular religious and cultural affiliations. We facilitate spiritual needs through our agency resources or when more appropriate, through the spiritual resources available in the community, including inter-faith groups and various religious leaders. We have an excellent working relationship with these religious and spiritual leaders and continually work to maintain those positive relationships.

Do the women who come for counselling openly state that they are victims of family violence?

The specific term "victim of family violence" is seldom used. In general, I think that women have a healthy reluctance to be labelled victims. Some abusive situations are not easy to identify even for the person suffering the consequences. They may also be fearful of not being acknowledged or worse being judged and shamed by others. As with many other sensitive issues in counselling, people have many indirect ways to communicate their concerns. Women and men may ask for help for problems with their children when the underlying issue is actually anger, control, and marital difficulties. Still, there are other women who clearly can name their situation of abuse and ask for help.

Some abused immigrant and refugee women staying in shelters have asked us, "Please help my husband. He is the only family I have in this country." Her perspective needs to be considered. It portrays a woman's view of the world in which caring and understanding are more important values than punishment or revenge.

Could you define "spirituality" from your point of view?

As far as we know, spirituality is essentially a human quality that allows us to see beyond narrow individualistic concepts. A person's spiritual dimension connects the individual with more holistic experiences, ideas, and ideals. Many people fulfill that need for connectedness and belonging in the notion and the experience of a transcendent being, God. Others find it in other ways, for instance in communing with nature, in identification with humanitarian causes, or in community work.

How does your own spirituality affect your work in this area?
You must be aware of your own worldview. You cannot suppress it. So be aware of it and be proud of it. For instance I am not a practicing Christian, but I am Christian by nature. I feel that my upbringing has taught me that all people are important. I believe I have universal values.

How does the staff at Catholic Social Services become aware of the needs of other religions and cultures?
Our clients originate from over ninety countries, from almost every region of the world. Our staff closely resemble that diversity in terms of language, ethnicity, and religion. The type of work that we do with clients includes communication and extensive co-operation with community organizations that include a wide variety of ethnocultural and religious groups. In addition, we have staff development programs that include intercultural education and information sessions where community and religious leaders are invited as guest speakers.

Our staff members are helped to understand and respect the multicultural dimension and religious diversity in the community by the very way they implement agency policy and the way they care for clients where they are at. We also provide annual spiritual retreats for agency staff and volunteers. We have a spiritual life and religious co-ordinator on staff who helps to sensitize staff to the spiritual needs of individuals while remaining sensitive to the pluralistic communities that they are a part of.

What are your thoughts on the roots of family violence?
I think family violence has many different sources. There are general factors that may influence the occurrence of family violence such as widespread violence in society, lack of social support for families, and lack of appreciation for women's needs and their contribution to society.

At the individual level, we should remember that violence is not necessarily an expression of power. It could be a manifestation of extreme frustration and weakness. Many people may be driven to violence as a last resort when they feel trapped by circumstances in life. They may also feel that they are isolated, are lacking in personal and spiritual connections, and are unable to live out a particular value system.

As a supervisor, how do you provide counsellors with support in their work?
In addition to case review meetings and staff development sessions, we provide ongoing supervision and ample opportunities for counsellors to consult about individual cases. There is also, depending on the case, a team approach to counselling where workers of different programs in the agency will co-operate to assist the client and support each other in the process.

How do you know if a counsellor is culturally sensitive or if he or she is giving culturally appropriate advice to an abused woman? How do you monitor this? Gender and culture sensitivity are some of the issues included in the case review and supervision meetings and a main topic in our staff development program.

Supervisory activities are carried out in a spirit of providing whenever possible positive feedback, support, and constructive criticism. Staff understand and support supervision, the challenges, philosophical bias, and client treatment methodology.

Mennonite Centre for Newcomers
Centre for Survivors of Torture and Trauma

As a professional I have
universal values
that I use in my work.
One of them is hope.

Johanna Bukczynska

Johanna is a counsellor and therapist who was born in Warsaw, Poland She has lived in Canada since 1988. Johanna's own faith is Roman Catholic.

What made you decide to counsel women in abusive situations?

Most of my clients have experienced political persecution and organized violence first hand. Some of the after-effects are lack of trust, anger, self-medication with alcohol and other drugs, and problems that affect control and frustration. Often these issues result in behaviours that are directed against one's spouse.

My interest and previous professional experience in working with trauma survivors and people suffering from post-traumatic stress disorder helped me in making the decision to begin my work with the ECSTT (Edmonton Centre for Survivors of Torture and Trauma Program).

Does your own spirituality affect your work?

I do not counsel people from one particular religious group. Clients I see at my work come from different religions and faiths or they may be nonbelievers. Therefore I cannot use my own religious beliefs in counselling.

As a professional I have universal values that I use in my work. One of them is hope. Its universal meaning and significant power in the healing process is widely known. I have to learn my client's values and operate at an appropriate level in his or her healing. Most of my work is focused on the healing process.

But what if you encounter a situation that conflicts with your own values?
As a professional I have to be objective. In any situation in which my objectivity might be in conflict with my own values, I am obligated by the PAA (Psychologists Association of America) Ethical Code to refer the client to another professional who would accept this type of client. There is one situation I might have difficulty with in this regard. I would prefer to refer a client who is a child molester to another therapist as I feel strongly about that type of offense. I know my limitations, and I think my objectivity might be impaired in this case. Being objective is paramount in my work.

Does the religious belief of an individual ever complicate situations of abuse for victims of torture and trauma?
Sometimes beliefs cause conflicts, and there are vast differences between different cultures. That is one of the problems for immigrants. One example of this is a young Iranian-Canadian woman in her mid twenties who left her parent's home to live on her own. This is a most unusual situation.

She was forced to hide from her father and brother as they were insistent that she return home. Although she loved and respected her family, she felt desperate to be away from this setting and to have her own apartment. The male members of her family stalked her and threatened to kill her. She refused to report the situation to the police out of loyalty to her family but sought help and comfort at a centre for immigrants.

The counsellor there talked with the father and brother who willingly came to the centre in hopes of convincing the girl to return home to them. They openly admitted their threats. The father's anguish was very obvious, and he told the counsellor that he loved his daughter very much but that she must return. After extended family counselling, the father began to understand his daughter's needs. However, the problem of saving face became the main issue. This conflict was only resolved through extensive negotiating and with each participant making the effort to understand the other's viewpoint. In the end this potentially volatile situation was resolved through compromise.

How do women in circumstances that involve family abuse find the strength to resolve their situation? They must feel completely lost and alone.
Most of my clients are refugees, strong inside, with a sense of direction and a purpose in life. They seek counselling only when their coping abilities are coming to the end. Sometimes they need to have emotional support and to reorganize inadequate coping strategies.

Do you know from the outset that these women are victims of emotional abuse or physical violence?

The program I am working in was designed to address the needs of women, men, and children who suffered trauma and abuse because of their political convictions, for instance, being a member of a family involved in democratic movements.

Women are very often the ones who come in first seeking help for themselves and their husbands. Yes, I do know from the start that they are victims of violence and abuse. The program's mandate is focused on this very specific group and often treatment for the entire family is necessary.

How are you able to help these families? What do you do for them?

As a therapist, I use four very important guidelines when I help abused and traumatized people. These are to:

1) recognize the general value of hope in people's lives;
2) attempt to help the client find the power inside herself, thus empowerment rather than providing prescriptions;
3) recognize that the classic client-therapist power relationship does not work with these people;
4) understand that their coping skills are completely worn down.

In many cases the existing coping skills need to be replaced by more adaptive ones in a new life situation. Many of these people come to the centre in a crisis situation. They need to be treated by people with multicultural training and experience.

Do you feel there is a role for religious leaders in family abuse situations?

Yes, I do feel so! Many of my clients claim that they have survived because of their hope and faith. Church for them has its authority. In many cases the very first support source for newly arrived refugee women and men is a church community. It is a safe place to ask for help and assistance. Spirituality plays a very important role in the human healing process.

Edmonton Community Services
A Partner in the Spousal Abuse
Follow-Up Team

Marie MacDonald

Marie is a social worker who was born in Canada. She describes her religious background as "Roman Catholic with a certain amount of Irish mysticism."

Even today,
self sufficient and independent,
I find my support and anchors
in my women friends.

Marie MacDonald and Colin Milton form one of the four city teams that are called upon to follow up family violence situations that require police intervention.

Could you tell me a little about your partnership with the police service ?
As a representative of Edmonton Community Services I work with Detective Colin Milton of Edmonton Police Service on the Spousal Abuse Follow-up Team. Part of our program involves public education. For instance, Colin and I are a part of the training program for police recruits and ongoing training of police officers. We also have a role in public education such as the presentations on spousal violence to the University of Alberta Faculty of Nursing as well as Faculty of Educational Psychology Graduate Studies. Other public education has involved conferences and talking to teachers. There is real potential in this area as sometimes there are identifiable symptoms that indicate there may be violence in the home. This a particularly important area because it may allow opportunities for early intervention. All of these activities mean that we have to be really up-to-date on current research so that we can have a meaningful involvement.

Another of my responsibilities on the Spousal Violence Follow-Up Team was serving on a committee consisting of women lawyers, agents, and people who worked together to bring protection and restraining orders into place without cost to the women who need them. As a result, funding is in place to hire a lawyer, and administrator, and to secure a location. Women in Alberta are able obtain free restraining orders.

Could you give me some idea of what the team does on a daily basis?
What we do on a daily basis is that we work from police files. Our first step is to read them. We then rate them as to seriousness. We have criteria by which we measure this. Colin and I both have to agree on the rating, and then we decide which ones are most urgent and we act on them right away. This gives us a window of opportunity to get to the people and to help them to look at alternatives.

Our task is to help them discover ways that they can change the pattern they are currently living in. That may mean various things to various people. In instances where charges are laid, which is quite frequent, sometimes we don't have an opportunity to work with the perpetrators. They are usually men but not always. Often their lawyers will tell them not to have anything to do with us. But, if we can, we try to help them to look at some kind of change in their lives, some kind of counselling or group work, then perhaps they can learn to live a different pattern of life.

Most of our work is with the women. We just had a woman here today who has been in an abusive situation for fifteen years and this is the first time that she has called the police. He has been charged. She is now living in fear because, although he was told not to go back to their home, it wasn't a legal order. She is terrified, she doesn't know where to turn, and there are financial problems. There are four children involved who are obviously doing very well in school. The family has kept the problem hidden. No one knows what they are going through. The wife doesn't want her own cultural community to know.

So Colin and I will try to help her, to direct her to others who can help, to give her some courage, and to challenge her to be strong enough to be able to handle this on her own without trying to focus on how to change him. Getting her to look at herself and what her needs are will help her to get her needs met, and the needs of the children. We were able to help her look at all the community resources available that she had no idea of. This woman has been isolated. She wasn't aware of the help that she could get. At the present time she is in school to upgrade her skills. So we spent a couple of hours sitting with her hearing all the pain and suffering she's been through and trying to help her look realistically at the situation she is in. During this talk she was finally able to tell her story, of exposure four times to venereal diseases, of all those inhumane things that have destroyed her dignity, and of her humiliation.

We are trying to help her to re-enter, to build some hope that she as a woman will be able to handle things on her own with the resources that there are out there to help her. We were just working with her this afternoon. Colin provides a lot of the help in matters pertaining to the law, but he's also providing emotional support and helping her regain her confidence. Coming from man (a different kind of man) this is very helpful. They talk about her gifts, her value, and her importance. Colin was stressing how she must make sure that the groceries are bought and not pay the husband's bills. He tells her how important she is and how important it is that she be physically, mentally, and emotionally healthy for the children. This is affirmation from a man you know, and a policeman is a very powerful image. You know, I have heard him tell people, "Sometimes I am ashamed to be a man." Words like this have a lot of meaning and help so much. It's very moving for these women to hear this from a male. His kind words mean so much to them. As a team we work together on helping to give those messages.

You said "building hope" and that's something that we've been hearing from others. The message is that there is help, that healing will happen, and that there is hope no matter how bad the situation. That is exactly what you and Colin are doing here.
In this particular case, I was able to identify her spiritual community and her growth and her needs, and she responded to that. I could just sense that she was in touch with her own spiritual identity, and I reinforced that and gave credibility to that belief. I tried to help her to see that she does have a spirit within and that she was losing so much ground.

We play other roles too. We also on occasion will attend court with the complainant, the victim, if she needs support. We connect the woman with appropriate training on how to be a witness and occasionally, as I mentioned, we'll go with her. We have one woman that came in yesterday. She goes to court on Monday. It's Friday now, and we don't really have time for the training because we were late connecting with her. She is so fearful of standing up there and seeing her former husband. Even though this woman has been divorced for six years, she's so afraid of him. At first she refused to even go, but we encouraged her to come and gave her some options. On Monday we will go with her because she needs the support so badly. She is terrified to tell what happened in the courtroom because of her fear of this man.

So the support of this team is very important for her? She probably couldn't or wouldn't do it without your help.
Those are the kinds of things that we do all the time, also all the legal advice. I've learned so much about the court process, the legal issues, the availability of help, and about the difficulties you run into with the system. And there are difficulties because our justice system is still in the growing stages.

That's an important thing to point out, that the justice system is in the growing stages and that it is still evolving.

Yes it is, and they need to hear from us. Our Spousal Violence Unit is also involved in another inter-agency committee known as ECAFV (Edmonton Council Against Family Violence). Most of the work that Colin and I do together involves working with people.

What happens to those cases that are not listed as the highest risk?

As best we can, we try to make at least a phone call on every one. We don't always succeed but we try.

How are you able to help those people with a single phone call?

We can help quite a bit on the phone. We do some resource sharing. We listen and we express concern about what's happening and always leave our phone number in case things should worsen. We make referrals to other aids in our department, to other offices and departments. We're looking now at being more of a consulting and referral resource. Our department is looking at change, so we're examining how we can take more of a consulting role and help other agencies in the community to develop more services. For instance, even now we will refer people to Catholic Social Services and other agencies that we know provide services. So we will continue to make these referrals as best we can.

It sounds very much like you're a link in the community that connects people up with help that is appropriate for their needs.

Yes and we get a lot a referral through phone calls, maybe not even police intervention. I get a call from someone who has heard about us from someone else, and I might help this person get to immediate safety. For instance, get them into a shelter. There may not be a police file, but there sometime is an obvious urgent need.

It's true, we often respond and act immediately on a phone call such as this. For instance, this week we had a phone call from a very concerned employee at one of the community colleges. This person was the class instructor, and she had a woman student who had five children. The husband was there at the door with all five children demanding that the mother go home with him. She was in one of the educational classes over there, and he was there threatening her.

So we got the police involved immediately. I called through and got them there. They took them all home, but for some reason he was legally able to stay in the home and because of this the wife refused to stay there. The police team had been in touch with me on phone the whole time and were trying to get beds for her and the children to stay in a shelter. They didn't have any rooms available that night. The excellent and caring instructor who was looking after her actually took her to her own home for the night with her five children. The next morning we were able to get her into a shelter. She went to class that day, and the children stayed at the shelter attending the school there.

If the teacher had not been able to take her into her own home, do you have any funds or resources to help her for the one night?
We don't but the shelters do, or Alberta Social Services, Emergency Services, or the Crisis Unit would provide us with something to put her in a hotel if she were in danger. In this case by the time they phoned me to say that they didn't have a place, the teacher had already offered to take her home. She was at her home with them. She did a marvelous job of handling a very touchy situation and went way beyond her role as an instructor.

We then got her down to legal aid the next day and got her a lawyer who came out to the shelter the next night. I inquired to see if this new program was going to be in place soon enough for her, but unfortunately it's not. The only way she can possibly go home is if we can get a restraining order to get him out of the home. So he's still there, and she's still in the shelter. That was just one of the cases that Colin and I handled this week.

Another case today involved a woman who had come to see one of our counsellors here. Her husband came marching into the police station looking for his wife. After we talked to him, he disappeared so we had the police come over to our office. We then had the principal of the school bring her children here to our office, and we stayed with her here until a police car came at 6:30 P.M. Then I went home with her to pick up her belongings and to a take her to the shelter. That's where she is tonight. So these things are always happening, and those are just two incidents.

A third situation this week involved a call from the Grey Nuns hospital. It was someone in emergency who knows me and has contacted me before. A woman was in because of a cat fight, and there was evidence of that. But she was in such an emotional disturbed state that she was a complete wreck. Our contact in emergency recognized that she was in distress and that she was afraid and desperate. She got the woman on the phone with me and we talked about her fears, the terrible situation that she was in. We acted quickly and were able to get her right into a shelter that same afternoon. So that was three this week. None of them originated in the police files, but the police got involved along the way. We like to think that our ability to act quickly might be diffusing situations that could end up much more serious.

It sounds like the community is realizing that you are here, and that's a real move in the right direction. Is this a typical week in the life of Marie and Colin?
Pretty much. Right now I am working on something a little different because it's not spousal violence, but I've just finished looking through the file with another

police officer. This is a woman police officer, and we are going to one of the education institutions whose clientele are handicapped. A social worker from this particular school called us because she strongly suspected that a student was being abused by someone in her family. And this is a handicapped student. I can't give you any more details. We do have translators and interpreters, and we have a police officer who handles sensitive situations like these. The police officer and I will be meeting at 8:30 tomorrow morning at the school with the social worker and the girl.

Do you anticipate that you may even be going to the home?
Yes, because it's clear that a family member has been abusive to this child.

Is the mother knowledgeable about this?
It's hard to say. Sometimes in a strange new country they don't know the rules or don't know what to do. So we're going to go into the home for an intervention. I would call it intervention right now, but it's quite possible that it will end up in charges.

Did this student tell her counsellor at school or how did the counsellor find out?
The counsellor began to notice a definite pattern of bruising and began to ask questions, but this student is not able to fully comprehend. By the time we are able to get to her, she will have a lot of fear.

And is she aware of the nature of the help that you're providing? Does she understand that?
I don't know how much she knows. She's afraid. I know she's terrified of the repercussions so we're going to have to handle it in a way that it doesn't focus on her having been the obvious informant. It started with her not returning home from school because the mother was not home at this time. She simply began to stay away until she knew her mother would be there.

Did she stay at school?
No, I don't know where she went. I don't know. But no, she didn't stay at school.

I think I have a much clearer idea of what it is that you really do as a team now. It's so much more than going to court and so much more than community education.
Yes, and the examples are very real and I think a very accurate representation of a typical work day. We start very early and we often work very late.

Yes, there are so many sad stories I could tell you stories, such as the woman with, what I call, "raccoon eyes." Real incidents of horrible violence and what it's like to work with them and walk with them and the many rewards of helping them grow. And this one—we've walked with for a year and a half—it's just beautiful to see her grow, to see her working towards independence.

That must be very rewarding. In spite of all the discouraging cases that you handle and all the discouraging situations, it sounds like there are rewards.
Oh, absolutely, I mean this woman today. She cried. It was so sad. But by the time she left her house, her home, she began to realize how many resources we were able to lead her to. She began to believe that we were going to follow up, that we're not going to abandon her, that we are going to be there. It was wonderful just to see her, to see hope in her eyes.

Mind you, sometimes that happens and then they go out and we hear later that they go back to the same situation without having changed anything. But even then, I can always say, "That's all right, we will be back, we will be there for you." And I'll phone them and say, "It's okay, I understand, I care, and you know we're here" and eventually they come back. So I never ever give up. I never give up hope because I know if they're back in that situation, it's because they need to be. And I can understand why. Most of these women believe that, first of all, they are responsible for making the marriage work and secondly, that they have to stay there to make it work. They often believe that they have a responsibility and that they have failed. They believe they must go back and try to make it work.

It's always the woman who has failed. It's seldom looked on as a contract or that someone else has broken the marriage covenant. And they see the need. They can't abandon the children. The children need the kinds of things that the husband provides. So they must make it work. They must go back.

Or fear. They stay for fear. That dependency, the built-in dependency because of the isolation that is happening. It's a built-in dependency whereby they believe that they cannot function by themselves. There are many reasons why but mostly it's because they feel they are responsible. They have to go back to him. They have to help him.

The nurturing woman.
That's part of it, yes. And there's been times that we had cases where the woman was the one inflicting the violence. It happens. We had one recently where, ironically, the woman was the perpetrator because she was angry at her spouse. She came home late and he had locked the door, and so she banged on the door and he finally let her in. They got into an argument and she became aggressive. She was so angry with him that she bit his back. She took a bite out of his back and that clearly was aggression.

It antagonized him to the point where he grabbed her, threw her on the ground, and mutilated her face so badly it was sickening. With his feet and his boots he caused such harm. The physical abuse to her body was outrageous. It was horrific, far beyond that of reacting to her aggression. And the police had to charge her for abuse as well as him. But the police statement clearly stated that his abuse was far more extreme and far more abusive than hers ever was and that he had to take responsibility for his reaction to her abuse. So there are cases like that also.

And how would a case like that end up when it's in the courts?
I can't really say but I think that this particular police report was so clear on the differences of the abuse that, I don't know, it hasn't gone to court yet. I don't know what the result will be.

Often what we will find is in instances where the woman will throw something at the male and hit him and the object will cut the side of his head or somewhere, he then punches her in the stomach or something like that, in retaliation. The judge will look at it, as both will have been charged, and if the police decide that they have visible grounds to determine that there has been an offense against the man also, that they can see some signs of injury, they have no choice. They have to lay charges. If they see it on both parties, they have to lay charges on both partners.

Because otherwise they're judging, aren't they?
That's right. Usually, in those cases where there seems to be a balance of abuse, often the judge will dismiss the charges.

So really, that doesn't solve anything, does it?
No, except that they have had the process of being charged. They now have a record and they've had to appear in court. They have to defend that. There have been a couple of cases where both have had sentences. Perhaps it would be probation for six months or something like that. It usually will end up to be an even sentence, but those things do exist.

And sometimes you know that the woman has been so aggravated by events and abuse that went before that…

Has your work in this area given you any insight into the source of family violence?
The contributors to family violence are global. The socio-economic situation, inequalities in the social system, and our male dominant society. This is a very significant factor. I firmly believe that change is needed and that the process of change is taking place right now, and the whole of society will benefit from it.

I certainly believe that the larger global picture of our economic, social, culture, and religious backgrounds has created an imbalance in our society.

In looking at present day society in Canada, do you find that drugs or alcohol play any part in abuse and violence?
If you are asking if alcohol causes abuse, then I would say no. However, if the perpetrator is abusive, it lowers inhibitions, but it does not cause abuse.

Do you find that violence against women is condoned in some cultures more than others?
No, and there is nothing written in law in any culture that says a man can abuse his wife. We must recognize that this problem is universal. It is not a characteristic of any specific culture and we, the mainstream population in this country, must acknowledge this. We must also remember that many of the majority population in Canada have British roots in their family histories. If we are going to look at various cultures for evidence in law, then let's consider the mainstream heritage. For instance, in 1767, English Common Law stated that a husband is permitted to "chastise his wife with a whip or rattan no wider than his thumb." This is the infamous origin of the "rule of thumb" measurement.

The history of economics has also been a factor. Society has evolved from an egalitarian hunter-gatherer stage, to an agrarian base (where women were the workers in the field), through to an industrial revolution, to a technological revolution. After all, it was the regulating of the poor that brought about the French Revolution. Historically, women have been in a weakened position economically and socially. Until true equality is achieved, there will be opportunity for abuse of power.

The hierarchy that has evolved in our churches in the major world religions has had a role in the perpetuating the idea that the male is the head of the household.

I agree and in the various religions we have looked at that has been the case.
Yes, and in the Catholic church, which I am a member of, I have been a part of a group that is reflecting on that, and of helping the church to see this. The church has grown a great deal, but it has hurt a lot of people too, and I am aware of that. So, it's a global thing that we're dealing with. Our value system is structured so that we're still not out of the woods. We have a long way to go. The still prevalent belief is that males are more important than females, and it's in our entire system.

What about religious doctrine? Does it ever contribute to the problem?
Religious doctrines must be carefully examined. For instance, people think that the Catholic church does not condone divorce, but if one was more aware of the teachings, one would know that God is just and loving. The annulment process is understandable when one realizes that the covenant is a commitment, a contract. When and if it breaks down, our Lord would not expect us to stay.

Through divorce you can leave as a good Catholic and a good Catholic priest can really help.

So the problem is that it's re-marriage that the church does not acknowledge, unless of course the marriage itself has been invalidated through an annulment. That's the church's teaching right now. It's being appealed and brought to attention. The recommendation put forth is to accept divorced people as full members of the church even without the annulment.

Does religion or a person's spiritual need arise in your daily contact with those who are experiencing abuse?
Spirituality definitely has a place in the treatment of those who are experiencing family violence. My belief is that we need to have a more holistic approach. Each one of us, each one of the victims, and each one of the perpetrators are players in the spiritual, emotional, and physical state of another human being. Therefore we have to look at the whole thing, all the contributing factors.

Now I don't even pretend to suggest that I bring religious or spiritual practice in any way into our work. But I may acknowledge or help identify the person's holistic self. I might respond in a way that acknowledges that this person has a belief system of her own. I just simply support the validity of the spiritual self.

So, you validate the spiritual component?
Yes, to validate that as a legitimate and meaningful part of her being. That has definitely been invalidated when she's been abused, when her body has been violated; her whole spirituality, her spirit within has been injured and abused and hurt. So simply recognizing this need and acknowledging the importance of it is as far as I go in my inclusion of the spiritual dimension of our work. And I don't know, I think it's enough and I think it helps, people seem to sense my support in this way.

It is very damaging for a woman to stay in an unhealthy relationship. Children are the real victims of family violence. This is evident in our summer camps for mothers and children. Even when the mother is free of the situation, the children are victims of the mother's guilt feelings.

Do you ever draw from your own beliefs to comfort women?
If the opening arises, yes, I would do that. The key to understanding other religions is to show respect for the beliefs of others. However, it is often useful to share one's own values. I might say something like, "The God that I know would not want me to have this much pain. God gave us all a free will."

It is important that counsellors and churches break the silence. There is a lot of truth in the quote, "Most men live lives of quiet desperation." Sometimes men feel that they are only valued because they provide material goods. This can create a lot of anger. But what is justifiable anger? The emotion of anger is not wrong but we really need to educate people about appropriate ways of expressing that anger. People need to talk about these things. One of our counsellors is fond of pointing out a somewhat truthful stereotype, "Women talk about their feelings until you wish they'd stop and men pretend they don't have any."

Could you tell me a little about what drew you to this line of work and of your own personal experience with marriage breakdown?
When my hard times came, it was my faith that carried me through. My own family would have thought I should stay in the marriage, but the church encouraged me to seek freedom. My parish priest, who was very supportive, helped to free me.

I take it then, that this support was a very important factor in your healing?
Definitely. When women are involved in abusive situations, it is usually this support system which is missing. There is isolation, and it is made worse by the partner's demands and by the situation itself.

In my own case, after moving out west alone with four children, I found support in the church and among other women. There was very strong support for me within my faith. I got involved in support groups over the years. Even today, self sufficient and independent, I find my support and anchors in my women friends.

Edmonton Police Service
A Partner in the Spousal Abuse
Follow-Up Team

Abuse touches and affects
the entire community.

Colin Milton

*Colin is a detective with the
Edmonton Police Service.
He was born in Canada.
Colin is a partner in the
Spousal Abuse Follow-Up Team.*

Colin Milton and Marie MacDonald form one of the four city teams that are
called upon to follow up family violence situations that require police intervention.
Colin is a police officer and the only male we interviewed in this project.

*Does a person's spirituality or religion come up in the situations you deal with?
What are your observations along these lines?*
Of course it does come up and spirituality is definitely a part of the healing
component. But the need for formal and organized religious counselling seems
to be minimal. At least it does not often come up in the context of the spousal
violence unit visits. Requests for formal religious counselling in this program are
only 2.5 percent of cases.*

In cases of Aboriginal women we have seen, they often don't want to go back
to traditional spirituality. They're not interested. The majority find their strength

---

* Safer Cities Initiatives, Edmonton Police Service & Community and Family Services, 1994.
Family Violence Follow-Up Team Implementation/Expansion Phase Research Report and Findings,
Edmonton: City of Edmonton.

within the realm of western religions or western counselling methods. The team's experience has not always been a positive one regarding the role of spiritual leaders in the Native community.

A recent case involved a woman who was advised by an elder to go back to her husband. The woman did go back—into alcohol, drugs, and abuse—and got hooked on drugs again. In this case the husband had been in prison and was receiving traditional Native spirituality counselling. He apparently told the elder about the counselling his spouse was receiving from our unit. The elder agreed to counsel the wife also and as a result she went back into a very dangerous and damaging situation.

Do you find that one's economic strata or self-sufficiency has anything to do with the incidence of family abuse?

The problem would more likely be brought about by isolation and the individual's belief system than the economic situation. In the area of the city where we are working, the south-east, there are more employable people than, for instance, the north-east section. The south-east spousal abuse unit sees approximately fifteen cases a week whereas in the north-east part of the city this number would be closer to thirty a week. In the north-east section, where I previously worked, many of the family violence victims are not employable or are in need of upgrading for employment skills. Many in the north-east are stay-at-home spouses. Approximately 80 percent of the people seen in this area did not work.

However, even though many of the clients in the south-east district may have had jobs, this does not necessarily mean they have economic independence. It is the dependency that is the problem. The issue of self-sufficiency is more than economic, and again, goes back to a basic belief system. There is often a very strong emotional dependency.

Another issue that arises frequently is that of the stigma of police involvement. For instance, one woman (from a visible minority group) chose to stay in an abusive situation because she felt she could not go back to her mother. The police who intervened in the crisis would have removed the woman from danger and taken her to her mother's home. However, even though the mother was willing to shelter her and to help, she did not want police cars in front of her house. She was afraid of what the neighbours would think, and based on this, the woman decided to stay where she was and not inflict her personal problems on her mother. It is often awkward for these teams in some of the more prosperous areas because there is this stigma regarding police involvement. In fact, many times neighbours in these areas don't call the police when they know there is family violence because this would bring negative attention to the neighbourhood.

How do you manage to respond to all the calls you do get? Do you ever turn people away because of time or budgetary restraints?

One of the strengths of our team is that we are able to determine our own work-load and that the entry point for women is very informal. Sometimes it comes by way of police involvement in a crisis, but other times it can be a simple phone call or referral because someone has heard that we can help. Also there is no limit on the length of time devoted to a specific case. One woman has been counselled off and on for the past three years because the abuser is stalking her. As long as the situation remains volatile, our team will be there to help. We get to every serious situation and will attempt to intervene in those that could explode at any time. Sometimes a phone call or two is enough to guide and counsel the person. Other times it involves the whole process including escorting her to court and court appearances.

What is the relationship of the police department with the shelters?

We have very co-operative and positive involvement with the shelters. Now that the program is well established, there has been a considerable trust built between the shelter workers, community services, and the police, and there is a good working relationship. Now that the shelter directors all know the team members involved, there are few communication problems. Sometimes it is the situation itself that is problematic.

In one case the woman had sought shelter with her baby for physical safety. The abuse was the result of involvement with a cult, and the baby was at risk. There had been a history of violence that had gone unreported by the woman. Both the woman and the perpetrator were cult members. In this case we had to evaluate the safety of the baby before that of the mother. In consultation with the shelter workers, we decided that the father may actually be a more appropriate parent than the mother. The situation brought danger from the mother as well, which is not uncommon. The strategies for dealing with cases such as these involve an integrated dedicated team working together to solve a very complex problem. Safety is foremost, but the question is for whom?

What type of experience do officers in the spousal abuse unit have?

Officers who deal with spousal abuse are chosen for their experience with and sensitivity to women's issues as well as a sensitivity to people of other cultures and backgrounds. In addition, they participate in various training programs including those offered by Alberta Justice.

My own experience includes positions in courts, education unit, major crimes section, child abuse, sex crimes, and Asian gang investigation. I serve on several community committees that are working on the problems of family violence. In addition, my work also includes presentations at local, provincial, and national conferences on the problem-solving model used by the Edmonton Police Service.

Could you explain a little about the partnership model that you and Marie MacDonald are working with?

Although the police officer and the social worker act as a team, Marie and I are both very aware of our differing responsibilities to our departments and clients. For instance, when a perpetrator wants to tell Marie, the social worker, about a fact in the case or about his (or her) behaviour in a certain instance, I will immediately warn him that he may be jeopardizing his legal position. I might tell him he has the right to contact a lawyer or might even stop him from discussing certain issues in the presence of the Law.

Our team, presently a team of three with the temporary addition of a student of social work recently interviewed abusers in prison who have a history of violence.

The team approach and a chance to talk through the subject has been very effective as a reality dose for these offenders. When Marie, as a social worker, was able to talk to these men about abuse from her own personal experience and demonstrate the effects, both short term and long term, some of these men expressed deep emotion that resulted in some serious reflection. Some of the men were so touched by the impact of their abusive behaviour that they had tears in their eyes and other definite emotional reactions. The combination of the intellectual exercise and the emotional impact resulted in touching at the soul level.

This Spousal Abuse Follow-Up Team is a unique project in Canada. Other police departments hire social workers for certain areas, but the difference here is the complete partnership that is involved. Two city departments, the Edmonton Police Service and Edmonton Community Services, work together as equal partners to provide very effective intervention, protection, and solutions to a serious societal problem. The pilot project has been written up in two manuals that are available to the public.*

Is there any particular group that is more touched by spousal abuse than others?

Abuse touches and affects the entire community. Although poverty and unemployment are obvious contributing factors, family violence is found in every economic strata, in various religious groups, and in groups or individuals of many cultural origins.

However, there is one area which is often forgotten or overlooked by those investigating this societal problem and that is the spousal abuse that is found among members of the gay and lesbian community. These groups encounter the same issues that the rest of the community does, but the problem is magnified by the social stigma often attached to these groups. The Edmonton Police have

---

* Safer Cities Initiatives, Edmonton Police Service and Community and Family Services, 1992 and 1995. *Family Violence Follow-Up Team Implementation/Expansion Phase Research Report and Findings and the Family Violence: Follow-Up Team Demonstration Project Research Report and Findings.*

a special group of officers, trained in and sensitive to issues within the gay and lesbian community, who are called upon when needed.

The gay and lesbian community is a segment of the population that must not be forgotten when dealing with problem of spousal abuse. As with other groups such as specific religions, immigrants, and cultural or ethnic populations, there is often a fear of exposure or of negative publicity that inhibits people from speaking out or from asking for help. It is the fear of being stigmatized and the fear of being labelled. Spousal abuse is not gender specific and it is not always an issue of male versus female.

The team approach initiated by the Spousal Abuse Follow-Up Team is an effective tool for educating the public and individuals in equality and justice. When people from various disciplines come together to solve a problem, they bring different perspectives and they see situations in different ways. Not only do all those involved learn new things, but they are able to view the situation from a much broader perspective. This has the potential of increasing understanding, empathy, and sensitivity among all concerned. This includes those who help and protect, the victims of abuse, the other family members who are affected by violence, and the abusers themselves.

Safe Place Women's Shelter

Heather Richards and Jean Hood

Heather is the executive director of Safe Place. She was born in Canada. Heather describes her own faith as being Protestant, the United Church.

Jean Hood is a child support worker at Safe Place and is on the Interfaith Committee for the Prevention of Family Violence. She was born in the Netherlands and is affiliated with the United Church.

We need to create an environment
to meet the needs
of the women we serve.
It is time to challenge ourselves.

Do you have people from various cultures coming to your shelter in this suburban community?
We have quite a few Chilean, some Muslim, and often Native women here as well as those from the mainstream population. In addition to our service for Aboriginals, there are three Native shelters in Alberta.

Is addressing spirituality one of your approaches in helping these women?
When admitting a woman in crisis to the shelter the priorities are safety, shelter, and the struggle. However spirituality is definitely a part of the process at this centre. It may not always be addressed directly, but it is an issue of concern to the staff.

The centre would like to be more pro-active in this area and we are exploring ways of doing so. One idea we are working on is the provision of a small quiet-room, intended for a woman to be alone and pray, meditate, or simply have some reflection time. At our centre there is a second interview three days after the woman takes up her temporary residence here. During this time, the counsellors are looking to find out about the woman's comfort level. We might be able to add spiritual needs to the interview topics that already include health matters and other matters of well being. This might be approached by asking the woman how we can help. Spirituality does not have to be addressed with every woman, but there are usually strong indicators that would guide counsellors in that direction. We could let women know that spiritual leaders or clergy are welcome to visit the centre.

We could begin to collect a small wellness library that would include items of a spiritual nature such as relaxation tapes and other resources of comfort. One of the young students who helps out at the centre could turn this need into a research project and collect the appropriate materials.

What are some of the problems you encounter at Safe Place?
Many women have to leave the community when and if they leave the situation. There are few housing choices in Sherwood Park for those with very low incomes. This community is predominantly middle and upper income oriented and very few women can stay because of the cost. This is very disruptive and upsetting for the mother and the children. When families have to flee to the city there are many new problems to encounter, and the chance for a smooth transition and relative stability is diminished. The local family and community support agency has been advocating for subsidized housing within the county for some time now.

How does religion fit in and what is the response of the different faiths to working with the shelters?
In a joint project initiated by Catholic Communication Centre, the Ecumenical Council recently produced a video called "Family Violence: It's in Our Church Too." The United Church and the Catholic Church have been very active in forming committees to deal with the problem of family violence. Many individuals throughout the province are working hard to make small gains, one small step at a time. The video "The Fire in the Rose" is the result of a two-year project on how the churches are dealing with the issue of spousal abuse. It was developed by the Church Council on Justice and Corrections. Fourteen Christian congregations participated in this pilot project to test, augment, and refine the material.

"The Silence of Men" was a researched article written for a local United Church by one of the males in the congregation. The author read parts of this article to the congregation making an impassioned plea for facing the problem. He stated that he was no longer satisfied to be a man and keep quiet about the violence. The author pointed out that there were basically three attitudes that males have regarding the issue of spousal abuse and family violence:

1) Some deny there is a problem or minimize it.
2) Some are strong advocates for social change to remedy it.
3) And then there are those who are beginning to say:
    "I see it, I recognize it, but I don't stand up and be counted."

Men are starting to ask how they can create an environment in the church where the abuser would not be judged or ostracized. Most men who abuse are afraid to admit it. So the question is, "How can the church create a safe environment for him to confess?"

What can you do? What can shelters do to move in a new direction?
As an administrator, I have observed that sometimes we hide behind our business. Maybe it's time for change. Staff could benefit by some additional training in this area. They do not have to be experts in every faith, but they should be able to use their abilities to access needed services and support. Some of our counsellors do stay right out of this area and perhaps that is not a good thing. Everyone should be capable of referring and supporting a woman who expresses spiritual need regardless of his or her own religious or nonreligious beliefs. A counsellor might respond with something like, "I recognize that this is a serious issue for you. I am not a Muslim, but let's decide together what you need and how we can help you meet this need."

The centre could create an environment for a woman to discuss spiritual need just as it does for medical issues, for instance, by asking about addictions or sexually transmitted diseases. So if a counsellor doesn't practice a specific religion, she should still be able to help and support the woman. Two resources currently available are *Keeping the Faith Questions and Answers for Abused Women* (Fortune, 1987) and *Violence in the Family* (Fortune, 1988).

I think it is time to challenge our own delivery of services. We need to create an environment to meet the needs of the women we serve. It is time to challenge ourselves. We need, and are working on, a code of ethics, a philosophy, and principles of practice. We know what it is we are doing, and we need to be sure we are doing it well. We know our business, so let's do it. We need to let everyone, including funders, know that we are doing and will continue to do quality work.

We need to work in collaboration with each other. To continue to defend core funding and to justify why we need to stay open is redundant. There is a need. It is well documented and yes, there is a need for documentation, but let's begin documenting the qualitative things we are doing instead of justifying and reproving the need for shelters. It's time we stopped worrying about filling every bed every minute and started to concentrate on quality care for the people we help. We need a sense of confidence. We need to challenge ourselves, within our shelters, to do what we do better instead of walking a tight-rope between staff, board, and funders.

What are some of the societal limitations that make your task difficult?
In looking at the role of the clergy, it is important to note that there are serious restrictions on the partners of male clergy. Changing the role of the church in family abuse means that clergy must look at their own family hierarchy. This

chosen vocation has great impact on wives and children. Afternoon tea with the ladies is not for everyone. Men who question these "modern" relationships tell a lot about their own. They speak of equality but forget about control.

We must look at what is happening to women globally, female genital mutilation for instance. And then, in our own country, there are the courts. The courts make some unbelievable decisions. For instance, in the Blair case in Alberta, the defense for assault was accepted as a valid one because the husband was drunk. This decision outraged the entire community, but the abused wife felt differently about the reversal of the judgment. This case illustrates how the victimized woman often feels about what is happening to her. It's the "if I leave this marriage then…" syndrome.*

We must address this also. What are our limitations as a safe house, to create a safe environment for a woman when she cannot leave? We should look more carefully at the models in other countries. For instance, in Russia to abuse one's wife is a crime. To abuse her while drunk doubles the crime.

In our country, the court system works against the abused women. For instance we have a client whose husband was charged with twenty-two counts. Plea bargaining brought them down to two counts of aggravated assault. He got six months. While she is on social assistance and not able to make ends meet she is charged because of social services fraud. She gets an eight–month sentence. In the meantime he gets out and he gets custody of the kids because she is in jail. This is what happens to the abused.

The husband does not qualify for legal aid so he is entitled to act as his own defense. In this position he gets all the court records and has access to her psychological assessment. She does not. At this point he applies for custody and guardianship. Now he has their attention as a parent, so on this basis the court will agree to anything.

In the meantime, both mom and dad have visitation rights (in this particular case). But since the mom does not have a car, someone in authority decides that the location of the children be kept from her (someone has interpreted that she has no need for this information since she can't get there anyway). She gets a friend to agree to drive her on visiting day but can't find out where they are. How strange. Does this mean that, because she has no car, she does not have a right to this information? When it comes to court again, Child Welfare points out that dad has been visiting regularly but mom is a "no show" so he gets custody and she is an unfit parent. It is Crown versus the husband (who is acting on his own). Everything that the Crown has must now be given to the husband to prepare his defense. Husbands can do this when they can't afford legal counsel. So he gets to cross examine her!

---

* Four months after this interview the wife did leave the situation and has since filed for divorce.

In addition he gets latitude from the judge because he is an amateur. He can say almost anything. He can intimidate his wife by physically invading her space in the courtroom, for instance, when she is in the witness box. He gets away with this because he doesn't know the rules of the Court and is, theoretically, not aware of court procedure and court etiquette. He gets latitude as an amateur and she gets terrorized.

Does this seem like blaming the victim? These situations are indicative of what our courts do for the victims of family violence.

WIN House Women's Shelter

When life is in balance,
one is different in the world.

Ione Challborn

*Ione is the executive director of
WIN House and a single mother
with one child. She was born in
Canada. Ione describes her
religious upbringing as Lutheran
"but not a positive experience."*

How did you come to work with abused women?
I was born a feminist, the eldest of five children and the only girl. I felt alone.
My parents were Lutheran so I had a strong religious background, but it was not
a positive experience.

The status of women became an issue for me early in life. I joined Canada
World Youth and left the country. During this time I met people from many other
backgrounds, cultures, and religions. I met and worked with Muslims and
Buddhists and made many other overseas connections.

How does your religious background and experiences affect you in your work?
As an adult, what is missing for me from my background is the ritual of the church.
What really bothers me about the church, for instance Christianity, is the blaming
and the anti-woman stance.

What I have found is that the faith doesn't matter. I find that spiritual people
are private. It's internal. It's how they live their life. When life is in balance, one
is different in the world. It is a different way one walks in the world. One's choices
and decisions are the governing aspect. In chaos there is order. In everything there
is meaning.

The more grounded the woman is in her own spirituality, not necessarily religion, the faster the healing. Of course these women are still wounded, clearly wounded, but the scar is not there. There is a meaning to everything.

How do counsellors and people who help battered women deal with the issue of spirituality?
People have a fear of entering this realm. There is a fear of emotion. We are bereft of spirituality. Counsellors are not in a position to reflect on their own spirituality.

Do you see any difference in working with women who are immigrants?
First of all, we have all immigrated here, except for the Aboriginals. In one way or another, at some time in our history, we are immigrants.

I don't believe we work very well with people of any other cultures. This is a criticism I have with Heritage Days. Simply eating someone's national food and watching their dance does not make us knowledgeable about their culture. I think what is effective is to be vulnerable enough to be open to another person's culture. In family violence, the woman is the expert. There is the stereotype versus the concern for communicating cross-culturally. In shelters, unfortunately, it gets focused on the stereotypes.

Those who are grounded themselves will be using their spirituality and their values in their work. Maybe things need to be calmer, but we could be more spiritual in our support.

How can shelters and shelter workers work to improve this area?
The images when you walk into a shelter are very violent—the government posters on the wall, the fortress. Even the art is cheap, make-do, anything we can scrape together. Shelters can't afford these items. So the environment is not a spiritual one. There definitely is room for it.

Funding space for a quiet room would be a start. The need has not been recognized. It has not been dealt with in the shelters. Even having someone on hand who can take care of the children while the mother has a quiet time is lacking. The mother is responsible in shelters for her children at all times.

How do you feel about spiritual leaders and their involvement with abused women? Do you see this as a positive process?
Many times it is handled poorly. There is some leverage in the Catholic church because they have had to become involved with issues of abuse. They have been repeatedly in the headlines for the child abuse that occurred in the residential schools and children's homes. Also the United Church has been in the headlines because of their fight for social justice. It is definitely an opportunity we should not let go by.

In the cases of the Hindu, Sikh, and Muslim communities, they are primarily institutionally based. The community is closing in on itself. There are general fears of discrimination. So the community does not want to focus on these problems and does not want them brought to the attention of the mainstream community. Public education is the solution.

We all carry our spirituality within us. As a shelter, creating a sacred place is all we can do. We have to leave choices open. A woman may choose to go back to the situation and not to see. You don't need to itemize spirituality. It happens in an ad hoc way, but indications are usually obvious whether a woman does or does not want this kind of help.

In the present economic climate, would adding this extra factor when exploring a woman's comfort level be seen as additional work by either staff members or funding agencies?

Not at all. It is very relevant. It fits right in with our mandate. Our priorities are to attend to immediate safety needs, to help the woman realize and know that she has choices, to discuss safety after she leaves, and to encourage her to find a sense of peace. It could be a special project such as," understanding the role of spirituality in healing." Now is the time.

Front-line Impressions

What we have learned from our conversations with these front-line workers is that family violence crosses all cultures, all religions, and all socio-economic stratas. It is not a condition specific to age, class, or gender. Family violence victims can be children, spouses, parents, and grandparents. Its contributors are universal, the socio-economic situation, inequalities in the social system, and the legacy of patriarchal societies. Family violence is a social problem.

The term violence is difficult to define in this context. Families are centres of intense emotional exchange. Where do you draw the boundaries between cultural practise, abuse, and violence? We have used the terms abuse and violence interchangeably because we believe that, whether psychological, emotional, or physical, spousal abuse is a violence against another human being. It is a violation of a woman's body, of her mind, and of her spirit.

And the community can help people who have been abused and traumatized. First, we must recognise the importance of hope in every person's life. Then we can help by listening and by encouraging women to find the power inside themselves. Even small changes can make a difference.

We need to think about culture, spirituality, and family violence in a global sense, learning to identify the positive as well as the negative effects of world-wide religious and cultural beliefs. Only by becoming more culturally sensitive and aware of each individual's spiritual needs can we expect to gain insight, provide encouragement, and offer hope for the future. Those who believe in helping, healing, and hope must seek a deeper understanding of others' beliefs and value systems—but as individual human beings, not as representatives of a cultural community or a religious group.

Where has
Lifelines Led Us?

Openings and Closings

5

OPENING THE DOOR

The collective experiences of the women who shared their stories in *Lifelines* are only a beginning of the exploration into the spiritual needs of survivors of family violence. With incredible candor these women, who refuse to give up on themselves, allow us into their lives by revealing their suffering and sharing their epiphany. Faced with the cruelty demonstrated by the one person they once trusted most, they continue to hope, in a time of their lives when everything they have trusted breaks around them. This is the time when their self-confidence is undermined, when their community recoils from them, and when their spiritual leaders seem to have run out of answers. We see these women striving to reach deeper into themselves to get the strength they need. This is an act of survival because the shelters and other refuges that our communities have provided as safe havens for victims of family violence, have no way of addressing a woman's spiritual need. Spiritual recovery demands more than safety.

The women who speak to us come from many different faith communities and play many roles. First, we hear the voices of women who have lived through humiliation and despair before finding their own strength and peace. Next, we listen to women of wisdom and faith who let us share in their understanding of women's strength and spirituality, drawing on their own knowledge of their particular religious tradition. Finally, we hear from women in the helping community who are searching for legitimate ways in our secular society to assist victims of violence in their search for spiritual growth. *Lifelines* attempts to give individuals the opportunity to hear, first-hand, what different women have to say about family violence and the regaining of strength through spirituality. We need to honour their voices, each speaking to us from a different cultural and religious community. *Lifelines* opens the door to understanding and invites us to explore within.

LIFELINES—A COLLECTION OF VOICES

Lifelines uses the language of the women who describe their journeys, their path to healing, and their way of helping others. The book relates in vivid and personal language the growing experiences of these women, in quite a different way from past accounts of family violence, that have often left us helpless, sad, and enraged. In *Lifelines* we hear from the women directly and in their own voices how strength arises from within, providing answers and guidance. The terminology commonly used to describe family violence, such as survivor, victim, healing, faith community and multicultural group has gradually evolved as society began to understand and describe the magnitude of violence against women in our communities. You will not find these terms used much by the women who describe their experiences in *Lifelines*. In some way, these terms represent a new language employed by those in the social sciences—politicians, scientists, helping professionals—and the media. As recorders, we are uncomfortable with this language because it depersonalizes the individual woman's experience. It serves to separate us. However, recorders and observers often use this language to describe others, who then become the objectified victims. Professional jargon also, all too easily, becomes the voice of authority. A counsellor of a victim of family violence becomes, when using this language and jargon, the one authorized to advise, to help, to heal others. In *Lifelines* we sometimes use these terms in default of other options, leaving the search for new language to future activists who may use this book as a catalyst. Some reports on family violence, including the exhaustive report by the Royal Commission on Family Violence in 1995, have been criticized for using women's life stories as evidence in presenting their material. This approach has been judged as being "too subjective," not using "proper quantitative methods," and being "anecdotal." The questions are: "How do you quantify misery and pain? How do you quantify life's forces to survive? How do you quantify the power of the spirit?" In *Lifelines*, we opted to use this method, one that is increasingly being used in anthropology and in women's studies. Namely, to collect life-stories and to present them as far as possible in the words of the speaker. This process validates the life experiences of the women, allowing the reader to reach her or his own conclusion.

If the writer takes over the women's experiences, telling them in her own voice, the result is more often more a reflection of the writer's style and interpretation than that of the story's owner. The questions we asked each woman are recorded in the text. Therefore, our own biases are obvious and you can easily identify them. Women do not speak with one voice. There are as many differences within each culture and religion as there are between them.

Canada, North America, and much of the rest of the world, have become increasingly heterogeneous socially and culturally. Two hundred years ago the state determined the religion of the individual. However, the twentieth century has seen huge shifts of populations. The pressures of industrialization, politics, wars, famines, and overpopulation, have all contributed to mass migrations of people from one place to another. North America became a destination for many. In Canada, a multiculturalism policy was implemented as a government tool to deal with the steady flow of immigrants into the country. This policy explicitly provides the opportunity to everyone to practice with dignity diverse religions, languages, and cultural customs. *Lifelines* draws on the richness of Canada's multicultural population. But it also provides each of us with more understanding of the difficulties faced by newcomers in adjusting to a new land where many life situations are handled in unfamiliar ways.

The women in *Lifelines* talk about searching for new paradigms for living their lives, both as believers from a distinct socio-religious tradition as well as members of specific ethnic groups. Within their marriages and their relationships, the tension caused by these realities often reaches the breaking point. The beliefs expressed by the women in *Lifelines* often do not mesh with our own beliefs. Frequently, the beliefs of the women clash with those of members of their own communities. The book's purpose is not to encourage readers to decide the religious hegemony of one religion over the other; nor does it validate one belief as more correct than the next. It simply attempts to show that women, from a wide variety of backgrounds, experience family violence. *Lifelines* demonstrates that many women have turned to their religions and their individual spirituality to gain the strength to overcome. As a result, we gain a deep appreciation for the honesty with which the participants allow us to see their reality and their struggle.

ADDRESSING HUMAN SPIRITUAL NEED

The secularization of the modern world has left many of us in a deep conundrum. Those who work with survivors of family violence are often left feeling unsure about the long-term effectiveness of our approach. How are we dealing with a woman who expresses spiritual need in her coping and healing process? Professional training gives us insights into the psychological, the emotional, and the mental states of these women. But what about the spiritual? We address legal issues, housing needs, economic concerns, child care, and personal safety. But what can we do with a deeply religious woman who feels guilty about leaving her husband, depriving her children of a father, in light of the marriage vows she has made? How do we address the view she has of her obligation as a woman, gleaned and internalized from her understanding of the sacred texts and their interpretation in her particular community and in her particular family?

Lifelines lets us in on the dilemma as experienced by individual women. The missing link in counselling, in helping, is spiritual need. The core theme in *Lifelines* is spirituality. What do we mean by "spirituality" at the close of the twentieth century? In *Lifelines*, we get a glimpse of the multitude of answers, the fractured consciousness in our multiple communities, and the various religious and cultural traditions. The "Women of Faith," in the third section of this book and the "Front-line Workers," in the fourth section, have personally witnessed that miraculous transforming power of the spirit within and found ways of exploring it with each woman they encounter. They regard their clients as their equals. Drawing on their professional training, their wisdom, and their understanding of the various religious and cultural traditions, they work towards individual solutions arising from each individual situation. These women, the care-givers, tell us that much can be done in the training of service providers, both within social service agencies and religious organizations, to better understand and respond to the spiritual needs of women experiencing family violence. Reading *Lifelines* may give individuals dealing with family violence the idea to test some of the tools that have been successful for women of varying cultural backgrounds.

Spiritual counselling is, at all times, dependent upon the readiness and willingness of the participant and the chosen counsellor. The tools for exploration appended to this volume are safe tools for initial intervention, until the woman involved can access a trained person. Spiritual need must be acknowledged by those who help and its importance in healing and hope must be reinforced.

LIFELINES AS A CATALYST

Throughout the process of recording *Lifelines*, many women quoted religious texts to explain how they felt about themselves and how these passages influenced their actions. Often, the exact passage was not known to the woman, yet existed subconsciously as a cornerstone to her behaviour in her community like an invisible stone in a stream firmly directing the flow of the stream. What are the specific words in religious texts, in the different belief systems, that have formed our view of what we are to be as men and women? How has history and tradition transformed those messages? From the participants in *Lifelines*, we hear a line from the Koran, a word from the Bible, a quote from a sacred Hindu text. As we assembled more of the whole text of *Lifelines*, we began to realize that each woman's knowledge of sacred writings is usually hidden in the subtext of her life, unconsciously forming her image of herself, guiding her in her actions. We believe that it is important for all women to follow the thread backwards to its source, the sacred texts and their directives to women and men.

An additional grant from the Government of Canada, Secretary of State, Women's Program allowed us to pursue a companion volume to *Lifelines*, *Sacred Stories: Healing From Abuse in the Global Village*. In it, we have laid bare the relationships of gender roles in Canada as formed by the diversity of religions and cultures in our society.

HOPE AND HEALING

Many women in the community have allowed us to listen to their life's darkest hours. In one sense *Lifelines* is a reflection of the depth and extent of women's suffering. It is not a monochrome of black and white gloom. It is a composite picture, made up of multiple voices that add colour and depth. It lets us believe in, hope for, and imagine happier times ahead. Multiple splashes of sorrow, suffering, and survival, all different, all potent are revealed as acts of abandonment and human kindness run side by side. Throughout the entire work, there is at first despair and then new found strength. We listen to the courageous voices of individual women in the community. We share their experiences, their pain, their progress, and their healing. *Lifelines* is a look from outside into the heart of experience and the survival of the soul. We discover our own personal connection to the voices we hear. The women, the participants, give hope to us all that life is deep and wondrous and that the power of our spirit can overcome all adversity.

Appendices

Tools for
Health and Healing

Appendix 1

A Few Tools for Beginning

Shelter staff and volunteers are rarely psychologists and should not attempt therapeutic intervention. They are also rarely trained in spiritual counselling methods. Despite this they often find themselves in a situation where women are seeking help in understanding their pain.

Often these searches are spiritual in nature. The following tools are meant to set a peaceful environment for both the worker and the woman in her care. Others can be added or substituted and the women themselves will have suggestions for things that work. These are but a few books, audio recordings, music choices, and films that can be used to broaden your perspective or enhance an environment.

The following materials are helpful when a woman is seeking a new understanding of her spiritual self.

WRITING MATERIALS

A personal journal

A comfortable pen

COMFORTS FOR BODY AND SPIRIT

Relaxing herbal teas

Incense or sweetgrass

Grounding stones, dreamcatchers, and other symbols of personal value

Uplifting images

Other symbols of a personal nature

Long walks

BOOKS

Blumenfeld, Larry, ed.

1994   *The Big Book of Relaxation: Simple Techniques to Control Excess Stress in Your Life.* Roslyn, New York: Relaxation Co.

VIDEO CASSETTES

National Film Board of Canada

> *One Hit Leads to Another.* National Film Board of Canada.
> Sylvie's Story. In *The Next Step Series.* National Film Board of Canada.
> To a Safe Distance. In *The Next Step Series.* National Film Board of Canada.
> Moving On. In *The Next Step Series.* National Film Board of Canada.
> *The Crown Prince.* National Film Board of Canada.
> *The Ticket Back.* National Film Board of Canada.

Read, Donna

1989   *Goddess Remembered.* National Film Board of Canada.

FILM

National Film Board of Canada

Loved Honoured and Bruised. National Film Board of Canada.
Up The Creek (Men). National Film Board of Canada.
Killing Us Softly. National Film Board of Canada.

Lamarsh Research

1994   *Breaking The Barriers: Reaching South Asian Abused Women
Multicultural Community Development and Training.*
Judy Lamarsh Research Centre, York University.

AUDIO CASSETTES

Fulmer, Colleen

Dancing Sophia's Circle. In *Original Songs Exploring and
Celebrating The Great Wisdom—Sophia Tradition.* Albany, California:
Loretto Spirituality Network.

Carczak, Carola

Listen to Your Body. Audiotape and Videotape Series.

Hendricks, Gay, PH.D.

The Art of Breathing and Centering. Audiotape. Audio
Renaissance/St. Martin's Press.

H.S. Khalsa and G. Fill

1985   *Pachelbel—Music for Meditation.* Invincible Music.

McDade, Carolyn, and Friends

Sorrow and Healing. Wellfleet, Massachusetts.

Appendix 2

Enabling Activities

In the process of writing this book we have listened to many women's voices, those who have suffered abuse in their families and those who have helped them back to themselves. The women interviewed came from a cross-section of Canada's multicultural and interfaith communities. Their voices are strong in their search for ways to strengthen their spirit and to help other women.

The activities described here are tools of empowerment for both women from abusive relationships as well as helping professionals. They are not to be considered as therapy but more like enabling activities that can assist women to stay grounded in difficult times.

They become familiar steps to be taken throughout life's journey to reach deeper into ourselves and to enhance spiritual growth.*

---

* Adapted from *Pathways to the Community* (1996). Ottawa: Correctional Services Canada.

Self-Affirmation

What Are Self-Affirmations?

Self-Affirmations are messages that you can repeat to yourself every day to help you care for yourself. You can also make up affirmations to send to other people (for example, to your partner or to your children) to help them know you care about them.

You can write them in your personal journal. You can make up stickers and post them. Read them. Say them. Listen to them.

Guidelines for Creating Your Affirmation

- Make the affirmation short and simple.

- Always use the present tense—
  "I am a strong woman" as opposed to "I will be a strong woman."

- Phrase the affirmation positively—
  "I am a good person" rather than "I am not a bad person."

- Repeat the affirmation to yourself whenever and for as long as it feels comfortable.

- State your affirmation in each of these forms—
  "I, Yvette, am strong and caring."
  "You, Yvette, are strong and caring."
  "Yvette is strong and caring."

- Continue to repeat the affirmation to yourself (even though you may not believe it at first, with practice your belief will strengthen).*

---

* Adapted from Women's Self-Help Network (1984), *Working Together for Change: A Women's Self-Help Handbook*. Campbell River, B.C.: Ptarmigan Press.

ENABLING ACTIVITY # 2

Visualization

A visualization helps you to create images or mental pictures that will change your feelings and reduce stress. To practice visualizing:

- Get relaxed and comfortable by sitting or lying down.

- Keep your eyes open (unless you are entirely comfortable doing the Activity with them closed).

- Take your time with the images and do not rush the visualization.

Here are some examples of visualizations to get you started:

- Imagine a ball of blue or white light shining on you, the light is cleansing and takes away any distressing feelings or thoughts that are there, the light moves down your body removing tension and distress until you feel relaxed and peaceful.

- Imagine a problem that has been bothering you, make it into a hard round ball about the size of a baseball, throw the ball into the sky and watch as the ball flies apart and turns into feathers, the wind carries the feathers off.

- Go for a walk in your mind to a safe beautiful place and spend some time relaxing and enjoying the beauty of nature.

- Create a visual picture of a positive memory of something that happened in your life, let yourself enjoy the feelings.*

---

* Adapted from Women's Self-Help Network (1984), *Working Together for Change: A Women's Self-Help Handbook*. Campbell River, B.C.: Ptarmigan Press.

Centring: Awakening Yourself

A Realization of Spiritual Questioning

Let us begin by being still. Sit back in your spirit. You do that by sitting back in your body. Let your reflections on "awakening" emerge from your inner self. Take time. Don't hurry. Try to spend at least a few moments with each question and with each of your responses before going on to the next one.

- When in your life do you find you are most awake?

- When are you least awake?

- To what in your life are you most awake?

- To whom?

- Are you awake to the presence of mystery, goddess, god, in your life?

- Are you awake to what is real but somehow beyond explaining?

- Do you ever feel touched by this mystery?

- Are you awake to other people, especially to their losses, their suffering?

- Are you awake to the voices of the earth, the stars, the wind, the rain?

- Are you awake to the possibility of joy, of hope?*

---

* Adapted from Harris, Maria (1991), *Dance of the Spirit*. New York: Bantam Books, p. 1.

Cultivating the Ability to Experience Joy

The world is filled with small and large things that can bring you pleasure. You can develop the ability to feel joy, even if it has been absent from your life.

Try noticing one small thing each day that brings you a little more joy (even the tiniest bit more) than you experience during other moments. Write it down in your personal journal. Reflect on the following questions and write your thoughts in your journal as you go.

- Think about what it was about that moment that brought you joy. Is there a way to make that part of your day each day?

- If so, do you want that for yourself?

- What else brings you joy, even a little bit? How can you put more joy into your life? Do you want to do that? And what will happen if you continue in that direction?

- What would need to happen to bring more joyful experiences or moments into your life more often?

- How are joyful experiences or moments different from your other experiences in daily life? What makes them better?

- Are there things you could do more of, so that you would have more joyful experiences or moments? Are there things you could do less of? What would be the results of those changes over days, weeks, months, years?

If you like what you imagined, you could do things differently. You're on the right track. If not, what would you add, subtract, or change?

Name a first step, one small enough that it's not too scary to try tomorrow.*

---

* Adapted from Dolan, Yvonne (1991), *Resolving Sexual Abuse: Solution Focussed Therapy and Ericsonian Hypnosis for Adult Survivors*. New York: W.W. Norton & Company Publishing.

A Self of One's Own

For each question, write down thoughts, images, or words that come to mind.

- Who are you, apart from others' expectations of who you are?
- Who are you, apart from your own expectations?
- If you were left alone but still nurtured and supported, how would you pass your time?

If your answers to the above questions are the way you really want to live rather than the way people expect you to be, or the way you might expect yourself to live, what productive or useful things would happen in your life?

How could you begin to make these things happen now? What would be the smallest sign that this is happening?*

---

* Adapted from Dolan, Yvonne (1991), *Resolving Sexual Abuse: Solution Focussed Therapy and Ericsonian Hypnosis for Adult Survivors*. New York: W.W. Norton & Company Publishing.

Choosing Your Mantra

A mantra is a short phrase that helps you to concentrate on your spirit. Mantras are repeated over and over again. Each one has its own rhythm. Your spiritual guide may give you a mantra or you may choose your own.

Choose a mantra that you can repeat to yourself every morning for a while. Repeat the mantra several times every hour later on in the day. By repeating the mantra you can recapture and reclaim the peace of your morning practice. Here are some examples:

"Here I am world. Here I am universe. Welcome me as I welcome myself."

"The time is now. The place is here."

"It is time for me to awaken from sleep."

"This is my spirituality. Waking up."

"At dawn you hear my voice. At dawn I bring my pleas expectantly before you."

A mantra can also be a word like *peace, joy, love* or a sound that is special for you. The word *ohm* is a common mantra.

My own mantra is*:

_____

_____

---

* Adapted from Harris, Maria (1991), *Dance of the Spirit*. New York: Bantam Books, p. 23.

Your Evolving Inner Spirit

For some people the crises that lead to awakening are crises in their religious lives, their spiritual lives. Here are some questions that can help you to understand your feelings in this area.

- Have you ever had an experience you would call religious or spiritual?

- Has that experience had any effect or influence on your life?

- Can you recall any particular moment or period when you had a feeling of awakening self-consciousness or of feeling yourself an individual with a degree of freedom and responsibility? Were these feeling connected to any spiritual feelings or ideas?

Some people see their childhood as clearer, more vivid, and more revealing of later life. Other people see their childhood as the first step in a gradual process of awakening that isn't completed until they are adults.

- Do you see your childhood in either way or is there some different pattern in your life?

- What do your thoughts and feeling about these questions mean to you?

- What do they tell you about your own awakening?*

* Adapted from Harris, Maria (1991), *Dance of the Spirit*. New York: Bantam Books, p. 23.

A Room of One's Own

This activity is a visualization to help you create a room of your own. It should take you about 20 minutes. If you feel uncomfortable or anxious when you're doing it, stop the activity. You will need your personal journal or some paper as well as pencils to colour with.

With your eyes open, imagine a safe room. It can be an actual room that you know or one that you create.

- Imagine its size and colour and its texture.

- Imagine the sounds or the lack of them in the room.

- Imagine yourself in the room and the place where you are sitting, standing or lying.

- Imagine the room clearly enough that you can describe it to yourself later in the day.

In your personal journal or on a piece of paper, draw the room you imagined. Sketch and colour in as many details as you can.*

---

* Adapted from Harris, Maria (1991), *Dance of the Spirit*. New York: Bantam Books, p. 24.

Praying Your Spirituality

Breathe silently and rhythmically, in and out. Allow your spirit, wherever it is, to emerge from within your own depths. Be quiet and attentive to it. Listen to it. Use your senses. Dwell on the four strengths. Incorporate your vulnerability, your emotion, your caring, your connection. Incorporate…incorporate…incorporate.

Have a gentle conversation with your spirituality. Give it all the time it needs.

- What does your spirituality give to your discovering?

- Are the discoveries you're making now mainly of what is within you or are they of what is outside you?

- Do you find your spirituality is a coming together of the within and the without?

Celebrate your spirituality.*

---

* Adapted from Harris, Maria (1991), *Dance of the Spirit*. New York: Bantam Books, pp. 26, 27.

Centring: Creating

The step of creating is an exploration of our power (ability) to create spiritual expression.

This is the step of creating, where we attend to the work of shaping our spirituality and giving it an artistic form. Let reflections on creating emerge from your inner self. Take time, don't hurry, and try to spend at least a few moments with each question (and with your response).

As you begin, take a few moments and remember (in detail):

- your childhood (an incident where you did something creative);

- your teenage years (something like writing a poem or planting seeds);

- your adult years (where is your creativity concentrated now?).

Pause for centring.

- Who are the most creative women you know, the first people you think of when asked to name someone creative?

- What is it about them that makes you call them creative?

- Are women more creative than men?

- Are children more creative than grown-ups?

- What about the women you know compared with the men you know?

- What about the child in you, is she still there in the woman?

- If and when you imagine a god, is god a creator or a creative spirit?

- What does god create, and how?

- Might a goddess, a god, or the sacred dwell within you, ready to guide you through this step of creating your spirituality?*

---

* Adapted from Harris, Maria (1991), *Dance of the Spirit*. New York: Bantam Books, p. 110.

A Garden as Dwelling Place

For this practice you need to be near a garden or some plants. After four minutes of concentrating on breathing, be present to the garden or plants and permit them to be present to you.

- In what way does this garden represent past gardens in your life?

- What things about past gardens in your life do you want to continue to cultivate in the present?

- In what way does this garden represent present garden dwelling places in your life?

Listen to what the garden has to say.

- What present circumstances of garden as a dwelling place do you rejoice in now?

- What circumstances sadden you?

Be present to the joy and the sadness.

- In what ways are you a garden for yourself?

- In what ways are you a garden for others?

- Are there any ways in which you experience spirituality as a garden?

If so, be present now.

End this practice by sitting quietly in the garden for at least two minutes, breathing the garden in and out as you return.*

---

* Adapted from Harris, Maria (1991), *Dance of the Spirit*.New York: Bantam Books, p. 111.

Comparison of Assertive, Nonassertive, and Aggressive Behaviours*

It is important to understand your own behaviour patterns and to identify those of your partner. In the chart below, under "Goal," state how you would like to communicate in an assertive manner (firm but not aggressive). Then go to "Sample Behaviours" and write down specific examples of how you presently react. Think about the consequences of each of the behaviours you have listed.

Use this chart often to analyze situations as they arise and to identify the most effective communication.

	GOAL	SAMPLE BEHAVIOURS	CONSEQUENCE
ASSERTIVE To express your needs, wants, thoughts, opinions, and rights without feeling guilty, anxious, or fearful.			
NONASSERTIVE To avoid conflict, to be liked.			
AGGRESSIVE To dominate over people and situations, to win, to control people and situations.			

* Adapted from *Pathways to the Community* (1996), Ottawa: Correctional Services Canada, worksheet 5–8.

Community as Dwelling Place

The community you are currently living within can be the place for acts of kindness by preparing meals, caring for those who are sick, or comforting those who are troubled. In this practice, you are to choose to do one of these activities as a volunteer in your community for at least one hour a week.

- Contact a community leader who might know of someone in need in the community.

- Ask what you could do as a volunteer.

- Make a commitment to this volunteer activity for at least three months.

- Keep a brief journal of diary entries about this work and its impact on you.

- Try and engage at least one other person in this activity with you.

Each time you engage in this practice, both before you go and after your return, do at least fifteen minutes of breathing or begin and end with a silent period.*

* Adapted from Harris, Maria (1991), *Dance of the Spirit*. New York: Bantam Books, p. 112.

Centring: Traditioning

The Actions By Which We Communicate Our Spirituality to Others

Pause and centre yourself. Begin by being still. Breathe gently, slowly, and easily. Let your own reflections on how spirituality has been handed on—traditioned— to you. Emerge from your inner self. Take time. Do not hurry.

- Is spirituality something that makes you feel comfortable?

- Has is always been that way?

- Have you ever felt that the spirituality you were offered or taught needed something more in order to fit you as a woman?

- Were there older women who assisted you, as a child, to develop a spiritual life?

- If so, can you remember what they did?

- Do you find yourself doing some of those things now?

- Are there women in your adult life who model spirituality for you, who you would like to imitate, women about whom you say, "I want to be like her"?

- If so, can you pinpoint what about them or their lives is alive for you?

- Do women younger than you, or girls, look to you for help in their lives?

- If you are a parent, have you thought about how you would or could introduce spirituality to your child or children?

- Is there anything about spirituality you would like to share with the men in your life, things you see missing from their lives?

- If so, where might you start?*

---

* Adapted from Harris, Maria (1991), *Dance of the Spirit*. New York: Bantam Books, p. 145.

ENABLING ACTIVITY # 15

Exploration of Spirituality as Traditioning

This practice helps us to explore what we understand as spirituality now and how that is influenced by traditions we grew up with.

First answer the questions by yourself. Then meet with a group of others to explore your answers together.

- What words or phrases do you think of when you hear the word "spirituality?"

- Can you remember the first time the word began to have meaning for you?

- What feelings do you have when you hear the word?

- Complete the sentence, "For me, spirituality is

- Describe an experience you had in childhood that is part of your spirituality. Are there any people who were part of this experience?

- Describe an experience you had as a teenager that is part of your spirituality. Are there any people who were part of this experience?

- If you could choose one woman, real or imaginary, who taught you about spirituality, who would it be?

- If you could choose one woman, real or imaginary, who mentors spiritually to you or whom you would wish as a mentor, who would it be?

- If you could choose one woman, real or imaginary, who modelled spirituality to you, who would it be?

- What aspect of spirituality do you most want to hand over to the next generation of girls and women?*

* Adapted from Harris, Maria (1991), *Dance of the Spirit*. New York: Bantam Books, p. 173.

Centring: Transforming*

Pause and centre yourself. Begin by being still. Sit back. This step is bringing together all you have journeyed toward—a birthing step—leading you to a new vision. This step is also an integrating one of all that has gone before. As you reflect, take time. Don't hurry.

- Where were you ten years ago?

- Who were you ten years ago?

- As you reflect on the last ten years of your life, can you pinpoint where changes or transformations have come from?

- As you have listened to your own life, have you recognized any experiences you need to mourn or grieve over?

- Are there memories or experience of which you say, "I have to let go of that" or "I have never really allowed myself to grieve over this."

- Do you resist mourning or do you make it a friend?

- Where in your life do you find you have made new connections or formed new relations?

- Where in your life have you created bonds with other women?

- Where and how are you bonded with men?

- In what ways are you bonded with the earth?

- How do these bondings or connections contribute to your personal transforming?

- Have you ever had the experience of feeling you have given birth (although not in a physical way) to someone else, perhaps by being

---

* Transforming—an exploration of personal change and how this in turn changes or transforms our world.

mentor, lover, model, or teacher, or given birth to a new relationship with the world?

- Have you ever had the transforming experience of giving birth to a baby? If so, can you recall the effect that giving birth had on your spirituality?

- Have you ever had the experience of feeling you had given birth to yourself? If you did, was it an experience of transformation?*

---

* Adapted from Harris, Maria (1991), *Dance of the Spirit*. New York: Bantam Books, p. 179.

Taking Time for Mourning

You can do this practice alone or in a group. Sit comfortably and easily. Focus on your inner self. Focus on your breathing—inhale—exhale. Be aware of your breathing. When you are feeling quiet, reflect on something within your life that needs to be mourned.

Locate that part of yourself that is aware of this need to mourn, that feels and thinks about it and that wishes to act in relation to it. Imagine this part of yourself as if it were a character in a book.

- What is she like?
- How does she spend her time?
- What is important to her?

Describe her as carefully as you can. Locate that part of yourself that does not want to mourn, that does not want to be aware of the need, that does not want to think or talk about it.

- What is she like?
- How does she spend her time?
- What is important to her?

Describe her as carefully as you can. Allow these two voices within yourself to be in conversation with each other. Hear them speaking to each other. You may want to:

a) write down the conversation;

b) describe it to someone else in your group;

c) role-play the characters yourself.

If you are in a group, you may wish to hear from each person after you have described the voices to them. Finally, decide on one step that will help you through the mourning process. Ask the group for whatever help you may need.*

---

* Adapted from Harris, Maria (1991), *Dance of the Spirit*.New York: Bantam Books, p. 198.

Our Experiences of Bonding

This practice may be more helpful if done with others (in a group) because everyone's experiences can both nourish and empower one another. Choose an image or symbol of bonding that has occurred in your life thus far.

- Share these images or symbols with others in your group.

- Name three times you bonded with other girls, for example, before you were fifteen years old.

  _____

  _____

  _____

- Name three times you bonded as an adult with other women.

  _____

  _____

  _____

- What did you receive from those bondings?
- What did you give in those bondings?
- What conclusions and resolutions does your experience of bonding lead you to make now and for the future?*

---

* Adapted from Harris, Maria (1991), *Dance of the Spirit*. New York: Bantam Books, p. 199.

The Experience of Birth

A mother writes the following after the birth of her daughter.

> The experience of labour and birth is still very much in my mind. I have
> never been that present in my life. All my senses and feelings were
> focused on that miracle going on. There was no room for any other
> thought. Past and future collapsed in that very moment. We still feel
> like celebrating and cannot be other than just full of awe toward this
> beautiful new life. Slowly, very slowly, I find my way back to reality, or
> better, to the other side of reality. I am starting to feel a deeper
> responsibility toward the future. It is as if the future has become
> personalized in our child.

Clearly, not all of us can describe birth as eloquently as this young mother. What
she offers us in her description is positive, encouraging us toward understanding
birth as miraculous, full of possibility and of hope for future living.

This theme of birthing has recently entered the realm of spirituality and this
allows us to enter the experience of knowing. We are changed by a spiritual event
in our lives. It allows us to know we are finally all we are meant to be. This life-
changing experience, one focused through all our senses and feelings, is the birth
of our spirit selves. For too long we have equated experiences of death to our faith
exploration. Birthing opens a whole new realm of possibility and hope as we
hunger to live our lives differently and well.

As you explore the practice of birthing or bonding, allow this eloquent description
to form and inform your reflection.*

---

* Adapted from Harris, Maria (1991), *Dance of the Spirit*.New York: Bantam Books, p. 193.

Labelling Emotions: Positive Words

adequate	determined	gratified	peaceful
affectionate	eager	groovy	pleasant
befriended	ecstatic	happy	pleased
bold	enchanted	helpful	proud
calm	enhanced	high	refreshed
capable	energetic	honoured	relaxed
caring	enervated	important	relieved
challenged	enjoyed	impressed	rewarded
charmed	excited	infatuated	safe
cheerful	fascinated	inspired	satisfied
clever	fearless	joyful	secure
comforted	free	kind	settled
confident	fulfilled	loving	sure
content	generous	loved	warm
delighted	glad		

Add your own words below or on a separate page.*

---

* Adapted from Myrick and Sorenson (1997), *Peer Helping: a practical guide*. Minneapolis, MN: Educational Media Cooperation.

Labelling Emotions: Negative Words

abandoned	distraught	longing	scared
agony	disturbed	low	shocked
ambivalent	divided	mad	skeptical
angry	dominated	maudlin	sorrowful
annoyed	dubious	mean	startled
anxious	empty	melancholy	strained
betrayed	envious	miserable	stunned
bitter	exasperated	nervous	stupid
bored	exhausted	odd	tense
cheated	fatigued	overwhelmed	tenuous
cold	fearful	pain	threatened
condemned	flustered	panicked	tired
confused	frantic	persecuted	trapped
crushed	frightened	petrified	troubled
defeated	grieved	pity	uneasy
despair	guilty	pressured	unsettled
destructive	intimidated	quarrelsome	vulnerable
different	isolated	rejected	weak
diminished	jealous	remorse	weepy
discontented	left out	restless	worried
distracted	lonely	sad	

Add your own words below or on a separate page.*

* Adapted from Myrick and Sorenson (1997), *Peer Helping: a practical guide*. Minneapolis, MN: Educational Media Cooperation.

Appendix 3

Inspirational Words

THE PATHWAY TO GOD

Prayer is a pathway to God
   which leads us to feel God's love,
      not only in the heavens above
         but within us
           and within those
              about us.

If we walk on this path
   with faith,
      we will feel God's presence
         here in this room,
           here in our hearts,
              giving us strength
                 guidance and hope.

from Central Conference of American Rabbis (1991),
Gates of Healing Prayer Book

A PRAYER FOR STRENGTH

O God, our refuge and strength and ever-present help in times of trouble, how much I need your strength and presence in my life right now. I feel weak, depressed, anxious, and fearful. I need help to face these hours and days.

So I claim your promise that I can bear whatever comes, that your strength will be sufficient, and that my despair will give way to your peace that surpasses all understanding. Amen.

from Central Conference of American Rabbis (1991),
Gates of Healing Prayer Book

I hereby forgive all you who have hurt me, all who have wronged me, whether deliberately or inadvertently, whether by word or by deed. May no one be punished on my account. As I forgive and pardon those who have wronged me, may those whom I have harmed forgive and pardon me, whether I acted deliberately or inadvertently, whether by word or by deed...May the words of my mouth and the meditations of my heart, be acceptable to You, O God, my Rock and my Redeemer. Amen

from Sha'arei Tshuvah
Gates of Repentance Yom Kippur Service

Note

Jewish tradition teaches that prayer and repentance can only atone for our sins against God. For sins against one another, we must seek forgiveness directly. Coming out of an abusive relationship, working through the anger and pain, it is often hard for us to forgive, but at some point forgiveness is necessary—in the end the anger becomes hatred and poisons our soul and not that of the one with whom we are angry.

Nevertheless, for at least a couple of years, this prayer was among the most difficult for me to say at Yom Kippur, our annual day of atonement. And yet, when the moment came that I could finally utter these words with intent and meaning, it was extremely liberating. By forgiving, I essentially gave myself permission to heal and to move on.

(Rabbi Lindsey bat Joseph, 1997).

PRAYER

come let us also raise our hands to pray
we who have forgotten how
we who know no god, no idol
only love
come let us ask life
to put the sweetness of tomorrow
in the bitter gloom of today
to lessen the burden of days and nights
for those who have no strength to bear it
to light a lamp in the darkness
of eyes that cannot hope
to see the face of dawn

come let us ask life to show a way out
to those who are lost on endless streets
to give the courage and the desire for truth
to those who worship lies and deceit
to give strength to those whose heads
are bowed in fear

love's veiled secret is in the fevered soul
let us make a pact and soothe this fever
let us accept the voice of truth burning in our hearts
so that our anguish is over
so that our hearts are healed

Faiz Ahmad Faiz

THE WOMAN'S DRUM*

So long, the Woman's Drum
has been quiet
while Women looked to Men
for the Teachings.
Now, the realization comes
to seek Women
for the Sacred Teachings
of the Creation.

Women, search out
the Sacred Teaching
of our Grandmothers.
Take up the Drum
sing the Women's Songs
of the Healing Ones.

So long, the Woman's
Drum has been alone
kept in the back of minds
silent in the Spirit.
Now, comes the time
to pick up the Drum
to sing the Healing Songs
of the Women's Way.

Women, sing out
the Healing Songs
of the Women's Teachings.
Take up the Drum
sing the Honor songs
of the Traditional Ones.

Too long, the Woman's Drum
has been silent.

Sky Blue Mary Morin (1990)

---

*   Sky Blue Mary Morin (1990) in *Writing the Circle: Native Women of Western Canada*. Jeanne
Perreault and Sylvia Vance, eds. Edmonton: NeWest Publishers Ltd. Used with the permission of
Sky Blue Mary Morin.

SARASWATI

AS SHE APPEARS AS WHITE RADIANCE OF KNOWLEDGE

She is whiter than white jasmine
She is more luminous than the white moon
She dazzles like the white snow
She wears flowing white silk
She holds a white lute
She is seated on a white lotus

All the high gods
creator, preserver, and annihilator
Sing her praise
May the great goddess
who is ultimate knowledge
Remove all the barriers to enlightenment

*Interpretation and translation from Sanskrit
by Gita Das (1996)*

Note

This is a vision of the goddess we see in our inner eye. In the state of meditation the practitioner gradually moves from the world of form to formlessness. Form dissolves into colour—colours dissolve into radiance—radiance dissolves into soft hues—and the hues merge into eternal glow that is neither darkness nor bright light. This is the light of wisdom that exists prior to the duality of light and darkness.

The lotus, in the creation period, is a symbol of the unfolding universe. The symbol of eternity is the white lotus within the sun.

SUNLIGHT

One day when all this raging sea has calmed
She too will find peace within herself
She will be calm like the sea
Big bright beautiful rays of sunlight. Her future.

She reaches for the stars
For she is the ray of sunlight
Bright, positive, regaining self esteem
The will to live, find happiness.

She has the strength to push herself ahead
And she will get there
One step at a time
Knowing that the Great Spirit walks with her.

adapted and condensed with permission from
"Sunlight" by Pauline Okemow (1996)

Appendix 4

What Places of Worship and Communities Can Do About Family Violence

UNDERSTAND THE ISSUES

- study the problem;
- talk with knowledgeable community people;
- educate the congregation.

BREAK THE SILENCE

- talk about family violence from the pulpit;
- form committees to address the issue.

SHAPE ATTITUDES

- tell the congregation that all people are equal;

- tell the congregation that abusive behaviours are not accepted;

- discuss and interpret the sacred texts that are contradictory to equality.

RESPOND WITH COMPASSION

When approached by those suffering from abuse

- ensure safety and provide necessities first
  (food, shelter, medical help, child care);

- then offer supportive counselling by helping women to:

  identify their strengths;
  know about the resources available to them;
  recognise the options they have;
  make their own decisions;
  empower themselves;
  understand that they are not to blame.

This is not the time to offer counselling to couples, this implies that the victims are contributing to their own abuse; it could increase the likelihood of further abuse.

GET INVOLVED IN PREVENTION

- strengthen family life education programs;

- focus on equality and nonviolent conflict resolution;

- discuss issues of anger, power, control, and the use of violence;

- advocate for the training of appropriate people who can recognise and respond to abuse in ways that are helpful.*

* Adapted from Alberta Family and Social Services, Office for the Prevention of Family Violence (1989), "What Can Churches Do About Family Violence."

Appendix 5

*The Canadian
Charter of
Rights and
Freedoms
Constitution Act
of 1982*

Everyone has the right to life, liberty and security of person and the
right not to be deprived thereof except in accordance with principles of
Fundamental Justice.

Every individual is equal before and under the Law (equality in
relationships is the fundamental right of men and women) and has the
right to equal protection and equal benefits of the law without
discrimination based on sex, age, religion, race, national or ethnic
origin, colour, or mental or physical disability.

Bibliography

Adams, Carol J.
1994   *Woman Battering: Creative Pastoral Care and Counseling Series.*
        Minneapolis: Future Press.

Angelou, Maya
1969   *I Know Why The Caged Bird Sings.* New York: Random House.

Ashraf, Sh. Muhamed
1974   *Islam in Practical Life.* Lanore, Pakistan: Ashraf Press.

Baldwin, Christina
1994   *Calling the Circle: The First and Future Culture.* Newberg, Oregon:
        Swan-Raven and Company.

Bass, Ellen and Laura Davis
1988   *The Courage to Heal.* New York: Harper & Row.

Blumenfeld, Larry
1994   *The Big Book of Relaxation: Simple Techniques to Control Stress in Your
        Life.* Roslyn, New York: Relaxation Co.

Brennan, Carla
n.d.   Sexual Power Abuse: Neglect and Misuse of a Buddhist Precept. In *Not Mixing Up Buddhism: Essays on Women and Buddhist Practice*, Deborah Hopkinson, Michele Hill and Eileen Kiera, eds., pp. 59–61. Fredonia, New York: White Pine Press.

Brin, Deborah, Rabbi and Liane Sharkey
1992   Jewish Women Creating Ritual, *Fireweed*, Spring 1992, no. 35, pp. 70–73.

Bushert, Joy
1986   *I Never Told Anyone: A Collection of Writings of Women Survivors of Sexual Abuse*. N.p.: Lutheran Church.

Cameron, Julia
1992   *The Artist's Way, A Spiritual Path to Higher Creativity*. Los Angeles: Jeremy P. Tarcher/Perigee.

Canadian Task Force on Mental Health Issues Affecting Immigrants and Refugees
1988   *After the Door Has Been Opened: A Report of the Canadian Task Force on Mental Health Issues Affecting Immigrants and Refugees*. Ottawa: Dept. of the Secretary of State of Canada, Multiculturalism Sector.

Carson, Anne
1986   *Feminist Spirituality and the Feminine Divine: An Annotated Bibliography*. Trumansburg: The Crossing Press.

Cashman, Hilary
1993   *Christianity and Child Sexual Abuse*. London: Society for Promoting Christian Knowledge.

Central Conference of American Rabbis
1991   *Gates of Healing Prayer Book*. New York: Central Conference of American Rabbis.

Cervantes, Nena
1988   *From Fright To Fight: Combating the Battering of Filipino Women and Children With Community Support*. Funded by the Ontario Women's Directorate. Toronto.

Champagne, C., R. Lapp, and J. Lee
1994   *Assisting Abused Lesbians: A Guide for Health Professionals and Service-Providers*. London, Ontario: London Battered Women's Advocacy Centre.

Chesley, L., D. Macaulay, and J. Ristock
1992   *Abuse in Lesbian Relationships: A Handbook of Information and Resources*. Toronto: Toronto Counseling Centre for Lesbians and Gays.

Christ, Carol, and Judith Plaskow
1979   *Womanspirit Rising: A Feminist Reader In Religion*. San Francisco: Harper & Row.

Church Council on Justice and Corrections, and the Canadian Council on Social Development
1988   *Family Violence in a Patriarchal Culture, A Challenge to Our Way of Living.* Ottawa: CCSD Publications.

Daly, Mary
1985   *Beyond God The Father: Toward a Philosophy of Women's Liberation.* Boston: Beacon Press.

Durrani, Tehmina
1991   *My Feudal Lord.* Lahore: T. Durrani.

El-Saadawi, Nawal
1982   Woman and Islam. In *Women and Islam*, Azizah al-Hibri, ed., pp. 193–206. Toronto: Pergamon.

Finson, Shelley Davis
1991   *Women and Religion: A Bibliographic Guide to Christian Feminist Liberation Theology.* Toronto: University of Toronto Press.

Fortune, Marie M.
1991   *Violence in the Family, A Workshop Curriculum for Clergy and Other Helpers.* Cleveland, Ohio: The Pilgrim Press.

1987   *Keeping The Faith: Questions and Answers for the Abused Woman.* San Fransisco: Harper and Row.

Fortune, Marie M. and Denise Hormann
1980   A Commentary on Religious Issues in Family Violence. In *Family Violence: A Workshop Manual for Clergy and Other Service Providers.* Seattle: Centre for the Prevention of Sexual and Domestic Violence. Rockville, Md.: National Clearinghouse on Domestic Violence.

Godin, Joanne
1993   *More Than a Crime: A Report on the Lack of Public Legal Information Materials for Immigrant Women Who Are Subject to Wife Assault.* Department of Justice Canada, Research, Statistics and Evaluation Directorate.

Government of Canada
1996   *Pathways to Community: Addressing Federally Sentenced Women's Violence and Aggression.* Ottawa: Correctional Service of Canada.

1993   *Changing the Landscape: Ending Violence, Achieving Equality. Canadian Panel on Violence Against Women.* Ottawa: The Royal Commission on Violence Against Women.

n.d.   *Working With Immigrant Women Survivors of Wife Assault: Towards Equal Access.* Ottawa: Education Wife Assault.

Hammond, N.
1989   Lesbian Victims of Relationship Violence. In *Loving Boldly: Issues Facing Lesbians*, E. Rothblum and E. Cole, eds. New York: Harrington Park Press.

Harris, Maria
1989   *Dance of the Spirit: The Seven Steps of Women's Spirituality.* New York: Bantam Books.

Jacobs, Gloria
1994   Where Do We Go From Here? In *MS*, September/October, pp. 56-63.

Jang, Deanna, Debbie Lee, and Rachel Morello-Frosch
1991   *Domestic Violence in the Immigrant and Refugee Community: Responding to the Needs of Immigrant Women*, Response, Issue 77, 13, no. 4.

Joyette, Donna A.
1990   *Considering the Impact of Culture, Immigration, Language and Race on Victims of Wife/Partner Assault.* N.p.

Kakar, Sudhir
1996   *The Colors of Violence: Cultural Identities, Religion and Conflict.* Chicago: University of Chicago Press.

Kuppuswamy, B.
1977   Rationalism and the Hindu View of Life. In *Life Divine and Spiritual Values*, C.S. Gupta, ed., pp. 34–40. Bangladore: Swami Sivananda Spiritual Centre.

MacDonald, Marie
1996   *Training Manual.* Edmonton Community and Social Services and the Edmonton Police Service.

MacLeod, Linda and Maria Shin
1990   *Isolated, Afraid and Forgotten: The Service Delivery Needs and Realities of Immigrant and Refugee Women Who Are Battered.* Ottawa: National Clearinghouse on Family Violence.

Mayor's Task Force on Community and Family Violence
1991   *Final Report: Section X: Immigrant Women: A Case of Double Jeopardy.* Calgary, Alberta.

Mitchell, Donald W.
1991   *Spirituality and Emptiness: The Dynamics of Spiritual Life in Buddhism and Christianity.* New York: Paulist Press.

Native Women's Association of Canada
1991   *Violences of Aboriginal Women, Aboriginal Women Speak Out About Violence.* Canadian Council on Social Development and Native Women's Association of Canada. Ottawa: Canadian Council on Social Development.

Newman, J.
1991   Review of Margaret P. Battin's *Ethics in the Sanctuary: Examining the Practices of Organized Religion. Canadian Philosophical Review* XXX, no. 2, pp. 85.

Nicarthy, Ginny, Karen Merriam, and Sandra Coffman
1984   *Talking It Out: A Guide to Groups for Abused Women.* Seattle: Seal Press.

Nicholas, Lee
n.d.   *Amor Sin Violenca (Love Without Violence): A Manual for Spanish
         Speaking Lay Counselors and Group Leaders*, translated by Iona
         Whishaw. N.D. Family Services of Greater Vancouver.

Richardson, J.
1991   Review of Janice Boddy's *Wombs and Alien Spirits: Women, Men and
         the Zar Cult in Northern Sudan. The Canadian Review of Sociology and
         Anthropology* 28, no. 4, pp. 557–59.

Ringe, Sharon H.
1985   A Gentile Woman's Story. In *Feminist Interpretation of the Bible*, Letty
         Russell, ed., pp. 65–73. Philadelphia: Westminster Press.

Roboubi, Nahid, and Sharon Bowles
1995   *Barriers to Justice: Ethnocultural Minority Women and Domestic Violence.*
         A Preliminary Discussion Paper. Federal-Provincial-Territorial
         Working Group on Multiculturalism and Race-Relations in the
         Justice System. Ottawa: Dept. of Justice.

Sabbah, Fatna. A.
1984   *Women In the Muslim Unconscious.* New York: Pergamon Press.

Sarkar, Ila
1991   *A Hidden Problem: Immigrant Women and Family Violence*, Briarpatch,
         19, no. 10, pp. 15–16.

Saussy, Carroll
1991   *God Images and Self-Esteem: Empowering Women in a Patriarchal
         Society*, Westminster: John Knox Press.

Schwertfeger, Ruth, ed.
1989   *Women of Theresienstadt: Voices From A Concentration Camp.*
         Oxford: Berg.

Spretnak, Charlene
1989   Toward an Ecofeminist Spirituality. In *Healing the Wounds: the
         Promise of Ecofeminism*, Judith Plant, ed., pp. 129–32. Philadelphia:
         New Society Publishers.

Talat, Ali
1992   *Empowering Canadian Muslim Women and Youth Through Parenting,
         Anti-Sexist, and Anti-Racist Education.* Funded by Multiculturalism
         and Citizenship Canada.

Walker, Barbara G.
1988   *The Woman's Dictionary of Symbols and Sacred Objects.* San Francisco:
         Harper & Row.

Women's Inter-Church Council of Canada
1988   *Hands to End Violence Against Women, A Resource for Theological
         Education.* Written and compiled by Gail Golding. Toronto: Women's
         Inter-Church Council of Canada.

VIDEO CASSETTES

National Film Board of Canada
One Hit Leads to Another. National Film Board of Canada.

Sylvie's Story. In *The Next Step Series*. National Film Board of Canada.

To a Safe Distance. In *The Next Step Series*. National Film Board of Canada.

Moving On. In *The Next Step Series*. National Film Board of Canada.

The Crown Prince. National Film Board of Canada.

The Ticket Back. National Film Board of Canada.

Read, Donna
1989   *Goddess Remembered*. National Film Board of Canada.

FILM

National Film Board of Canada
Loved Honoured and Bruised. National Film Board of Canada.

Up The Creek (Men). National Film Board of Canada.

Killing Us Softly. National Film Board of Canada.

Lamarsh Research
1994   *Breaking The Barriers: Reaching South Asian Abused Women Multicultural Community Development and Training*. Judy Lamarsh Research Centre, York University.

AUDIO CASSETTES

Fulmer, Colleen
Dancing Sophia's Circle. In *Original Songs Exploring and Celebrating The Great Wisdom—Sophia Tradition*. Albany, California: Loretto Spirituality Network.

Carczak, Carola
Listen to Your Body. Audiotape and Videotape Series.

Hendricks, Gay, Ph.D.
The Art of Breathing and Centering. Audiotape. Audio Renaissance/ St. Martin's Press.

Khalsa, H.S. and G. Fill
1985   *Pachelbel—Music for Meditation*. Invincible Music.

McDade, Carolyn, and Friends
Sorrow and Healing. Wellfleet, Massachusetts.